A young woman's journey of self-discovery

A Free Spirit

Lorraine Walton

Co-written by Yvonne Walton

Lorraine; A Free Spirit
2018 © Lorraine and Yvonne Walton

National Library of Australia Cataloguing-in-Publication entry (pbk)

Author: Walton, Lorraine, author.
           Walton, Yvonne, author.
Title: Lorraine; A Free Spirit / Lorraine and Yvonne Walton
ISBN: 978-0-6480888-6-8 (paperback)
           978-1-9256807-9-9 (eBook)
Subjects: Non-Fiction--Autobiography
           Lorraine Walton--Family Story
           Lorraine Walton -- Diaries
Published by Yvonne Walton and Ocean Reeve Publishing
www. lorrainefreespirit.com
www.oceanreeve.com

OCEAN
REEVE
PUBLISHING

Contents

Dedication

I dedicate this book to my daughter Lorraine. It was her dream to write and to see some of her work published. In compiling this book, I hope I have made that dream become a reality.

Acknowledgements

Firstly, I would like to express my extreme gratitude to Ocean Reeve, of Ocean Reeve Publishing, my mentor and friend - I acknowledge with grateful thanks his unerring guidance, expertise, support and motivation. A true Super Hero, and behind every super hero there is a super heroine. Thank you, Vicki Jane Reeve.

In those very early days of compiling Lorraine's story, I was grateful to receive much support and encouragement from friends and family. Two people during that time shone for me. Elizabeth Kyle, thank you so much for your support, advice and hands-on help at the computer. Bronwyn Frazer, a chance meeting at a writer's seminar in Sydney leading to much appreciated advice.

To Professor William McCarthy, for his invaluable advice and support during the early 1980s, for which I will be forever grateful, and for his permission to include his letters in this book.

To Peter Allison, and his sister Lori, and to Peter Lindeman of the Sun Herald Newspaper for their permission to include Karen Allison's article 'Fighting Cancer'.

To Maxwell Swart, Lisa and Ward Lemons, Jacques and Jill MoraMarco – thank you for the love and support you have given Lorraine and myself, then and now. I will be forever grateful to you all.

Lisa Lemons, Denise Hawkins and Suzie Drew, I thank you for your memories of that time in Paris.

I would like to thank my wonderful Beta Readers, some from the early beginnings to those more recently, for their very constructive critique and encouragement - Annabel Norris, Thomas Jones, Dilek Young and Kristina Mitic.

I would also like to thank my editor, Daria Costello. Working from a distance with a novice writer, who was basically compiling a book already written from diary and letters, must have been a unique experience to say the least. I'm so grateful for your expertise and patience.

A huge thank you to my grandsons, Andrew and Lindsay, who have supported and encouraged me throughout this journey. Even though he was on the other side of the country, Andrew was always there to rescue me and manuscript, when I hit a wrong key or sent documents into the unknown.

And last, but by no means least, I acknowledge my daughter, Barbara, without whose encouragement, help and loving support, Lorraine's story would not have been told.

I apologise to those who have been with me over the course of this endeavour whose names I have failed to mention.

Introduction

This book is the story of the last four years of the life of one of my beautiful daughters, Lorraine, told by her through her diary and letters to her sister Barbara and me. It is a true story - a story of life, of love and laughter, faith, happiness, despair, hope and courage, and the many challenges and experiences encountered on life's journey.

On the 3rd of January 1980 my daughters Rainey, twenty-six and Barbie, twenty-three, boarded a KLM flight to Amsterdam, and leaving behind their boyfriends David and Jeff, they departed on the first leg of their adventure of a lifetime. They had always talked of travelling in Europe ... to live and work there, to experience different countries and cultures in everyday life rather than as tourists. Their student exchange experiences reinforced this desire.

Rainey had always dreamed of living in Paris, even during her childhood, and this was to be the beginning of the realisation of that dream.

Through her diary and letters, Rainey has written her own story and compiling it has been a highly emotional journey for me, punctuated by much laughter, wonderful memories and many tears.

Rainey was thoughtful, sensitive and intuitive. She had a great depth of feeling, a wonderful sense of humour, loved life and approached it with enthusiasm. She loved to write, and it was her dream to one day see some of her work published. I hope this book will make her dream become a reality.

This is her story.

Yvonne Walton

Chapter 1

Diary, 25th March 1980

Barbie leaves tonight. We've done our last-minute shopping here in Amsterdam. I've covered all my books I'll need in Paris. Hope I'll get to use them. I'm looking forward to living and working there and settling down.

I keep getting these very strange feelings that everyone will read my diary. Not that I mind – I don't because I think it would be rather fun, but I just get these strange feelings that I'm going to die over here and never see anyone I love again. It's very real. It's like I have a secret no one else knows. But whatever happens, I know I'll be fine, and I want you to know that too. Maybe I'm just feeling fearful or apprehensive. It's strange ... I feel like I'm writing this for someone else to read. Well, read on.

We had a long talk about the end of an era finally rearing its ugly head and making you tear yourself away from it. Quite a conflict; almost as if you are an unwilling victim of circumstance in a realistic and necessarily fateful way. I know that feeling. I've had many such eras already. I feel I'm now on the verge of another; who knows what it will bring. I wonder. I feel sure it will be something intensely traumatic. Not sure which way, though.

But for now, we're back in Amsterdam after three incredible months of travelling. It's so nice to smell the welcoming aroma of Mr

Schroder's hotel … staying in the same place with the same lovely man and his beautiful dog, a Weimaraner named Herta. Mr Schroder serves a wonderful breakfast and sitting in the dining room is like being at a meeting of the League of Nations. It's almost like coming home – so nice to relax into. I love being here.

The weirdest thing happened today. Barbie and I were in the *de Bijenkorf* department store looking at leather purses when a guy came up behind us. "Do you find those very practical?" he asked. And from there I launched into the pros and cons of this purse before realising we were talking to a guy we didn't even know, about a purse we didn't even want. He was a student studying French and photography in Paris. He lives in an apartment that overlooks the *Seine* to *Montmartre* and the *Eiffel Tower* … *and* I have the key to his place in my purse!

He told me I could crash there for two weeks or a day, or however long. He would be back in two weeks on April 15th and "please to stay." It's probably safe, and I'd love to stay, but anyone who gives their keys to a stranger in a department store in Amsterdam has probably given keys to all his friends and other complete strangers. Who knows? Maybe something good will come of it, even if I don't stay there. Although on second thought, I should have my brains brushed for even entertaining the idea of taking that key.

I shouldn't have, after that experience in Paris a few months ago. That should have taught me not to trust anyone again. I had more reason to trust Ari than this guy, and look what happened. But I just thought here was I, this very day, wondering where to stay, and always wanting to be in an apartment in Paris. I'll probably be the only person staying in a sub-starvation place, sharing it with five or ten others while having a key to a free apartment in my purse!

We left on the bus at 4 pm. I couldn't believe Barbie was leaving. Arriving at the airport, she checked in and we went upstairs to have coffee. I just couldn't say much because I was too choked up.

After going through the departure gate, she walked back twice to and from the customs area waving and blowing kisses. I must have been the only person carrying on like it was the arrival bay each time I saw her. At 8 pm I went up to the observation deck, watched the KLM flight take off, and I wept because Barbie was leaving and I too could have been that close to David.

I think I was in shock on the bus, still not truly realising that she had gone. Arriving back in Amsterdam, I went to our favourite brown café and had a hot chocolate and ham and cheese sandwich with our friend, the restaurant's cat. Gave him my ham and he sat in Barbie's chair. I crossed the road to our hotel. Mr Schroder heard me coming up the stairs and asked if Barbie got off okay.

Diary, 26th March 1980

Woke up at 6 am to a cheery, "Good morning lady!" from down the hall.

I managed to come forth with, "Good morning, Mr Schroder," born out of habit at that time in the morning, I'm sure. Got to the station at 7 am and waited for the 7:50 train to Paris.

A very sweet lady helped me on with my bags. The Dutch are beautiful people – so friendly. She reminded me of David's mum, a lovely lady. Hope I'm like that when I'm older. I didn't want to talk to anyone on the train. I felt strange.

I wrote some more of my letter to Barbie. I miss her so much. Slept for about three hours and woke up when the train jerked to a stop in Brussels. With me in the carriage were two Dutch ladies, a Frenchman and a Belgian. The Frenchman offered me a sweet, so I wrote in Barbie's letter, "If this ship crashes, I'll save him first!"

Slept some more, I was so incredibly tired!

The train finally pulled into Paris at *Gare du Nord* ... and then the fun started.

Here, I think I need to give you, the reader, some background and insight, which I will do as best I can throughout.

Rainey was born in Sydney on Mother's Day, Sunday, 10th May 1953, and Barbie on 1st August 1955.

In 1958, I moved with my daughters back to my home town in country New South Wales after leaving my husband, and a very distressing and abusive marriage. I brought the girls up on my own, and the three of us were very close.

In 1971 Rainey completed her Higher School Certificate, with excellent results in all subjects, including French, and gained a scholarship for her chosen degree in Education. She was then selected for the Rotary Student Exchange program, and in 1972 travelled to the United States where she lived for twelve months.

There, she attended a further year of school in Seattle, Washington, and later moved with her second host family to Baltimore, Maryland. During her stay in Seattle, she had the opportunity to work as a teacher's aide in several schools outside her normal school hours. She returned with some wonderful references and experiences; as did Barbie, who was also selected for the Rotary Exchange Program, spending a year in Brazil in 1974.

On her return from the US in 1973, Rainey commenced her Diploma of Education at Mitchell College of Advanced Education in Bathurst, (now Charles Sturt University). She graduated with excellent results in 1976.

For the next four years, she taught at Rosehill Primary School in Sydney. She loved the children and loved teaching. She also loved the sun, the beach, nature, sunsets, her family and friends, and life itself.

During this time, she met David, and they were in a relationship at the time the girls left for Europe. He continued to be an important part of her life.

Diary, 27th March 1980

I knew I would be lonely, but God, not this *alone*! Oh! I cried till I made myself sick and couldn't stop. That's when I got my room in a student hostel without having any proof of being a student. I suppose I *was* a bit suspect. Then when the lady at the desk told me I needed to give her a traveller's cheque, okay, but to *sign*! That was the last straw because the value of the cheque was so much more than the cost of the accommodation. I was so tired, upset, didn't know who I could trust, and threw a tantrum ... told her what I thought, grabbed the pen, signed it, and oh, did I have the poos. She didn't like me, and I don't blame her. No student ID card, no cash, and a tantrum to boot. I suppose I'm lucky to be here.

The room looked very much lived in, but I was too tired to care. I didn't have the energy or the incentive to get my bags from the train station locker, so in time-honoured tradition, I fell into bed and slept in my clothes.

I'd never felt so hopelessly alone. God, how I wanted to ring David. I was too sick to go out, even if I *did* have the cash. I know he said to call collect, but under the circumstances of his last angry call, I couldn't. How I wanted to, so much. If ever there was a time it was last night. I felt hopelessly alone.

Crawled into bed at about 5 pm and woke in a semi-conscious state to a knock on the door at 8 pm. The guy who rents the room permanently wanted to get his books. Nice guy – a student who is currently on holidays. Then I went back to sleep ... a most confusing sleep. Couldn't work out where I was, or whether I was alone or not.

Woke early today and didn't even have to get dressed! Arrived at the breakfast table and asked, "What's the procedure?" even before I said *bonjour*. How rude!

It was a lovely breakfast with a bottomless pot of coffee, and I kept a bread roll to have for lunch.

I must be some weird individual to do this on my own. That's what I thought last night when I was so upset. I thought, *What the hell am*

I doing here? I want out ... home. Well, thank God for a new day and for the sunrise. It's true – things *do* look better in the morning. They couldn't have looked much worse than last night, I can tell you.

After breakfast I went to the train station to collect my bags and managed to talk to the taxi driver in my high school French the whole way. That was good. He was surprised that I didn't know anyone here in Paris.

I came back, showered and dressed ready for interviews with some prospective families for *au pair* , then rang Mum and Barbie from the post office. I needed that.

Found my way to *Alliance Française* and enrolled. I start French classes on Monday 31st March. Found out a six-month working visa is needed even to *au pair*. I hope I can get one tomorrow... and I must ring David and send a telegram for his birthday. Then I did some grocery shopping because in this room you can cook yourself ... no, not yourself ... the food. Tonight, I'm writing, listening to music, saying a big prayer that the embassy people will be kind to me tomorrow, and having an early night.

Diary, 28th March 1980

As I write I'm sitting in a little restaurant near the Opera Metro Station and American Express to rest my feet. These boots are killing me.

I do so hope I can work here. I knew I needed a visa to work but didn't think I needed one to be an *au pair*. I guess you do if you get a job through agencies like *Alliance Française*, but maybe I'm meant to get one outside of them.

I can stay here for three months or for ages, but not to work. God how I need the money! Maybe that employment agency contact will have one for me. I hope so. Maybe she knows a family who needs an *au pair*.

Today I've been to no end of trouble to visit the Australian Embassy, Prefecture of Police and the Department of Foreign Affairs for them all to say *no way* to a six-month working visa – my key to legal work. Not just *legal* work, but the *choice* of work. Anyway, when the guy in the Department of Foreign Affairs told me no, it was the last straw. I burst into tears and had to make a quick exit. I mean, I knew I didn't have a visa, and I couldn't get one but figured if I went and made my final plea, there may be a chance. It was just that I'd run around all day going to places on the Metro – some of the places had changed addresses, and I was tired - no, exhausted, and I just cried. I'm itching to start working and to settle in properly. Maybe I'll have to go through a back door somewhere. Anyway, I'm still hopeful. I'll keep looking, and try not to be as upset as I was today when they all said no. It's just that it has always been my dream and goal to live and work here; even while I was at school. To have it threatened at this point would be devastating.

So here I am at the restaurant. It's been raining for two days now. I bought Easter cards for Barbie and Jeff and David and will post them tomorrow. I wrote and told David how I was looking forward to calling him. I hope it's a nice call, don't think I could cope with another call like the last one.

I usually try to avoid the subject, or even thinking about David … not always but often, because it hurts terribly. At least when Barbie is sad it's a definite quantity to be sad about, but with us (David and me) it's so indefinite, but with the same feeling of caring. I suppose I'm pretty confused really, and that doesn't reduce the feeling to any lesser degree – just the validity. But who's to say what feelings are valid and what are invalid? No … I think it's simply a matter of being true to yourself in terms of feeling, acting and valuing. I know David wanted me to go home with Barbie. He was so angry when I told him on our last phone call that I'd be staying longer.

"Well, goodbye and have a good trip, and don't you expect me to be waiting here with open arms when you *do* decide to come home!" he'd said.

I know he's hurt and angry that I'm not going home, but he knows how much I want to live and work here. How am I supposed to cater for my need in staying here? I'm trying to be fair and trying to be true to myself in doing this, and I want him to understand that I must. I want him to understand that he must give me this time before we can move on and continue our journey together. Perhaps it would be different if we were engaged, but time still does things without you being considered, even though you are given a choice that may be yours if you reach out and take it.

At about 6 pm I went up to *Montmartre* to *Sacré-Coeur* when it was still light and came out of the church about 8 pm. It was beautiful; so nice not to go there just to 'ave a look' like tourists do. I went there to sit and pray and think.

Before I went inside the church, I was standing at the lookout. It's very high, overlooking the city, and the view from there must be the most spectacular in all of Paris. It looks more like an artist's impression on canvas. And the light! The light that surrounds this city is mystical, but then again, almost tangible. It's so completely different to any other place I've seen. No wonder Paris is called the "City of Light." I think this is what drew so many of the old master painters to Paris.

The clouds were so low and moving so fast. Parisian skies are hard to describe. It was so beautiful, and I was inspired to write about Time in relation to those clouds, so I wrote a poem right there and then in about five minutes. Then I went into the church through the little door with the sign that read, 'Enter here only if you want to pray.' I wanted to feel apart from the visitors. I know it doesn't matter *where* you pray, but it seemed better there.

I love going there, even though I'm not Catholic; not for the ceremony of it all, but for the simple communion with God. I find that inexplicably beautiful. Doctrine ... yes, I have doctrine ... taught beliefs. In fact everyone does, depending on the direction of their upbringing. That differs mostly from person to person, religion to religion, but the one thing that holds us together is our faith. No one can dispute what you have inside you – that's a very personal thing between you and your God.

I cried, I prayed, I thought, and I lit a candle for David. It was dark when I came outside. I went to the post office on *Rue de Louvre, Metro Louvre*, and called David for his birthday. And yes, it was a gentle call. Then I came home.

Clouds

The clouds are so low you can all but reach out
To touch their elusive silence
And like time, their intangibility is stunningly visible.
Oh, to be able to grasp and hold their beauty
For a time,
Forever.
Love and beauty can never be
Strong enough to hold their timeless impetuosity

- Lorraine, 1980

Letter, 28th March 1980

Dear Mum,

I've now officially joined the thriving ranks of impoverished students. It's so expensive to live in Paris, and I still don't have a job. I really do love it here. Never thought I would fall in love with a city so much. I can find my way around well and ask for things, etc., so the language doesn't bother me for day to day living. I even held a conversation with a taxi driver the other day when I enrolled with *Alliance Française*.

Now for the bad news. I knew you had to have a six-month working visa to be able to work here. I had originally thought about working in

England, remember, but changed my mind. If I'd known, I would have applied for a French working visa before leaving, just in case; and no, you can't get one for me as you have to apply in person in your own country.

Today I went to the Australian Embassy, Prefecture of Police, and the Department of Foreign Affairs and they all told me what I just told you, so I have to go through a back door somewhere. But I'm still hopeful. I'm ready to start working and settling in properly.

Now let me tell you about my room here at the student hostel. I know I like to picture someone in a place … not just have an idea of what they're doing. This place is for full-time students. Everyone here studies something full time, so when I'm asked, 'What do you study?' I suddenly become a student teacher from Australia on leave. I have to remember to write 'student' on papers that may bounce back too.

My room belongs to a guy who lives here all year-round, (he's currently on holidays) so as opposed to other temporary bare rooms, this one has all the mod cons like radio, coffee-making facilities, bookcase crammed with books, and walls crammed with posters. There's a desk under the window complete with reading lamp, and carpet on the floor. It's a private room with unlimited free hot showers. The guy is very nice; I've met him several times. He just knocked on the door and said, "I suppose you notice that I sleep on a board. I have a bad back. You can take it out if you like."

I felt like saying, 'You better believe it. That bed is not a bed; it's concrete!'

When he left, I checked it out – pulling it out with brute strength. Do you know what he had under the mattress? A bloody two-inch-thick wooden door! I couldn't believe it! Well, I could really, I've been trying to sleep on it! So, I'm standing in the middle of the room holding this door, and wondering where the hell I was going to put it. It's huge! I was laughing because it was so funny, trying to find somewhere to store it. It's longer than the bed because now the mattress is flopping over the end. No wonder he has a bad back! I finally wedged it against the wall at the head of the bed. Hope it stays there. I have visions of it falling and squashing me in the middle of the night.

Breakfast here is a bottomless pot of coffee and huge bread rolls that, for me, double as lunch. Pretty good for Paris if you ask me. I mean even to sleep in the park you have to buy a newspaper, and that costs eighty cents!

These last few days have been go, go, go. Admin things like finding this place, enrolling at *Alliance*, the visa drama, looking for a job, and incidentals. The days are beginning to have no name – just a continuum of time, day and night. This morning when I woke, my first task was to find out what day it was. No one at breakfast seemed to want to come forth with any hints, so I spared myself the embarrassment of asking, and bought a newspaper. Yes, I do believe it's Friday, so the papers say. The alternative was, "Excuse me, do you have the time, and can you also tell me what day it is?" and, "No, I don't wear a name tag."

I can hear Jeff saying, 'My God, no wonder she hasn't got a job yet.'

About jobs … with no visa, and the few channels I have open to me (i.e., agencies that require you to have that six-month working visa), I had to look for another plan of attack. Now it's a matter of *who* I know. I went through my diary and sifted out all the people and acquaintances I knew in Paris, and the grand total came to four; all of whom Barbie and I had met, ever so briefly, while travelling during the last three and a half months:

1. *The Hotel des Balcones* Manager and Manageress
2. The hairdresser we met at the Vidal Sassoon training salon in London
3. The Dutch lady's sister at the employment office in Amsterdam (I don't know her, but I soon will)
4. Randy Garret (who seems to have his finger on the pulse of Paris)

I've met some of them only once, some never. Not to worry, I can't afford to have any class in my predicament. So, I donned my best clothes and shoes and made a personal visit to all. No class, heaps of flair, but definitely no class. I figure I have to reach out and grab because no one here is going to come to me.

Well, Randy wasn't in his den. He lives in the basement of American Express and is rather *au fait* (just practising my French) with all the legal and not so legal deals going around town. Now *there's* another story for later.

Then I went to the hairdressing salon, which would be the French salon of your dreams. This lady, Vivienne, had cut Barbie's hair in London at the Vidal Sassoon College for hairdressers. Barbie knew her, I didn't really, but I was getting desperate. She was pleased to see me and called her husband over to introduce me. She's so sweet. Their salon is out of this world … all white with flowers everywhere, and all the staff dress in white. She even said, "Why don't you let me wash and trim your hair for free, just as a souvenir?"

Guess where I'll be going back to? She is lovely. I gave her Barbie's regards, told her about my situation, and she asked, "Would you be interested in teaching English to adults at the Berlitz School of Language?" Inside I was ecstatic!

I managed a very dignified and positive, "Yes, I would be most interested." It almost killed me to remain composed.

Vivienne is a friend of the principal of the school. She told me they only have French teachers of English and would welcome a native speaker. But the visa still worries me. The money would be very good, but I don't know. I should have applied for a visa before I left, but then I had every intention of working in England, remember? I couldn't stand working in England now; I'd go mental. Even if worst comes to worst, I'm going to offer my services as an aid in conversational practice classes for free, just as a 'foot in the door.' I know I'd enjoy it, and I would meet people too.

So, you must be anxious to know what happens there. Not half as anxious as I am! In positive anticipation, I went to *Saint-Germain* post office and made copies of all my references. Now is when I need to have my teaching diploma with me. I can fake it; I've had heaps of practice recently, but hope so much that something good comes of it.

I also have another contact given to me by the Irish girl - the travel agent who Barbie and I had met on the train to Italy.

This morning it's a Catholic organisation. In my best French on the phone, I explained then went to see them. They are an *au pair* aid organisation – very prim and strict but very nice. They wanted to know the ins and outs of how I came to find them – ME, not even a Catholic! One of their first questions was, "Are you a Catholic?"

I felt like saying, 'No, I'm an atheist,' but because I had my best clothes on, I had to play ladies too. I've left my name and phone number and feel sure they'll call. I think they thought I was okay for a Protestant. Told them I had just come from visiting an elementary school down the road as I was a teacher, etc.

I had. I invited myself in because the door was open, and spoke to the teachers in my best French. I'm sure my best high school French has a heavy accent and questionable grammar. I must sound like that all the time. But they understood me ... at least I think they did. Maybe they just nodded their heads in polite amazement that the words, let alone the structure of it all, could possibly fall out of anyone's mouth like that. They were so nice. I left my name with them, and I hope they'll call. I hope someone can help me.

Haven't managed to get to the *Hotel des Balcones* yet but I was thinking that wasn't bad going for only knowing four people in Paris, was it? I was happy with the success of my day.

Lectures at *Alliance* start on Monday 31st for two hours per day. What I see as being ideal, (hope I'm not dreaming too much) is *au pair* five hours a day, lectures two hours a day, and work at the Berlitz language school. That's heavy considering I have my acupuncture to read, study, and review, and my French class homework and study. I *have* to because *Alliance* costs $65 a month and I want to do it well. I'd also like to *live* somewhere in there.

I find it amazing to think that most of the events that led me to these contacts happened outside France before I even got here. The way I see it is, the past is forever working towards a *related* something in the future. I mean things just don't happen without rhyme or reason. It's amazing, isn't it, that the past can be so incredibly in touch with the future. I tend to think that there's no such thing as 'past' or 'future' *per se*; it's almost as if everything has already happened at once, but for the sake of living, it's all just been spaced out in time somehow.

All very illogical I'm sure, but I'm very wrapped up in Time as a subject. Most of my poems have been about Time. I'm glad you liked the last one. It's nice when someone gets a little pleasure or meaning out of something I wrote. It's so easy to be subjective and insular where the meaning is so totally related to the writer, and so un-meaningful to all else.

Now I've got that little outburst out of my system …

I also find my English spelling is becoming progressively worse. I have to stop, think, and say the word to get the sounds in some sort of order on paper. Very strange … then again, what else can you expect from someone who doesn't know what day it is?

This evening I went up to *Sacré-Coeur* again. It was lovely. I just love going there. I'll go at Easter too, I think. That's where I'll celebrate all the special occasions like birthdays, etc. I know I'm a bit crazy, but I feel closer to home when I'm there.

It must be lovely to see Barbie. It was better for her that she went home. Her place isn't over here; I know that now. She wouldn't enjoy it at all without Jeff. But I do miss her so much.

I was constantly amazed at the serendipity of how Rainey's needs were met in the way of accommodation, contacts and unexpected events during her early days in Paris. She achieved much in that time due to her positive attitude, belief and determination. So many things just seemed to fall into place, though not without some varying degrees of stress and pressure.

Letter, 31st March 1980

Dearest Barbie and Mum,

Guess who I saw in the subway today Barbie? Christopher, the busker we met in the metro and who we had invited for coffee. I heard this singing that sounded familiar, so I just stood by until he finished his song. He has a fantastic voice. Then I asked, "Do you remember me?"

He didn't straight-away, as I had worn a head scarf that day; then he actually remembered. He asked about you and what we had done on our travels, and if we had visited his friend in Amsterdam at the address he had given us. No, he didn't ask, he said, "You didn't visit my friend, did you? I knew you wouldn't."

He lives with his girlfriend and invited me to their house for dinner, which was nice. He also suggested I put signs up at the universities in both French and English, for English tutoring, private lessons and/or group lessons, so I'll do that tomorrow.

Went to see Mr and Mrs '*Hotel des Balcones*', who were very nice; they remembered me (the infamous one) and took my phone number and address.

Then I went over to the Luxembourg Gardens across the road from where I live. Being there is just like walking through a painting. They are so beautiful now in the spring. But it was cold and started to rain, so I left and will come back on a sunny day.

After leaving the gardens, I went to *Jeu de Paume* in the *Tuileries Gardens,* a little *musée d'art* near the *Louvre* … a wonderful place! You know I'm not an avid lover of art, but to go into these places to see the originals of the greats – Renoir, Monet, Gauguin, Van Gough, Toulouse-Lautrec – it's quite breathtaking. The paintings are so beautiful; you just wonder what sort of talented, creative mind could capture a thought or a vision and place it so perfectly and so beautifully on canvas. I was there for about two hours. Kept saying to myself, *I'll just go back one more time and have a last look at that one,* so it was ages before I left. It's only a very small place, two floors, but fantastic.

I can remember as a little girl at the infants' school in Dubbo; there was a painting on the wall that I just loved to look at … that one of Renoir's - a garden scene, bright and happy. I loved that painting, and to see the original was a strange feeling indeed.

On my way to *Jeu de Paume,* I was fined twenty francs for riding in the wrong metro carriage. I couldn't believe it! The controllers (all ladies) were out in force on Saturday, briskly and almost coldly going through their paces of physically escorting people off the train! As they came into my carriage, the number of people who bolted for the door was unreal. But the doors lock automatically, remember? I figured I'd be okay because I had my ticket and thought it was all quite amusing watching people dashing for the locked doors, and watching others being removed and presented with their fines – until we got to the next stop where, on having my ticket checked I was also physically escorted off the train and had to pay the fine.

I felt like a criminal and was so upset. Didn't think it was very funny then, I can tell you! Apparently, (I didn't know this) the carnet of ten tickets, which 90% of the people buy, is for *second* class travel. There are always a couple of carriages dispersed through the train that carry the No 1 (second class is not numbered). So, guess who watches what carriage she travels in now?

That night I came home and cooked tea in the community kitchen with everyone else. I have two special friends here. One is a Mexican guy, Anton, a real scream; we get on very well. Another guy, Gabriel from the Dominican Republic, helps me with my French. He's a student at the Sorbonne. We ate tea together then went to a soiree where I met and talked with so many people. The punch was red wine and orange – just up my alley! Had a great evening and got to bed at 2 am. I do like staying here; it's just like a home away from home.

The next morning I was supposed to go to the flea market at the end of *Porte de Clignancourt* with Anton and Gabriel, but I didn't surface until 11:30 so I went to the *Georges Pompidou* Centre. We should have gone there Barbie, it's incredible! Outside, the buskers have to be seen to be believed. Inside there are musées d'art, films, plays, expositions, a library and an incredibly lovely view from the top. It's open from 10 am to 10 pm.

I arrived there at 1 pm and left at 9:30 pm. The Salvador Dali Exhibit was incredible! I was so amazed and thrilled when I read about the film that he and Walt Disney were to make, a surrealist film about what time does to love – just what I write about. It's said they had a falling out, so only a short segment was recorded. What a shame, but knowing Dali's work, I probably wouldn't have been able to understand it anyway.

Thought I'd go to the top and work my way down; got half way down after four hours of looking at everything. Got to the library and stayed there for the next three hours, sifting out books on acupuncture. I read one through and took heaps of notes. It was so interesting; it was a layman's book with many wonderful explanations that clarify so much. I've been wondering when I'll be able to complete my acupuncture course. Maybe I could complete it here.

Anyway, this was one of those rare occasions when I'd not taken any note paper with me. All I had were the paper bags from my postcard purchases. The French girl and her boyfriend sitting opposite kept looking at me (between their amorous kisses) as I wrote notes on my brown paper bags. I think it got all too much for her because she offered me some of her paper.

I have this habit of going somewhere in the daytime and becoming so immersed in my surroundings that it is night when I come out and I don't know where the time has gone! Had tea – boiled eggs which my friend Anton cooked with some of his beans, bread, pâté, orange and milk. What a mixture! Had a late night again – sat up talking and laughing with Gabriel. I want to get up early tomorrow so I can find my lecture room at *Alliance Française* before the class starts.

Next day now and today I went to my first French class. It was great. I loved it! I feel sorry for those who've had no grounding in structure, grammar and pronunciation. It really helps me. I understand it very well so far. I've just done an hour review of the lesson. I've been speaking French into the cassette recorder. The first try I had might have been too much for the little recorder. It collapsed all over my desk in a little heap and shouted, "Please! Why me? No more!"

I've improved a little now. I think it just humours me. It has its little chuckles.

My lectures are from 10:30 am to 12:30 pm. I barged into the wrong class this morning (true to form), and the teacher invited me to stay. I was in another class, more advanced than mine, for half an hour before my class started. The teacher asked one guy a question in French (it's all in French), and the poor fellow didn't know the answer. Then the teacher looked at me and raised his eyebrows. I took the cue and answered it in French, at which point he started jumping up and down on the spot and yelling in French – very dynamic, not cranky, just dynamic.

"She's been here ten minutes, and she knows. What's wrong with you?"

At that stage, I was wishing I had waited outside.

So my high school French is an incredible help. The method here is oral – conversational, and even though the students can say it, half of them, or most, don't know what it looks like on paper or the structure. Fortunately, I have that advantage.

Tuesday 1ˢᵗ April

My accommodation here is like a house full of family. I'm so glad I didn't take that apartment offered in Amsterdam - I wouldn't have met so many nice people. I'll be sad to leave here when I find a job. At the moment I have so many channels open to me to find work. It's quite amazing. Every day incredible things happen – unexpected things. I told you about the hairdresser with that opportunity to teach at the Berlitz School; I'll see her tomorrow.

You might say I got waylaid a little today – had a wonderful day!

Went to collect my mail from American Express and who should be there propping up the client's mail counter but Randy Garret, an American ex-pat who has made Paris his home. He's the guy who told us to "go out and live life" while we were here, and who gave me a lot of contacts to follow up. During our conversation when we first met him in January, I remember he had said to us, "So, you have someone at home? Are you going to say, 'No, all I want is a purely platonic relationship'? You could be missing out on a worthy friendship or experience for someone at home who will be there if it's right when you get home. Ride with the wind … go with the tide … go with your feelings … with discretion of course, and live life to the full, with respect to yourself and others."

That seemed like okay advice.

Well, I was standing there with a grin from ear to ear. It was so good to see him. He kept staring at me. "Do I know you?" he asked. When I began speaking, he said, "Of course! What have you done to your hair? You look so chic!"

When we first met Randy in January, my hair was very long. Now it's short, all one length and in a pageboy style. I love the new cut Vivienne at the salon has given me.

Randy and I talked for an hour over coffee in a little sidewalk café. He wanted to know what you and I had been doing on our travels Barbie, and gave me more helpful advice on job hunting and contacts. He told me what I already knew.

"You don't need any visa," he said. "You can do it. You have to *sell* yourself to the right contacts. Make special note of your qualifications to all, dress well for the interview, be … how do you say … confident, well presented, and make them think, 'Here's a special lady – good profession, etc.' and visa or no visa, if they want you they will make provision. You must *sell* yourself, of course. I know you can do it."

I've been putting my best foot forward, as it were. He seems very cluey.

We were deep in conversation when we heard an Australian voice at the next table ask, "Do you have any sausages and gravy?" In a sidewalk café in Paris! I almost fell apart laughing.

"My God - who said that?" asked Randy.

That's how we met this couple. The lady was ready to leave Paris; she hated it. She was a nervous wreck, a real case. Her husband was a high school teacher – both very nice. She was a compulsive worrier and told me she was on valium – just couldn't cope and believed she was going to fall apart. I would venture to say that she was on the way to a nervous breakdown. After a while, Randy and I decided we should go and eat. We invited them to join us, and they happily agreed.

Remember the restaurant Randy had invited us to, Barbie? Well, that's where we went. It's like walking onto the set of an old movie … so old, so beautiful, *and* so cheap! In the early days, some of the restaurants in Paris didn't supply cutlery. The regulars brought their own and kept them in little boxes in the wall for when they would return, and the boxes are still there today!

Anyway, on the way to the restaurant I talked to this lady, Margaret, about worry and she said, "You are very understanding. You know exactly how I feel – I can't believe it – I'm so glad someone understands."

She really couldn't believe it and said it made her feel so much better to talk to me. Said I was a real tonic. I told her of some things to do to help herself – relaxing things, positive thinking, etc. And Randy… well, you know what he's like Barbie. They couldn't believe him.

We had a wonderful time. They had eaten, but came anyway. Randy talked to the guy the whole way to the restaurant, and I talked to Margaret, who couldn't believe I was here in Paris on my own.

Well, as they had already eaten, she just ordered an entrée and when the waiter came to ask for our main meal, Margaret (and I'm serious) almost fell apart because she thought she had to order a main course. The waiter kept pressing her for her order, and she really didn't know what to do, so I said to her, "Margaret, don't worry, just don't worry. The worst they can do is pick you up and throw you out of the restaurant, and they won't do that. Besides, if they did, Randy would have them plastered all over the walls in one hit." Randy laughingly agreed.

She looked at her husband and said, "Aren't they wonderful? They cope so well."

We had a great time, and they enjoyed it. We talked about the locals, and Randy agreed that when the French are put out, you have never seen or can't imagine how cold they can be, so you either ignore them or stand up for yourself.

I couldn't believe this lady – worry and fear totally controlled her; she told me it just engulfed her. We had a good talk, and she said we had saved her day. Randy had them in disbelief with his stories; they were so "go by every rule in the book, regardless." After lunch, she was a completely different person.

When I asked, "Now what will you do this afternoon?" She replied with a wave of her hand.

"Whatever - who cares!"

Diary, 2nd April 1980

Today I went again to *Alliance Française*, then to the American Église to see about au pair work. They have a notice board full of ads for live-in au pair positions. I made a list of names, phoned some, and made an appointment for 6 pm with a couple at *Ponte d'Auteuil* at their apartment.

First, I went home to change and freshen up for the appointment. On the way I met a friend, and we sat for an hour over coffee in *Le Café de l'Odéon* on the corner. That cafe has a lovely, lively atmosphere that reminds you of what Paris is all about. Then on to the appointment.

The other *au pair* was there, but I don't know – I'm not sure. Think I could get a better job, like teaching. This one might be too restrictive. I'll ring them tomorrow. Maybe they'll say no. I don't mind … sort of hope they do. They have high expectations. Working five to six hours a day for $15 a week, plus lodging ... I can't save on that, so I think I must wait. I feel it. Yes, I must, and trust that I get a better job.

I got home and talked with my friend Gabriel. Then we were ousted from the kitchen, so we sat on the stairs and talked 'til 2 am.

Diary, 3rd April 1980

Went again to *Alliance Française* then to see my friend Andrea for lunch and we had arranged to meet another girl for coffee. Later, I went to

American Express to cash a cheque for Easter. I did some shopping at *Uniprix*, met up with two people from the hostel, and then went home.

As I was entering the front door, a man suddenly came up behind me and told me not to carry those parcels like that. He helped me carry them, and suddenly he was inside on the stairs – where I entertain all my men friends, it seems. Well, I'm going to have coffee with him tomorrow! *Je ne sais pas!*

Tonight, I have to write my resume for work, on Saturday I'm going out with some friends to walk in the gardens, on Sunday I'll meet up with Randy, and tomorrow I'll have coffee with Henri, the parcel guy.

Diary, 4th April 1980

Well, today wasn't my day. I went to sleep at 2 am after talking with Gabrielle and woke late this morning for *Alliance*. I then caught the wrong metro in *Châtelet* and to top it all off, I couldn't concentrate in class. The teacher always asks me questions.

I met Henri at the *Café Grande Cluny* at 2 pm. He was waiting. We talked for four hours over coffee – the proverbial rendezvous. I just knew he was married, but I didn't ask, even when he asked me if I was. He's a maths teacher and is married with two boys, aged twelve and ten. My God, later he told me all about his marriage, and I still don't know whether his situation is as he says it is. I don't believe it, I just don't. It just doesn't gel with me. I like him, but with some reservation.

"Same place, same time," he said, and told me to think about what he said and that he would be waiting in the café at 4 pm.

"So, you like adventure?"

"Yes, but that's not why I'm here with you."

Venice would be wonderful. Good story for a movie, great setting. Someone should take it up … took it up. I write in riddles because I think I know my diary will be read in my absence. I've got nothing to hide and never do anything to be ashamed of, but some things are very hard to explain.

Anyway, here I am, two weeks in Paris but it feels so much longer.

Diary, 5th April 1980

At 4 pm today I met Henri again at *Grand Cluny Café* where he was waiting. We had coffee. He looked different in jeans. I don't believe this, I just don't, don't, don't. Seeing a married man? *Mon Dieu - c'est pas possible.*

We drove to *Versailles* and spent time walking through the gardens. Saw the small *Trianon* palace. It was wonderful, so wonderful. It was a bit like a movie set but very real. We kept walking for a long time until it was dark, crossed moats, ponds, fences, walls, and finally had to scale the huge front gate!

About Henri – it's almost as if he is two people. Unsure, almost clumsy, timid, and then frightfully mature like a father. We had dinner at a little restaurant in *Versailles.*

He told me, "Lorraine, choose carefully a husband. You need a father in a husband, strong enough to support you psychologically, then for the father portion to go away and then remain the husband." And I thought I was the strong one.

He said about David that two years together is more than enough time to be sure of a relationship and you can't leave if you love. Maybe he's right ... maybe not.

We drove back in comfortable silence, went to a couple of jazz clubs – great music – and then he dropped me home.

A note to you, the Reader; you may find some repetition as you are reading. As Rainey tells her story through diary and letters, I have omitted parts that are repetitious, but she speaks more freely in her diary. There, she is more open, and I feel that including both letter and diary in these instances is necessary for the reader to truly understand her thoughts.

Letter, 6th April 1980

Dear Mum and Barbie,

Now, where to start? I've been running around after jobs all week. You know I've been a lady of leisure for the past four months, and honestly don't know how I'm going to handle work. I mean, I'm really looking forward to working, but I'm not sure about *au pair*.

I had another offer of an *au pair* position. Went for the interview and they wanted me for six hours per day (sometimes longer), with occasional evening babysitting during the week, and they ask an occasional day on weekends. I would do all housework and take care of a two-year-old. Had visions of being shut away, with little money and no time. They had high expectations and wanted me to stay for six months, so again it was 'no thank you.' I'm trying for a job that pays. It's very hard, but I have contacts now. I'm writing letters in answer to ads and have some people looking out for me too.

Had a lovely week last week; kept running into people I know from the student house and we would end up having coffee, sitting for ages in those wonderful sidewalk cafes, talking and watching the passing parade. The weather is still crisp and fresh, and everything is blooming or about to. Spring in Paris is just beautiful. Honestly, the clichés about Paris in the spring aren't just clichés, they're actually true.

Just now I'm waiting in my room for my friend Anton, and we'll go over to the *Luxembourg Gardens* to study our French. It's beautiful there.

You would never believe yesterday ... a wonderful day. I have a lot of friends here, it's nice, but I also like to be by myself if you know what I mean – I don't like being suffocated. Anyway, I had coffee with Henri near the *Musée de Cluny*. Do you remember, Barbie? It was across the road from where we had our first meal in Paris. From there we went to *Versailles* – not into the palace but walking in the palace gardens. Oh, they are a picture – I wish so much we could have gone there together.

We drove to *Versailles*, arriving quite late in the afternoon and became so engrossed walking around the gardens, palaces and pavilions there. They have to be seen to be believed. Oh, so gorgeous!

By the time we were to leave it was twilight, it was magical … like walking up to the *Heidelberg* Castle at night. Remember that? Yesterday I felt like I'd been back in time.

We were in there so long that the gates had been closed and we were locked in. To get out we climbed walls, contorted ourselves around fences and puddled through moats and ponds. It was such fun and so beautiful to be there at that time of the evening. We left from the front of the palace and had to scale over those huge wrought iron gates. My God, I'm sure I could climb anything now!

Now Tuesday 8th

My days are cram-packed between lectures, study, looking for work and meeting and talking with friends. I've met a lot of great people staying at this hostel.

Actually, what I love is *not* being a tourist in Paris. It's so nice. Yesterday a group of us from the student house went to the *Bois de Boulogne*. It's a wonderful place at the end of one of the metro lines on the very outskirts of Paris. It's huge – 850 acres of beautiful woodland with waterfalls, ponds, streams, lakes and swans – the essence of spring. Families, complete with their dogs, were boating on the lakes (the French take their dogs everywhere). It was so relaxing.

These woods were originally a hiding place for bandits in the early days and later became a hunting ground for the kings and the aristocracy. The Duke of Windsor and his wife, Wallace Simpson, lived in the *Bois de Boulogne* in the Villa Windsor, and it's where they both died.

We just walked and talked and sat and laughed. Quite frankly, the French seem a lot more sophisticated than Australians. That's not necessarily either good or bad, but they are very different. Then that night I went with two friends (a German girl and an Italian guy) to the movies. We saw *Kramer vs Kramer* – wonderful movie, you must see it. It was in French with no subtitles, but strangely enough, I managed.

It's rather exciting; it's all coming back to me – the French language I mean. It's all in my head, and I can follow conversations well enough now to understand most and also speak a little. It's weird; when I first arrived here almost three weeks ago, I barely knew enough to get a room, but now I know and understand so much more.

I really enjoy my classes at *Alliance Française*. I go every day, of course, buy the paper on the way to the lectures and scan it on the metro. This morning I found something! "English Sales Assistant Wanted."

After the lesson I went home, changed and donned my good gear. It's a French perfumery. There are two shops, one near the Opera and the other near American Express, and they want someone for their American tourist clientele. They gave me the third degree, and asked me back tomorrow to watch me work and be interviewed by the manager! Have to rustle up a few 'let's play ladies' manners between now and then.

I do need a job with a wage – it would be impossible to live here otherwise. *Au pair* would be okay, but I can't survive economically on $15 a week here in Paris and save for other things. I'd have to work two jobs, and I wouldn't have much time for anything else. So, I look now for a regular job.

I've also written letters to language centres that require your whole educational history. It's amazing what one can concoct with a little imagination! Well, now I wait, and tomorrow when I go for the interview, I must remember to 'ave me best manners.'

It's now April 13th and this letter has taken ages to write. I'm having a lovely time and ... *I have the job*! Yes, I'm working at the French Perfumery, Eden! They also sell leather bags, suede, beautiful scarves, but mainly French perfume. It's a very classy and elegant shop about three minutes' walk from the Opera.

The five girls working there look like they've just stepped out of *Vogue* magazine, especially Caroline on the make-up counter. We are required to be well groomed and well dressed. The manager told me that I have the manner, the looks, and all else will come with experience. Oh, the perfumes are wonderful. We were each given a bottle on Saturday –

we could choose whichever one we wanted. I chose *Vivre* and received a huge spray bottle. I really enjoy selling perfumes.

Fifty percent of their clientele are the *haute couture de Paris* (classy French ladies), and the others are mostly English and American tourists. I work with the English-speaking clientele. All the girls in the shop speak French to each other and to me, so I'm getting plenty of practice there too.

My lectures at *Alliance* are from 8:30 to 10:30 am, and from there I go straight to work at 11 am to 6 pm. It's great!

In the afternoon, we have aperitifs – drinks, salami, olives and cheese. I have to keep practising my elegance because the shop, Eden, is *très chic* and everything for their clientele must be beautifully gift wrapped. So now I get $130 per week, plus my stock of French perfumes. I can live comfortably on that. With *au pair* work I would have been getting $15 per week, plus lodgings.

My friends at the student house are stunned that I have a well-paying job and no visa. They all say it's impossible, but I just *knew* I could find one and I did! The manager doesn't require you to have a visa, thank God. I didn't tell at the interview, and he didn't ask. Later I think I can slip into a teaching position when I have a little more French. This job means I have no preparation to do after hours, so I have time for French study and going out socially.

I told you about Henri. He's the one I went to *Versailles* with. Since then we've been to *Chartres* to see the beautiful 12th-century cathedral and to *Rouen* where they burnt *Jean d' Arc* at the stake. She was only nineteen. We walked around the towns; the French countryside is lovely, the buildings there so quaint and so old.

The other day I had lectures from 8:30 to 10:30 am and then worked from 11 am to 7 pm. Met Henri in a café on my way home from work as planned and I was absolutely exhausted ... so tired. So instead of going outside of Paris, which is a nice change of pace, we sat for a long time over coffee just to relax and rest.

Wow, a week has passed and its Sunday, my day of rest, and believe me I deserve it. It's been 'go, go, go' looking for work ever since I arrived here. I go out a lot with people from this hostel, attend my French lectures, study, work at Eden, and I see Henri a little too. I'm also doing two extra night classes at *Alliance* with two friends from the student house.

Today I slept till Anton knocked on my door, so got up and we went over to the gardens to study. The sun was lovely; we just sat and relaxed. I'll do something tonight; don't know what … might go for a walk. It stays light now until 9 pm with daylight saving.

I haven't been to collect mail for about five days. By the time I finish work the American Express office is closed, so I must see if I can hurry and go before work. It's hard, because I don't leave the *Alliance* till 10:30 am. With the metro it's quick, but I think I can find a quicker way by studying the metro map.

I'm so excited that you'll be coming over. We'll have to plan your trip. There are so many places I want you to see. I have this job until the end of summer and seeing that good jobs are so few and far between (especially the well-paying ones) I want to stay there for as long as possible. I can leave whenever I want I suppose, but I need the money and I want to settle for a while. Not to mention how much I'm enjoying it. So why don't you come over in about three or four months? It wouldn't be so good to come when I was working as you would be stuck in Paris by yourself. I'll leave the job in about four or five months so that when you come over, we can travel. May as well make the most of it and not be limited just to Paris, as lovely as it is, so I think that's better.

There are not enough hours in the day for me. I had to work yesterday, Saturday, as there are squillions of tourists now. Eden is an incredibly classy shop, and you always have to look glamorous. I try hard. The other day the manager told me I looked "a million dollars," so that was encouraging. All the Australians who come into the shop want to know how I got such a lovely job. I'm still trying to work that one out myself. There was a couple from Taree in the shop the other day. The Aussie accent sounds so funny to me now. When I hear it, I think, *My God, do I sound like that?*

The manager told me that Mrs Nixon, President Nixon's wife, does her perfume shopping here when she comes to Paris, and proudly showed me the photo. Very classy! I'm familiar with the French currency and giving change too. The shop has its own cashier on the till, so we just hand the docket to her, but we have to count the change back and work out the difference in English, American and Australian currencies.

Now, what else can I tell you? I'm still at the student house. I still have my own room (very comfortable), free hot showers (as many as you like), and all for $8 per day, including breakfast. I buy at the markets and cook my evening meal with everyone in the community kitchen. I like it here, and it's just like a big family.

I've been away from home now for nearly four months and only about three weeks here in Paris. It's just gone so fast. I look back and wonder where the time has gone. It's about 8 pm now and still very light. I love living in Paris and feel like I really belong here.

My cassette recorder is so good; I'm always playing my music, and I practice French with it too. You know I'm so busy with people, work and going out, that I look forward to being on my own occasionally. I would never have thought that would be the case. I spent this morning studying in the gardens, and tonight I might go for a walk, stop for coffee in a café, and have an early night.

It's spring in Paris, and it's beautiful – so green, with everything in bud. Paris in the spring is truly a picture. All the cafés and restaurants have moved a lot of their tables outside now onto the sidewalk – it's lovely. Well, I'll close now and go for that walk.

All my love, always.

Diary, 14th April 1980

I mentioned before that Henri and I drove out to *Chartres* about fifty miles out of Paris. It was lovely. He gets so incredibly immersed in all the affectivity of it all. I feel that sometimes he's in a different world. I still can't get used to the way he's so absent-minded with everything except culture. We had to leave the *Grande Cluny* early so that we could find where he parked the car. It's an adventure in itself looking for it. When he's driving and doesn't know where to go, he stops in the middle of the road and figures the guy behind him has to stop too. When they do, he gets out of the car and asks them for directions! Heaps of style but no class! Then in a block or so, he's forgotten. Incredible!

Henri is like two personalities – sensitive and strong, yet so absent-minded and 'in another world,' but he has something special. He wanted us to spend the night together in *Chartres*, but no thanks. Been there, seen this, done that. No thank you. Well, we must have arrived back in Paris at 5 am. Needless to say, I went to sleep in the car.

The next day we met again and went to *Rouen*. There I learned Henri was thirty-nine, not thirty-four. He has to analyse everything culturally, logically, and emotionally. I analyse, but only in terms of feeling, and not consciously.

Well, I slept on the way home from *Rouen*, and we got home at 5 am again. I had to change my *Alliance* lecture time from 8:30 to 10:30 am. I had a bugger of a day at work, and fronted up at the *Café de Cluny* at 7 pm, very tired. We just had a drink and I went home and got my gear. I didn't feel uncomfortable at all. I knew, but still, I should have had my head read. Why! After my last little episode! But it was nice just being close.

Fancy being married – I don't suppose it makes you feel that much different. I don't believe it – here I am in Paris almost three weeks; top job, busy with friends, and seeing a married man to boot. Well … I hope when someone reads this I can explain, because it's not quite as deadly as it reads.

Diary, 21st April 1980

Well, it's a week since I last wrote in my diary.

Today I got up, treated myself to breakfast of coffee and croissant, and then went to work. Henri couldn't see me yesterday, Sunday, because his family was coming home from holidays. I had a case of the downs in the afternoon and only wanted to be by myself. I suppose I was realising the change that had occurred with Henri. I sort of expected it, but it was very abrupt. I suppose I naively thought differently. One thing I do know, the French attitude toward many things is confusing.

So, I spent the morning with my friend Anton. He knocked on my door and woke me at 11 am, and we went over to the gardens to study our French. It was good until I got sick of feeling cramped and closed in. I just wanted to be alone. I wonder what's the matter with me.

I told Anton I wanted to be by myself. I felt so suffocated that I almost ended up in tears. I was tired and had been working all week too. I just wanted to be alone. Told him we would catch up later, and then left to walk to the *Notre Dame la Seine* and around that area. Had tea at *Cluny* and enjoyed being in my own company.

When I got back to the house, Anton confronted me with, "What happened?" and he walked off in a huff. I don't blame him, but I know what I want. I'm a little crazy, but sanely so. He ignored me again at breakfast this morning. Bugger him – that's all I can say. I'm not here for hassles. He's a lovely person though. But then again, so am I. It doesn't work when you always try to bend to another person's needs and neglect your own. I just have to have the space to breathe.

Today I worked at the other perfume shop – Eden on *Rue de Rivoli* near the *Tuileries Gardens*. It's much more relaxing and not so busy there. Tonight at the *Café Odeon* on my way home from work at 8 pm, I read my mail over coffee and sat there for about an hour. I bought an alarm clock and shopped at the *Monoprix* for food too.

Tomorrow I move to *Anvers*.

It was at this point, for some reason, Rainey stopped writing in her diary. The next and final entry was dated 21st October 1980. Perhaps Henri was the catalyst for no longer recording her thoughts and feelings in her diary. They were no longer seeing each other as before, but remained friends for a time.

She expressed much in her letters to me and also in her poetry and prose. The rest of her story is told through her letters, the many loose pages of her writing I have found, our talks and time together, my knowledge of what was happening in her life from this point, my intuition as a mother and later, speaking with some of her friends.

Letter, 5th May 1980

Dear Mum,

Happy Mother's Day! I hope you have a lovely one because I'll be thinking of you all day.

I'm tired today because Henri drove me to Dover, crossing on the ferry; I needed to get a new re-entry stamp in my passport. We left Paris Saturday after work at 6 pm and arrived in Dover at 5:00 the next morning. We spent a lovely day there … so relaxing. Left Dover at 9:30 pm to return to Paris at 4:30 am … all in the one day, and still alive to tell the tale.

I had to hurry because of the expiry date on the stamps in my passport. So now I have my re-entry stamps to France updated. I'm still here illegally as of May 4th but it's a chance – better than nothing – so I'm pleased.

That was Saturday night and Sunday. I'm having an early night tonight.

I'd like to go there again. Actually, it felt very strange to be where I felt at home. Not that I've been out of England that long, but the time in Paris has been completely different to anything, and so intense, that it seemed ages. Anyway, I know I sound strange, but I enjoyed speaking in English. It was like a little game for me; such a different feeling to be able to speak English with ease and to know that you will be understood and get a reply.

I enjoyed that. Dover is a little country border town, very nice, but it was good to return to Paris. I love living here.

I hope you get this card on Mother's Day Mum.

All my love always and especially on Mother's Day.

Postcard, 11th May 1980

I'm sitting on the bank of the Seine, soaking up this wonderful sun. Boats go past all the time – it's very relaxing here. I bought some bread, salami and cheese and had a little picnic. I also wrote another poem. I must write them up. I think I'm getting sunburnt!

New leaves are covering the trees and some already have blossoms. It's so lovely here in the spring, so fresh, clean and new. I just love the flowers and the new growth this time of year, so much. On the bridge a little further along, a man is playing a piano accordion and singing French songs. I walked very far this morning. I really feel like I belong here now.

Love you.

Chapter 2

In 1979, about six months before the girls left for Europe, Rainey had sought a doctor's advice about a mole that was causing her some concern. The GP excised it, and the pathology result reported a melanoma. The doctor said he had removed it all – no need for concern – but to have check-ups every three months, which she had started in Australia. The GP did not refer her to a specialist, and general knowledge regarding melanoma was not as widespread as it is today.

Over the next few weeks, there were no letters and no diary entries, so she does not speak of her break up with Henri in late April, her two moves (firstly to Anvers then to Montmartre), her medical appointment in early June, nor of David's arrival in Paris.

Letter, June 1980

Dear Mum and Barbie,

Sorry about the joint letter but it's better I think. I'd be telling you the same things anyway. Love you both. Wrote some postcards a few days ago and when you said on the phone you hadn't heard from me, I remembered that I hadn't even posted them yet!

Work is becoming busier and more intense as the tourist season picks up; some days it's nothing short of a madhouse. The manager, Monsieur

Riccard, has two shops here in Paris; one near the *Louvre* on the *Rue de Rivoli* where I work on Mondays, and all the other days I work at the Opera shop on *Rue de Helder*. I've never really told you much about the shop, have I? Except that it's *très chic* and that I have an inexhaustible supply of perfume and makeup. Haven't had to buy any since I've been here, and I've had quite a lot of tips. It's my poise and graciousness, you see.

Yes, my French continues to improve. I understand and speak well, and now always serve the French clientele. The language doesn't sound foreign to me, as it used to – normal I suppose; just reflects the change or rather the ease of learning and being able to understand more.

It doesn't get dark here till 10:30 or 11 pm now. It's summer, with daylight saving. I love it, especially on the days when I finish work at 7 pm, and there's still four hours of daylight.

It's Sunday today, and David and I went to *Luxembourg Gardens* which is just like walking through a painting. We went there to write letters, but it started to rain so we took refuge in a café, and then went up to Sacré-*Coeur*, which is just two minutes' walk from my place if you run up the steps behind the church.

Barbie, you know the street going from the church to reach the painters' square … well, that's the street my little flat is in. Not exactly there but it's the same street as you follow it behind the church and down the long flight of stairs – *Rue de Chevalier de la Barre*. You can see the *Sacré-Coeur* bell tower and part of the church as you enter my front door. It's an old and very beautiful area, one of the oldest sections of Paris - cobblestoned streets, lots of atmosphere, and you can hear the church bells ring.

Sorry I haven't written to you for so long pets. I only went to American Express to collect my mail once last week. If I don't go there before work, they are closed when I finish. I think I'll have you send my mail here:

Home Montmartrois

Chambre No. 45

6 Bis Rue du Chevallier de la Barre

Paris 18, France

Write still to American Express and maybe one postcard to this address just to see if it gets here okay. When it does I'll tell you, then you can write always to the new address.

Tuesday

Today, before I started work at 11 am, I went to collect my mail at American Express. I love the skirt; it's so smart! Thank you, Mum.

I got your aerogrammes. I loved reading them. I also got Barbie's aerogrammes that she had written on the plane on her way home three months ago. They were the ones she had asked someone to post on her stopover. Well, they must have arrived by sea mail! They were so funny. Barbie writes such good letters.

Letter, 8th July 1980

It's taken so long to write to you. Sorry. Love you.

Let me tell you about the doctor's visit and check-up. Last year I was told that most people just leave it and wait for something to happen – that's what I *wasn't* going to do, remember? Even though I had the check-ups in Australia, then was cleared.

Well, after six months of being away I wanted a complete check at a proper cancer hospital. I found the name of a prominent cancer specialist (not only in France, but in Europe), and went to see him. He ordered tests, all of which proved safe, with no immediate cause for worry, meaning that all the blood and allergy tests proved negative. But, as he explained, it may take a long time, or a short, sudden time, for a cell having already escaped, to show up – then you have cancer. The chances of a cell escaping before I had the mole removed depended on the depth of the melanoma. He went on to say that while the tests he did here in France were okay and all proved negative, it was necessary to have all the Australian slides sent to Paris.

When they arrived, he examined them with other cancer specialists and dermatologists and came up with his diagnosis. He explained that what they first look at is the depth of the melanoma under the skin. Melanomas are all basically skin cancers, depending on and varying with the depth, although not as serious as one in a muscle but as *potentially* serious. It's this potential that they look at, using the pathology reports.

Keeping in mind that nothing has shown up physically in my body, it's all a matter of how great is the potential to metastasise. Actually, the potential they talk about is the possibility of one of the cells having escaped before the removal of the mole. As I said before, that depends on the depth; that is, how many layers the thing penetrates the skin. The deeper it goes, the greater the possibility.

He gave me a grade 4, meaning that even though it was only a skin melanoma and not a muscular one, the thing removed had penetrated through two or three skin layers. So, with the possibility of a cell escaping *before* the mole was removed and given the depth, I was placed as grade 4, which means I don't have anything. But these escaped cells are incredibly small, and even though they may travel and grow, it's not until they're detected that it's too late. When they are young, it's impossible to detect. Well not too late – there's surgery, but then who knows if other cells have escaped.

Anyway, he said that given the grade, it would be unfair not to treat me. He said that chemotherapy was necessary. It costs $250 per month. He also talked to me about that and asked if I had insurance. I don't think they cover pre-existing stuff – they might, but he said he could arrange it so I didn't have to pay.

I've thought it over a lot. He said if I was a grade 2 or grade 3 I would have been advised of the treatments available and would have had a choice – a medically accepted choice, as it were, to treat or not. However, with grades 4 and 5, he is sure of the line of treatment. So, I figure he probably knows more about it than most doctors in his field.

I have two nurses who look after me at the hospital. The treatment is a drug given intravenously over five consecutive days per month for seven to eight months.

Australia wrote a letter back to him when he called for all the information. Buggered if I know why no one told me in Australia – I was just told by the G.P. to have another check-up. But being in the field or area of medicine that it is, with so many uncertainties and grave possibilities, everybody from the street sweeper to a specialist has an opinion regarding what may or may not happen and what you should or should not do. I think when it's regarding what "may or may not happen" to you, one starts to think of doing positive things towards it. I hope I'm doing the right, positive thing. I think I am. I feel sure I am.

Nausea is one of the side effects, especially initially. The first three days of the five were the worst, with vomiting, nausea and pains but they say that's normal anyway. The first day I managed to get home on the metro and bus but was vomiting for some hours, then fell asleep.

The next day, David arrived. How glad I was to see him. Well, as David said, "The Metro will never be the same after this."

We had plastic bags, and I came forth with heaps for about three metro stops, then a horrible walk home. We crossed the road out of the metro when I began throwing up again. I hate it when people stare.

Well, I'm fine today. Yesterday was my sixth day, and I was back at work today. When I'm having the intravenous, the doctor usually comes in and asks how I am and how I was the day before. I told him about the metro trip home, so the next day he had an ambulance take me home. It drove very fast (so I wouldn't make a mess in the van, I think). If I'd been in a more comprehensive frame of mind, I probably would have enjoyed the 'flight'. They have little blue lights on the ambulances here. The next morning, David and I got a lift in the ambulance again. I believe the initial five days of chemo is a shock to the system.

David was really good … cooking things at all hours and making things for me to eat that I could keep down, as I feel like eating at odd times and should take the opportunity to eat and drink. Well, those five days were pretty bad, so I think … I hope … the worst is over. I hope next month won't be as bad. I don't know what I would have done without David, coming home on the metro with me on the second day and looking after me. Whatever I managed to mumble in the line of food was always there. On the days I was going to the hospital, he was up early making breakfast, so it would digest and I wouldn't waste it by looking at it twice.

I can't say all this over the phone, and after an $80 phone call, you would be even more worried because you wouldn't understand. So now I've explained. I'm happy, or at least satisfied that I'm doing this and not sitting back hoping nothing will happen.

The doctor's name is Schwarzenberg. People I speak to want to know how I managed to be treated by such a well-famed specialist. On Saturday, as David and I were walking out of the hospital grounds, he was driving in and screeched to a halt when he saw me. He backed up and asked me how I was and if I was okay to go home today.

Well Mum, Paris is still lovely. It's officially summer but still raining on and off. Where I'm living now is a lovely area with *Montmartre* so close. When the bells of *Sacré-Coeur* chime, always you can hear them.

I love you and love getting your mail. Tell Barbie I love her and miss her. I love you both so much. I'm going to send you a care package … not food, but miniature bottles of French perfume. You'll love them. And please don't worry; I have a phone in my room now, which is a good contact.

It's Bastille Day on the 14th and all Paris closes. Eden Perfumery will probably be open. Monsieur Riccard has dollar signs for eyes!

If I don't stop writing now I'll never get to sleep, and I won't be able to afford the postage. The next letter will be more news pet; this one is for the information and to tell you that I love you. Please take care.

All my love.

At this time, I was hospitalised for six weeks following surgery on my feet. When I learned that Rainey was having chemotherapy, I remember asking the hospital staff, "What is chemotherapy?" They, of course, did not speak about the side effects — just that it was a treatment given to cancer patients intravenously.

Rainey had not confided in either Barbie or me about the appointment and chemotherapy before that letter. I believe she chose to make this decision herself and confide only in David because she knew I was going to hospital and did not want to cause me any worry. In retrospect, this was tragic as had she done so, it would have been discussed and an alternative opinion presented to her from doctors here in Australia. When I look back, I still agonise about this. If only she had told us ... but I will be forever grateful that David was there with her for most of that time.

Letter, 27ᵗʰ July 1980

Dear Mum and Barbie,

The enclosed postcard shows the street where I live. My little flat is behind the *Sacré-Coeur* where the street curves – you can't see it in this picture. Fancy, a postcard showing a picture of my street. I thought you might like it. I do.

At the moment I'm sitting in one of the big lake parks on the outskirts of the city. There are several here, all so gorgeous with waterfalls, lakes, and breathtaking walks among the oak and chestnut trees. This is a very beautiful city.

Today is my first day out after the second month of chemotherapy, and I'm so enjoying the sunshine. There are about four little islands in the middle of this lake and people splashing about in rowing boats. A couple just came by and asked if I would like to go rowing with them, but I came here by myself expressly to read and reply to all your and Barbie's back-mail. So, I told them no thank you. They said, "Maybe when we pass by on the water, you will have finished."

I felt like saying, 'If you would like to help me read all these letters and reply, we just might be in time for work on Monday morning.'

Yes, I can hold a conversation now. David and I went to a Chinese restaurant a few nights ago, and I was talking with and understanding the people at the next table. As long as they don't launch into a profound account of the state of the nation, I'm okay. At work, I can serve the French quite competently now so I'm improving. I don't feel like a stranger here anymore.

Last night David left to go to Italy for a week. He is meeting his mum and sisters in Rome, and they will travel to Florence. That will be a good break for him. I really hope he has a good time. He asked me what I wanted from Italy, and I couldn't decide between a cute Italian or a pair of leather gloves. It'll probably be a surprise! Bloody big surprise if he brings back the cute Italian, I can tell you.

David and I had a wonderful time in Amsterdam – we did heaps – I told you, I think. I'm sure there's nothing closer to fairyland magic than walking around Amsterdam and along the canals at night, and nothing closer to 'fairies' than the two who run a restaurant on Mr Schroder's street – at number 48 *Haarlemmerdijk*. Oh Barbie, the head guy (the big man who owns the cat) is married to the gorgeous male blond waiter … the one who talked to us that night. It's a great place to go – good food and lots of fun.

All this and I haven't answered anything. Mum, I think of you all the time and hope you're taking good care of your feet. I'm taking care of myself. I'm going to the hospital for my check-up after each lot of treatment, and David wants me to wait till he gets back from Italy before I start the next lot, which will be due then.

We're having a champagne party at work on Saturday because the manager of the smaller shop is leaving.

I've been surreptitiously watching two guys rowing on the lake. They were so busy looking at me over here and making eyes, they've just crashed into another two boats. Now there's lots of shouting and laughing and a mangle of barking dogs and kids, (just the dogs barking). I was going to point to warn them of the impending disaster, but I wanted to watch the fun. The couple who invited me to go rowing are having a water fight with two other boats now, oars and all, and everyone drenched. Glad I didn't go with them. Who said the French aren't friendly? Crazy but friendly.

Fancy you and Barbie getting lost on the way to the hospital. Mum, I can remember when I was eight and went to the hospital to have my appendix out. You made a special red checked dress for me to wear home and a matching one for my Wendy doll. I loved that and still remember it so well.

I'm glad you changed your holidays to come earlier in October, Mum, that's much better. Take care of your feet, won't you? It's so important; you'll have some walking to do when you get here!

Will close now, with all my love.

Postcard, 28th July 1980

Dear Mum,

Today I'm working in the other Eden shop on *Rue de Rivoli*; I much prefer it here, it's much saner. Always they speak French here, so I must too. The shop at number 3 *Rue du Helder* near the Opera is good but gets a little crazy at times.

I'm glad you're feeling better, do get lots of rest. Your care package is ready now; I can send it tomorrow. It's just a little something for you because I love you and because you are feeling poorly. If I were there, I'd make you take long, soaking, relaxing baths, but instead, this care package might encourage you to do just that. You don't need a lot of the fragrance, and it stays with you as there's no alcohol to make the perfume evaporate.

You just rang me here at work. It was so good to talk to you. I'm fine Mum, please don't worry. You must take care of your feet. Get plenty of rest and eat properly.

I sound just like you!

All my love.

On my discharge from hospital in August, I arranged to see Professor William McCarthy at the Sydney Hospital Melanoma Unit. Before meeting with him, he requested and reviewed Rainey's pathology slides and results. After the interview, I called Rainey with the information and advice he gave me.

" I have spoken with Professor McCarthy, and after reviewing your pathology slides, he said there is no doubt in his mind that your condition does not warrant chemotherapy. The lesion was only 1.5mm which means a minimal degree melanoma – there is at least an 85% chance that it won't recur. He is very concerned that grave genetic damage is being done to blood cells and everything else.

The chemotherapy will damage ovarian cells – a long term thing perhaps. He said that if you became pregnant, deformity may occur in the foetus. He strongly advised that you must cease the chemotherapy immediately.

He said that in Europe not much is known about this type of melanoma because they don't have much experience of it in those cold climates – only occasionally, and by then the condition is usually in an advanced stage; therefore, they would hit all such conditions hard.

He also consulted with the pathologist who is of the same opinion as himself – that you should not be having this treatment. Professor McCarthy seemed very concerned that they were giving you this treatment and wants to know the names of the chemotherapy drugs they are using. Please ask and let me know this love, as soon as you can. He asked that you call him."

Letter, 11ᵗʰ August 1980

As I write, David and I are in the Metro on our way to the hospital for the fifth day of this month's treatment. The doctor wrote down the names of the drugs, which I'm enclosing with this letter. He said they are international and would be understood by all medics.

Next day now and I feel very tired – thought I'd stay home today and go to work tomorrow. I received the three aerogrammes you mentioned on the phone, and the photos of everyone were lovely. That's a nice one of Barbie and Jeff. Are they any closer to getting a place to live?

Love you, Mum. I do hope you are taking it slowly, resting and exercising your feet so you can use them when you come over. Just remember pet, when you start to pack: pack, throw out half, repack, throw out two-thirds, then bring what's left-over in your pocket. It's warm here – no woollies allowed; just a bag about the same size as Barbie's.

David's Mum and his two sisters are coming tomorrow for a week, and then David and I are going to take a trip together. We haven't quite decided where yet, but I'll ring you before then. I'm including a list of the chemo drugs for Professor McCarthy.

Love you.

Letter, 21st August 1980

Dearest Mum,

What a wonderful surprise the parcel was! The dress is gorgeous, and it fits perfectly. I love it – so chic and simply elegant. Thank you so much, Mum. You always pick exactly the right size! And thank you for sending the vitamins too.

Tell Barbie I got her letter, and her little house sounds so wonderful. See, it's true ... when one door closes, another one opens.

I get tired more quickly these days since starting the chemotherapy. When I first arrived in Paris, I was never home, and when I did get home it was usually in the early hours of the morning around 2 am. Back then I could go, go, go. Now I realise that I need sleep.

What can I tell you? It's late summer now; can't say it's been an Aussie summer but it's very warm, more like our hot spring days.

Yes, I can understand more French now. I think David was surprised to know that I understood so much; so am I. It sort of clicks suddenly. Sometimes I had to ask him if I was speaking in French or English because the French language sounds so familiar to me now. No, I'm not fluent but I understand so much, and it's not a problem for me.

David has a job offer in Australia that he can't refuse, which means going home early if he wants to accept. It's a very good position and not one that comes around often, so he must take it. He's very excited about it, and so he should be. We are going to Amsterdam next Thursday for ten days. We had a fantastic time there before, and David, like me, adores the place. It is a picture, isn't it Barbie? I'm really looking forward to that.

I should stop eating this liquorice – I think my feet are turning black! I bought it on the way home and it's nearly all gone!

I've lost more weight but I'm eating properly now. Don't worry that I'm not because I must, but I can't eat much during each five days of the chemo. It's usually about now that I pick up and start eating again. It's strange how my tastes have changed since the treatment began. Now I like more fruit and vegetables … not so much meat and I can't handle the taste of wine (shock of shocks) nor pastries, so I find it's just simple natural food. Liquorice is a simple natural food! My next treatment will probably start September 8th.

Monsieur Riccard has been encouraging me to stop work and rest as I usually work ten hours, sometimes seven or eight per day, six days a week. He told me he was concerned about my health. I think it's because he sees me just a few days after the treatment when I know I do look terrible. Anyway, he's been very good with me. If I ring in sick, he says, "Don't take one day, take two. You need rest."

I'm grateful for his concern but I also know him very well. He's a businessman and a crazy one at that. I couldn't help feeling that he wanted me to leave for some reason. I'm certainly not looking my best, and the treatment is taking its toll. He's given me ten days off to go to Amsterdam with David, but can't promise any work when I return as the summer is coming to an end and there will be fewer tourists. Also, the police have been on his back about some of the girls working there without working papers. Another two girls are also leaving.

No, I'm not sorry I'll be leaving … I'm actually looking forward to the change of pace. But I'm glad I was able to work there for five months. I loved it, although the hours were too long. I learned a lot – everything you want to know about French perfume but were too afraid to ask. I know all about it. I have squillions of free stuff, and I'm buying about $100 worth at 40% discount next week before I leave. I know I can find a job just as good, if not better in terms of time, when I come back. I think I might do some part-time au pair work just until you come over.

I can't wait till you come, Mum! There's so much of Europe I want to show you between treatments. Try to arrive early October as my five-day treatment for that month will start on the 8th. If you arrive in Amsterdam, I could meet you there, and we could have a few days looking around before coming down to Paris for the next five days of treatment. I know you'll love it here. I can't wait to show you this beautiful city. Don't worry; I'm not going to rush us around Europe or run you off your feet. You'll relax over here; we'll take it easy, but you'll see a lot too.

Well, yesterday was one of *those* days for me. Got up at 6 am to be at the hospital for the BCG injection, *Levamisole,* which only takes five minutes (it's just a stimulant), then met David at the station to see him off to Amsterdam. I arrived at work at 11 am and felt lost all day. Also when M. Riccard told me I may not be needed from September.

I left work early to collect your parcel at American Express and unfortunately didn't have my passport with me. I couldn't wait to collect it and felt I'd been ripped off all day. This was *my* parcel, but they wouldn't give it to me without my passport! I had all other ID but no passport. Well … it was all too much, so I just burst into tears right there and then. The man was sympathetic but not the ladies. He kept saying there were so many thieves, so I just said *merci* through my tears, and went home. They were right. I'm glad they're careful, but it was all too much. The French are incredible. I understand them more now; I don't excuse them but I understand. Live and learn.

Actually, it's observation time. It's interesting … I find the French extremely individualistic. They mix primarily in their own circles and seem basically aloof from other French. But at the same time, as individualistic as they are, you would expect them to be intolerant of others. But they're not intolerant; they're just simply indifferent in many cases.

I find them to be a whole range of contradictions … hard, aloof, and yet I've had conversations in restaurants with French people who act as though they've known me all their lives. I find also that they're completely unpredictable, straightforward, never beat around the bush, know exactly what they want, are very definite, and expect the same of others. Of course, I can only generalise toward a national character, but I feel that's it.

I believe a little of that may have rubbed off on me. I have somehow 'slipped in' as it were. I looked at my reflection in the window of the metro today, and I looked just like one of them hurrying home – my mind seemed to be thinking the same. I no longer look at them and think, *Oh, French; different. I'm a foreigner from another world almost.* I don't feel that way anymore. I think Barbie, from her twelve months living in Brazil, can understand that.

Now it's Sunday, August 24th and as I write, I'm at the indoor pool with two friends from work, Denise from the UK and Lisa from the US. Actually, it's a solarium where you can lie in the spring sun. The French think it's hot, but I've got news for them, and it's all bad. This is the first time I've been for a swim since I left Australia eight months ago. The closest I've come is standing under a cold shower!

Last night I went with Lisa and Denise to another friend's house for dinner. We had a good time; talked about ghosts, tarot cards (one of the girls can read them), and all things spiritual. We got up from the table at 1:30 am and were too scared to go home so stayed the night. Then this morning after breakfast we all came here to the pool for a swim. I'm wearing a blouse over my swimmers - I must be careful now.

Bought a magazine the other day, *Télérama,* and flicking through it I saw a familiar face. My doctor (Schwarzenberg) was interviewed on the power of the mental attitude; how the will to fight serious diseases is just as important as the actual physical condition. It's very interesting reading.

Oh! Before I forget, Monsieur Riccard now wants me back casually after my holiday. I know it's because he's a bit concerned, as too many girls are leaving now. Well, I need the job, so I'm going to stand down the road, wait till the shop is crammed with tourists, and then walk in. He has an address to give me. I'll pick my time and knowing how disorganised he is, he'll ask me to pick up a book and help.

On Thursday, August 28th I'm going up to Amsterdam to meet David for ten days. He leaves for Australia on Thursday, September 4th. I might stay an extra few days then come back and go straight into my next treatment on September 8th for five days. After about the eighth day, I'll go into the shop. I'm sure I can pick up the job if I work my timing right, and then work for three weeks before I meet you in Amsterdam.

Please don't worry about me and the treatment because Lisa will be here to take me to the hospital and bring me home. I've already explained to her what to expect, but she says it's fine. (Poor girl, she doesn't know what she's in for!) Must go now and have my shower.

Love you both so much.

Postcard, 27th August 1980

Dear Mum,

Just thought I would write to you before I go to bed. Tonight, I washed and cleaned my room because while I'm in Amsterdam with David (he's already up there) Lisa, my friend from work, will move in and share with me just for September. I've finished packing now and will leave tomorrow at 3:30 pm straight from work. The trip takes six hours. It's so exciting to think you can be in another country in so little time, and it's only sixty dollars on the train to Holland.

Today I splurged and had my hair cut; it looks really nice, all the one length now – very chic. I was going to get it cut before but thought it would have been a waste of money seeing it was going to fall out like everyone else's at the hospital, but so far I haven't lost a lot. Can't believe I still have most of it. I was proud of myself today; I could tell Vivienne, the hairdresser, how I wanted it cut … and all in French too.

Can't wait till you come over!

Love you lots.

Amsterdam, 4th September 1980

Dear Mum,

I really can't believe its September already, autumn! Time goes all too fast. By the time you get this card David will already be home in Australia. We are going out to the airport after breakfast. When he leaves, I'll catch the 2:30 pm train back to Paris. It's been lovely here in Amsterdam. This postcard is exactly what Amsterdam looks like at night. Just magical. Amsterdam and all of Holland must be my favourite place to visit.

Love you.

Letter, 8th September 1980

Dear Mum,

Remember the *au pair* job I had applied for in *Saint-Tropez*? Well, I have it! They told me to come around the morning of September 15th with my bags. Just imagine, Saint-*Tropez* on the *Riviera*! They are a young, handsome couple and I'll be looking after their two-year-old daughter. She's lovely. I've already had a talk with her; she's said okay to all the bars, discos and general events around town! I'll 'tame' her gently.

Her parents drive a huge, shiny, black 1937 Rolls Royce and he drove me to the metro station after the interview. It was incredible. There we were … the husband and the little girl on my knee (not both, just the little girl) driving down the *Champs Élysées* in this incredible vintage Rolls. I felt like royalty. I think we'll be driving down to *Saint-Tropez,* as they showed me photos of their last holiday there and the first thing I noticed was the car.

They live on the elite side of Paris. He's French, she's Scandinavian, and has done what I'm doing – travelling. She's been to Australia. He makes perfumes, and I sell them. There's nothing like an insight into the upper crust of Paris.

So, I'll be back from *Saint-Tropez* about September 30th. I'm going out to the hospital today to see if I can have my treatment brought forward so I can go. I had accepted the job before I began my treatment, so I hope Doctor Schwarzenberg lets me start this month's chemo today or tomorrow.

I'm so very grateful to Lisa; she won't hear of me going to the hospital by myself. I tried to talk her out of it by telling her what she was in for, but she won't hear of it. If I can start this month's chemotherapy today – 8th, 9th, 10th, 11th and 12th then leave for *Saint-Tropez* on the 15th – I should be fine by then. I'll have to give myself the immune stimulator injections. I'll just close my eyes and be brave.

Now I must run. I have to go to the bank, to American Express and out to the hospital by 3 pm. I don't have an address in *Saint-Tropez* yet – I'll just write to you from there.

See you in three weeks' time!

Love you.

As it transpired, the treatment dates could not be changed, so Rainey was unable to go to Saint-Tropez. She was alone for the September treatment as Lisa's parents had come to Paris and she went with them on their travels. I can only imagine what it must have been like for Rainey being alone during that time, for the five consecutive days of that month's treatment.

Letter, 15th September 1980

Dear Barbie and Jeff,

Finally, I'm writing a letter addressed to your little house! Can't wait to visit you, pet. You must be very happy there. I was so glad when you rang, Barbie; it was the fourth day of my chemo. The treatment days go by number, indicating the degree of survival. I found this month very, very hard and was glad to see today come – the eighth day – but still I am without energy. I ate today, so am feeling a little better. Just wrote to David and filled him in on all the highlights of this month's treatment so you can ask him for all the gory details if you like.

In retrospect, it's really quite funny in some places. On the last day, Doctor Schwarzenberg drove me home ... I was so grateful for that. I've been very tired this time and once even fell asleep in the taxi going to the hospital and the taxi driver woke me when we got there. He was so nice. Then I went in and crawled into a bed in the hospital. I was all under the blankets because the smells of the things they use always make me feel like throwing up. I was so very tired, so I just curled up and had a little sleep. Then at the end of the drip, Doctor Schwarzenberg came in and very slowly pulled back the blanket ... 'to see what it was,' he said. He thinks I'm an okay patient.

So, today was the day I was to have gone to *Saint-Tropez*. There was no way I could have done that. I'm so glad they found someone else; the two-year-old probably would have ended up looking after *me*.

In a few days, I'll be back to my normal self and I won't be working. I know Monsieur Riccard will ask me back to work, but I'm going to be a real culture vulture these next couple of weeks until Mum arrives. I'll go to all my favourite museums of art; revel in those a little. Go for aimless walks in the gardens and along the banks of the Seine, wander around *Montmartre* at night – it's just magical. I want to go to *Sacré-Coeur* and to the houses of Dior, Chanel, Yves St Laurent and Ricci for their fashion shows, go to a few movies ... just relax. Visit the woods around Paris, have late mornings and early nights ... what bliss!

This is beginning to sound rather droll, and I'm letting my imagination run wild ... or is it just wishful thinking? I'll have to review my plans when I'm feeling a little more energetic, then we'll see what we can come up with. Admittedly you may never hear about those plans.

What else can I tell you? I'm getting tired now. I don't think I've got the energy to go for a walk, and I'm sick of bed. Had thought of sitting on the toilet and wait to see how long it would be before someone knocked. I don't know – I'll think of something. I was going to ring myself up at one stage but the lady at the other end asked me what number I wanted, and I couldn't remember my own number so that canned that.

But really, some days after the treatment, I feel like I have a new lease on life. I feel more aware of my surroundings and appreciate them more. I'll probably start feeling alive again tomorrow. Haven't lost *all* my hair Barbie, so I'm pretty much intact. Send me a photo of your house with you and Jeff in front. I love you so much, and I'll be able to write a more exciting letter next time.

Letter, 17th September 1980

Dear Mum,

It's now four days after my treatment and I'm beginning to feel alive again. No, I didn't go to *Saint-Tropez* as my treatment dates were unable to be changed, and knowing how much time is needed for my recovery, I had to cancel. At least they had time to find another *au pair* – she was only sixteen.

I was in bed for two days after this lot of chemo, just sleeping, no energy, then on the third day went to do my grocery shopping. We had almost forgotten what food looked like – my stomach and I, that is – took us ten minutes to figure out how to use those funny things you eat with. I've lost more weight, but I'm eating again now – can't keep me away from the stuff.

Yesterday was my first day out after the chemotherapy, so I took myself up to *Montmartre* and lost myself in its rustic atmosphere.

Whenever I go somewhere like that by myself, it's a ten-to-one chance that I end up spending the afternoon with someone I've never met before. That happened yesterday. He (Marc) was French – very nice – doesn't speak English, so it was good French practise for me. We went for a walk, and he told me about the history of *Montmartre*. There is so much to see there, its old vineyards and incredibly old cemetery, so much more interesting when you have a walking tour guide.

Did you know that *Montmartre* was built over quarries – gypsum plaster quarries? Hence the name Plaster of Paris. I had heard that the cemeteries in Paris are absolutely unreal. I had never been to one because you don't usually say, "Oh, what a lovely day – I might go to the cemetery."

So, when he asked, "Would you like to see the cemetery?" I lit up like a Christmas tree.

"Oooh, I'd love to!"

While he was looking at me as if I had two heads, I realised what I'd said with such enthusiasm and thought to myself, *A little self-control here wouldn't go astray, Lorraine.*

I learned a lot about the *Montmartre* cemetery from my tour guide. It's out of this world – calm and peaceful, yet sometimes a little eerie. It's behind the *Moulin Rouge* and was built in the hollow of what used to be an old gypsum quarry. Some of the tombs are very elaborate, some crumbling with age, and the graves of many of the great artists and musicians are there.

I had a wonderful afternoon. When I left Marc, I went into the church and thanked God for taking special care of me and asked him to take special care of you now, with so much to do. If He's not there Mum, He's on His way! He sure had His work cut out for Him this time taking care of me.

Letter, 23rd September 1980

Dear Barbie,

Just a quick note because I'm going out soon and I want to post this.

It's strange here with the language, Barbie. I understand most things now and speak with ease; well, that's to say, buggered if I know if they can understand me! But really, I *am* becoming more fluent.

It was funny the other day. I was walking in the woods on the outskirts of Paris with my friend Marc, and of course we speak always in French as he doesn't speak English. Some English-speaking ladies approached us to ask directions. I didn't know the directions, so I repeated their question to Marc in French. He gave me the directions and I turned to the ladies to translate. But I find it confusing sometimes to translate from one language to another, and I actually told them in French, the directions. They looked at me, Marc looked at me, and then I realised what I was doing. I turned to Marc and spoke to him in English! He couldn't understand a word of course, and I was totally confused and embarrassed. You know I think it must happen when French is becoming more natural, but English still has the upper hand.

Sometimes I find myself thinking in French unconsciously. I can read without problem the magazines. Between reading, understanding, and speaking, my reading is the best of the three. Enough of that; I know you understand Barbie, because of your Portuguese.

Tomorrow I go again to the hospital for the BCG stimulus injection. They are okay but they leave scars, so I have them on my leg. I'm so happy to see the end of each month's treatment – really, it's like having a new lease on life. I've lost a lot of weight of course because for seven days every month I hardly eat at all; then after that, very little, as my stomach has shrunk. My tastes have changed too. I mostly eat vegetables and fruit now and can't handle even *looking* at pastries – shock of shocks.

I'm really mixed up and confused at the moment. I want to stay here so much but wonder whether my place is at home now, instead of traipsing around the world at my fancy, doing whatever I want to do, whenever I want to do it. It's important to me, my independence and that self-direction that you want and have with Jeff. I want very much to share all with my choice too. I need that.

When David was here we talked a lot. I know now he does love me, very much and deeply, and as he said one day, my problem is that I want a written guarantee that everything is going to work out. Anyway, I told David I would come home with Mum when she comes over in a couple of weeks' time, and I meant it then. I don't know … I think sometimes

I'm my own worst enemy. I made a decision to come home, but my God, a little taste of freedom and I'm off again!

Well, at the end of these last four months here with David I decided that even though I wanted to stay for another year (because I had been here by myself for only eight weeks when he first came over) I didn't want to lose him, so I thought I should go home.

A hell of a lot happened in that time too. David knows almost all there is to know now because he read my diary while I was at work one day. On looking back, I don't hold any ill feeling for that, but the aftermath was, well … something I don't like to remember. Consequently, I haven't written in my diary since. Anyway, I must do something about it either way, and soon. I'll probably see you in December Barbie … I don't know. Well, my final decision, as they say, is a "definite maybe." That seems to be the story of my life.

So, pet, it's nice being a lady of leisure for the past three weeks, having late nights and being able to sleep in, and seeing more of Paris while trying to sort myself out.

It will be so exciting to see Mum at the airport. It will be fantastic for her. I'll show her a really good time. I'll try and keep her out of trouble too. You know Mum … keep her away from pastry shops, lolly shops and dress shops.

Today I went to the Eden perfumery to see if there was any work, but the tourist season has finished and business is slack. The manager still tells me my place is at home in Australia because of my health. I really do look terrible, both during and for some days after the chemotherapy.

So now I'm 'playing ladies' and relaxing. It feels so good to relax and not work. Ten hours a day *was* a bit much – even though I now know perfumes, make-up and leathers inside out. I probably even have enough perfume to start my own shop! Well, not quite.

Take good care Barbie, I love you and think of you often.

P.S. You never cease to amaze me with your letters. Today I received a letter saying you'll be moving into your new house soon. I got one three weeks ago that said how wonderful it was to be in your new house!

Is it me, or you? That's okay; I'm not complaining. This letter only took you … yes … just under a month to write. I do believe you're improving! Like the letter I got that said, 'In three weeks I'm going for an interview for a job in operating theatres' then on the same line, 'well, I got that job.'

What a little pet you turned out to be.

I love you Barbie.

Letter, 2nd October 1980

Dear Barbie and Jeff,

Well pets, today is my quiet day where I unwind and write letters and generally catch up on things. I spring-cleaned this little studio from top to bottom yesterday, and it sparkles. Everything is back in its right place and now I'm completely lost – can't find a thing! Hang on until I do the washing up and get my life into gear – if only I could remember where I put the detergent. My little flat is only one room you know, so it has to be here somewhere.

Finished – and the place almost looks like a bought one.

Well, where to start. Thank you for the telegram, Barbie. The concierge called me to go down and get it about an hour ago. It took six hours to get here; that's pretty good. I plan to go to the airport tomorrow. I've worked out the times already; I'll get there about 7 am and wait.

It's raining today so I spent the morning consoling myself with old books, and magazines I've read over and over that have crumbs of long ago meals hidden between the pages. It's a welcome change of pace, even perhaps a little overdue after the last few weeks of high-paced living, attributed to my treatment I think. I usually feel like I'm dying in that week and waste no time in making up for it as soon as I can. So today I was almost thankful for the rain, it gives me a chance to practice being sedate, sensible, and sophisticated for when Mum arrives tomorrow. I need the practice. Needless to say, some of my friends have gone into hiding and others – well … who knows.

I find I can read French quite well now. At the moment I'm reading Albert Camus' book, *L'Étranger* (The Stranger). It's a little heavy, but a good exercise.

I'm so looking forward to seeing Mum tomorrow. She'll be here for two whole months – I can't wait! I plan to take her to Italy and Greece first, then to Spain, Austria and Switzerland, through Germany to Holland.

Holland is my second love after Paris – it's only six hours to a completely different world in living, culture and language, and ever so beautiful as you know, Barbie. Summer nights in Amsterdam are exquisite. David and I went twice while he was here. It's possible to unwind completely there.

Always the re-entry to France is a problem for me because of my illegal status here. As you know, my tourist visa expired in May. I have no work permit, and as in Australia, semi-permanent residency or anything over a three-month sojourn is extremely difficult to obtain. Here it's practically impossible unless you are a full-time student or have residency in a French colony elsewhere.

I'm ever aware of this and so far have been fortunate. Always gendarmes are patrolling the streets and metros, checking the passports of obvious imports. My only redeeming factors? I'm white and well-dressed. It's sad but true, happily though for me. Unemployment here is high and opportunities are abused by the many illegal imports, mostly from Africa, Tunisia, and the Arabian countries. I could be deported along with all the other illegal imports next week.

I've been lucky with work too (It's my regression session now as I don't work there anymore). Eden Perfumery really was a beautiful shop and a great place to work, all things deluxe, at deluxe prices. Behind the scene, the story was a little different. Monsieur Riccard employed girls for their language and of course paid us the legal minimum wage. It was possible to live on that comfortably though. The last few weeks were spent in the basement taking famous brand names off cosmetics and loading them into trucks – box after box – to be smuggled across borders, then return to the shop, don our most inviting smile, and in our best French, ask, *"Bonjour Madame, vous desirez?"*

I could write a book on my time in the Eden Perfumery. The girls were nice, and we all became close friends. I share my little flat now with one of them, Lisa from California. She came back from Austria last night. I haven't seen her yet but will catch up with her tonight, hopefully.

I learned a lot of French while working there, and still miss having aperitifs in the afternoon (once a wino, always a wino – isn't that what they say?).

Now that brings me to the next enlightening saga of my life here … my neighbours. Jeff is always saying 'Tell me about day-to-day things'. See I'm trying hard.

Where was I? Oh yes, my neighbours ... a middle-aged couple who live in a perpetual state of intoxication. I learned all my worst French from them. The only time I see them is when they knock on my door asking me to unlock *their* door. I've never seen anyone so highly unco-ordinated under the influence. I could perhaps understand if it was only occasionally, but they are stoned every night. They seem happy enough, however, having found the rich fulfilment of life and fruitful channels for their energies in a four-franc bottle of red.

It's really sad, there are so many down and out stories walking the streets here. It's almost a way of life. Prime accommodation goes to the metro tunnels where it's warm, safe, and cheap. Next in demand are the air vents for the metro on the footpath; they're warm and cheap, but not that safe. But when you can't afford a newspaper, it's cheaper than the park. No, not so illustrious but *c'est la vie.*

Where I live now is rather wonderful, immediately behind *Sacré-Coeur, 6 Rue de Chevalier de la Barre*, very rustic, very beautiful, with lots of trees and narrow, winding cobblestone streets. It's full of history and in summer, full of tourists.

Tourist season, happily, is almost over. I'm sure they forgot to give Paris summer this year, and we had just three weeks of beautiful, warm, spring weather when the Parisians thought all their Christmases had come at once. There was a mass exodus to all the beaches and Paris practically closed down for the month of August. That happens every year. The tourists come to Paris in the August summer and wonder why everything is closed! The Parisians are not as silly as we thought they were.

But it's true – generally speaking they are cool, distant, blunt and not particularly helpful. It's one place where, to slip into the lifestyle, to absorb it and appreciate it, you must have the language and of course, the time. Did my good deeds in the summer and helped many a frustrated tourist tackling a defiant Frenchman who had no intention of telling them anything.

It's really lovely being a lady of leisure for a change, although I'm fast becoming a *poor* lady of leisure. But it's time to stop and smell the roses, and I'm enjoying the change of pace.

I've learned to appreciate the sun here, really. After I had gone to the *Musée d'art* on Sunday (a glorious day), I walked home along the bank of the Seine. The summer colours are so beautiful: the trees, the buildings and the sun reflecting on the water. It's hard to explain, but the air is tingling with lively energy. No, it's not me – it's Paris. I don't know how else to describe it. But yes, the air just tingles with an energy and life source of its own.

Saw Randy yesterday when I went to American Express to collect my mail. He keeps telling me how I've changed … how I used to be so prim and proper and keeps saying, "Now look at you!"

Don't quite know what to think of that, but I suppose the chemo-therapy *has* made a difference. Maybe I should keep practising being 'prim and proper' tonight and stay home. Anyway (doesn't take much to get me sidetracked), I walked home along the Seine and bought some posters from the vendors there.

Just ran down to the shops to buy bread, fruit, etc. That guy Marc, who I told you about in my last letter, has invited himself around tonight so he'll probably come right on tea time. He's really very nice. He wanted to take me out tonight but I want an early night so I can be fresh for tomorrow … up early and out to the airport to meet Mum. Can't wait!

Marc speaks no English so needless to say my French has had to improve. I even had a dream in French the other night and woke myself saying something that wasn't English. Lisa will be here tonight too, so she won't go hungry either. She is lovely. She bought me a box of beautiful Austrian chocolates from Salzburg. She's been back two days and I haven't seen her yet. We keep missing each other.

It's a strange day today, very sombre outside. I hope it's nice tomorrow when Mum arrives. Can't believe she's on her way. It's the same as when David came; I went through all the motions of getting organised to go to the airport to meet him, never really realising he was coming, and I was so surprised to see him! It was sort of like starting over and felt somehow strange … like I had to get to know him all over again. When he saw me he picked me up and whirled me round. When he left, we were both very different. I understand a lot more of him now and of myself; we are both more mature and have mellowed toward each other. (I don't mean as individuals – I mean towards each other).

There was more understanding and he was not so emotionally aggressive. Yes … that's it. Here, we had time to ourselves, to live, to talk, to relax and to learn. I didn't think it would ever be any different to what it was like at home, but it was. You can't rely on a place, but I know we *did* change. Then of course toward the end of the three months the same problems arose, not, 'when was I going overseas and for how long' as in Australia, but, 'when was I coming home and for how long was I staying,' and I just felt pressured.

I just feel so terrible sometimes because it's been *me* pulling the strings and making all the decisions for *me* that have affected us like this, and even at times without realising it if you know what I mean. That's just a reflection from now looking back, but it's necessary. Otherwise, I wouldn't be here – I would never have left Australia. You know the horrible thing is that I'm getting it out of my system, that's for sure, but at the same time it's equally as contagious. It's at this stage, I have to say, "Okay – been there, seen this, and done that – am I going to wander, or settle, or what?" I know it's not something you have to think of consciously – it's natural, it's life. If you want something you take it, and if you share it, it's there. It's not complicated; it's very simple. I always seem to make things so complicated.

Sometimes I don't understand myself. You know, I can spend a lot of time with a guy I really like and then suddenly – I mean suddenly – we can be eating lunch or whatever, and I just have to get out, get away, be by myself – be free. That happened last Sunday. I really enjoy whomever I'm with; it's always a pleasure for me to talk and to share, but this feeling just grabs me sometimes.

Marc and I were having lunch, and suddenly I just wanted to leave, so I picked up my bag, and he asked, "Where are you going?" I told him I had to keep an appointment. It's suddenly so urgent with me, and I can't explain it (No class, but heaps of style).

"I'll call you tomorrow," he said.

"OK," I replied. Then I was out of there.

The next day he asked me to call him, but I didn't – that's the day I went to the *Louvre* and spent hours in the *Musée d'art*. I had a wonderful day. He had been calling all day, but the phone doesn't operate on Sunday, only at night. When I got home, the concierge rang and said there was someone waiting downstairs to see me. He wanted to know what happened. What could I say? Oh, I've always got something to say, but I must sound like a raving sixteen-year-old. It's not so much what happened … it's me. I never thought I was like that. I don't particularly like being like that, but I've been like that ever since I've been here. Or maybe I just realised it here, and acted on it.

Well Barbie, it's 6:30 pm now, and Mum will have been flying for eleven hours already, she must be exhausted, she'll have to come down for a pit stop soon – her arms must be killing her! I hope she didn't bring too much luggage. I wonder what she'll get up to on the plane. You know Mum, always has a funny story to tell. Remember that time we were waiting at the Sydney Town Hall for her and the bus didn't stop to let her off? It just kept going, and she looked out the window at us and made that funny face. I have visions of her boarding the wrong plane in London and looking out the window with the same funny face…
"Rainey, I wanna get off!"

I hope Jeff had a lovely birthday on the 17th. I thought of him but then forgot because I'm always a nervous wreck in anticipation of the next five days of chemo, and once into the treatment I can't do anything. Give him my love and a belated hug and kiss for a happy birthday.

Lots of love to you both always.

Chapter 3

*I*t was wonderful to see Rainey when I arrived in Paris. It was as if I had been waiting to see her forever. I was shocked to see how tired and drawn she looked. She had lost so much weight, but her bubbly personality and positive attitude had not changed.

Her studio apartment was very small but cosy, situated in a lovely area just behind Sacré-Coeur in Montmartre, a very old, rustic area, with many trees and narrow, winding, cobblestone streets infused with an essence of the past. The apartment was just one small room and there was a shared bathroom down the hall.

"But where is the kitchen?" I asked.

"You'll never guess," she said, throwing open a cupboard door in the wall no more than 40cm wide.

"Voilà!" she exclaimed, and we burst into laughter. Inside was a single gas burner, two saucepans, a frying pan, a few plates and some cutlery.

We spoke about the chemotherapy, and I gave her Professor McCarthy's letter. It must have been so confusing to be presented with a completely different opinion, one so completely in opposition to the French doctors. I could understand her dilemma, but with his letter, I was able to impress upon her Professor McCarthy's opinion. We made an appointment with Doctor Schwarzenberg, and Rainey had decided to tell him that she was going back to Australia and would continue the therapy in Sydney. She did this just to simplify matters. He asked that we come back the next day when he would have a letter for her to take to Sydney.

My priority was to help Rainey in regaining her health and strength after the months of chemotherapy, and the physical and emotional turmoil she had endured. She needed rest, a good diet, plenty of TLC, love and laughter and a mother's ear. She knew I wanted her to come home with me, but it had to be her decision. She still felt her place was there in Paris and she wanted so much to stay. She was a free spirit, and her independence was very important to her.

On our first day out, Rainey took me to her 'most favourite place in all of Paris,' up a long flight of stairs from where she lived, to Sacré-Coeur on top of Montmartre. We strolled along the cobblestone streets to Place du Tertre (the painters' square) with its arty and Bohemian atmosphere, and now Rainey's letters came to life. We spent the next few weeks just relaxing, going for leisurely walks along the Seine and through some of the beautiful gardens she had often spoken about in her letters. She was so keen to show me Paris, to experience its atmosphere, its living history, its light, its colour and movement. We spent hours just sitting in sidewalk cafés, sipping coffee, talking and reminiscing while watching the passing parade. To me, this seemed to be one of the most popular pastimes for the people in this beautiful city.

Those few weeks seemed to make a lot of difference to Rainey. She became more relaxed and began looking more like her old self every day. We went to visit Eden Perfumery. She looked really lovely that day, having taken special care over her makeup and dress, and everyone was surprised to see her looking so well and so healthy. I watched as she spoke with the manager and to the staff members, oblivious to their admiring glances. Yes, she was strikingly attractive. Tall and elegant, she moved with a natural grace and poise. She radiated serenity and a natural charm.

Among her friends from the perfumery were Denise, an English girl, and Lisa from California, with whom she had shared an apartment in the home of Madame Gaba. Madame was a wealthy and eccentric French widow, who, when learning that Rainey was to have chemotherapy, did not allow her to stay, believing that her condition was contagious. I didn't know about this until after I arrived. It must have been a very stressful time, but

Rainey seldom gave space in her letters to any negative experiences, always making light of any awkward or heavy situation.

I also met Lisa's friend Ward, a U.S. Marine sergeant stationed in Paris on Embassy duty, and Sammy, a warm and sincere young man who was Denise's boyfriend.

One of Rainey's friends, her mentor and advisor in her search for permanent work and residency, was Jim Wilkes, who had been advising her on how to overcome the many obstacles she faced without a visa or working papers. Jim was advisor to the many who sought his help as he was familiar with the French legal system. Rainey was so very fortunate to have met him. I don't know how that came about, perhaps through Randy Garret, but I see it as one of the serendipities of her early days in Paris.

One day we were out walking, and Rainey was showing me some of the quaint streets in the older areas of Paris. We turned a corner and came upon a film crew shooting a street scene for a movie. It was interesting, so we stopped to watch the proceedings. By now a small crowd had gathered, and the director called for the scene to be enacted for the third time. On his call of 'ACTION!', the scene became alive again with the main characters alighting from a car, intent on their dialogue, and the 'extras' hurrying along the footpath in both directions. The director looked at Rainey and shouted, "Allez! Allez! Allez!" (Go! Go! Go!)

"Mais, je ne suis pas l'une des extras," she said. (But I'm not one of the extras.)

"You're not?" he said. She shook her head.

"Wait here!"

We waited, and eventually he came and spoke with her. He gave her his business card and asked that she make an appointment for an interview. However, she didn't follow this up as we were leaving the next day to begin the trip she had planned for us.

Our first foray out of Paris was Amsterdam where I was introduced to Mr Schroder and his dog Herta. It was wonderful putting faces to the names I had so often read about in her letters. We stayed at Hotel Schroder for a week – so relaxing for both of us. I loved Holland, and Rainey's letters came to life here too. She was a great tour guide and took much delight in showing me the places she knew and loved, and sharing them with me. It was wonderful to see it all through her eyes ... to spend that time with her and to watch her health and vitality gradually return. After Amsterdam, we returned to Paris for a few days before travelling to Italy.

Here I will include her last diary entry dated October 21st, 1980, written during those few days in Paris after our visit to Holland. This was her first diary entry since April, six months earlier.

As to her deepest feelings during this time, I can only imagine. It seemed easier for her to pour her true feelings onto paper.

Diary, 21ˢᵗ October 1980

Since my last diary entry, 14ᵗʰ April, I've moved twice and so much as happened. I promised myself I wouldn't write in my diary ever again. It wasn't hard. I didn't even want to look at it ... and now David has been and gone, and in a month or more Mum will be gone. Time is so incredible, how it passes in spite of all things and all men. Mum has a migraine now. I've given her some acupressure, and she is resting.

In the interim, Time, Fate, Destiny and Circumstance got their heads together and ordered a stop to my treatment. I could write a book on that little number. Funny how it found its way into my life just as anonymously as it disappeared again. Can't say the interim was too anonymous; it sure made its presence felt and my hair is *still* falling out!

I can't begin to explain it on paper. It remains for me to feel, and for David to remember. I sometimes start to cry when I think of that ordeal; I never did cry then, but once or twice. I know I *did* find the strength to endure it. No one will ever know how it felt, especially the last lot when I was alone. Then I used almost to cry because I didn't have David there, but always stopped myself because it was necessary to keep mentally strong through it. That was my whole strength through those four months ... my attitude, and David.

Amsterdam has seen me twice since I last wrote in my diary … the first time a little happier than the last. I spent a mixed birthday, but a lovely one that I will remember always. In retrospect, I think perhaps it was *adieu,* for that time, place, person; *adieu,* for that time alone; *adieu,* for those feelings, left in its own space in time. Just like a book, you read it once and close it. To open it again would never be as it was *au debut,* so for this, I am quietly accepting.

I wanted to write tonight on David. That was the motivation for resurrecting my diary again, six months after my last entry; the difference being that this time I looked a little further than my name and address on the first page. I still haven't read the account of my affair with Henri in the diary, because it pains and hurts me. I find myself turning away if I cast my eyes on it; to think that David read my diary one day when I was at work. Not that I'm ashamed of anything I said, did, or felt, because it was only ever feeling, but for the hurt and disbelief that David must have felt on reading it.

It was too much hurt I know, and it didn't stop there either, and hasn't stopped.

I'm crying now. I want to assure David that I love him and that I care. It's a hell of a way to show it.

What the hell do I want, drifting from day to day, thinking as far ahead as 10 pm tomorrow, when I ring Claude, the insurance agent, for my illegal claim to work? You can't expect someone to wait that long. You can't change your mind like you change your clothes. It's people you're dealing with and someone you love dearly. Then why change? My God! And God knows I had decided to come home with Mum when David left. That's what I told him, and told myself … and I believed it. What's happened? Time has given me the chance I wanted with David. I act now on what I know. There's no one else, before or now. The reason I haven't been out with Marc for ages is that I would rather be with David in thought than with anyone else in person. Even the other night watching TV at Marc's place, I just didn't want to be there. I was twenty-four thousand miles away.

69

Why do I put myself into situations where I would rather be somewhere else? Or do I just tell myself that God and I expect, or hope, that David understands me? Shit, I don't even understand myself half the time. I love him and care for him so much.

Please help me to sort myself out, being true to myself and others. Please help me to see the things I can't see now for my future. Please help me.

From Paris we travelled to Italy, visiting Florence, Rome, Naples, Pompeii and Capri.

Pompeii made an everlasting impression on me. Walking through the ruins, one could almost feel the history, and I tried to imagine what it must have been like for the people on that horrendous day.

We arrived on Capri in November and stayed in a lovely pensione there. Rainey had arranged to have a special breakfast sent up to our room on the morning of my birthday, and I remember the breakfast tray, decorated with flowers, was beautifully laid out. It was a lovely surprise and is one of my many treasured memories. We spent wonderful days on Capri relaxing and exploring the many wonders of this beautiful Mediterranean island.

From there we travelled to Venice, Innsbruck and Zermatt, soaking up the beauty and grandeur of the Alps … nourishment for the soul and for the spirit.

While in Zermatt, Rainey wrote the following letter to one of her uncles.

Letter, 24th November 1980

Dear Uncle Len,

To-day I was inspired to write to you. I think of you often of course and wonder how you are, both in your life and your work. So, congratulations! You have now joined the ranks of the privileged few who are fortunate enough to receive a letter from me! I only really write to Mum, Barbie and Jeff, and David, but manage to send others the occasional postcard from time to time.

As well as having this good fortune, you now have the added *misfortune* of trying to decipher my writing. As my French improves, my English spelling and structure become progressively worse.

Mum and I are in Switzerland now, staying in Zermatt, the little village at the foot of the Matterhorn surrounded by majestic mountain peaks. It truly is breathtaking. We travelled up to Zermatt on the Cog Railway which wound its way up the mountain to an altitude of over five thousand feet. This place is awe inspiring ... a world on its own.

We had a wonderful day today. From the little township, we walked to the base of the Matterhorn and took a cable car up for even more magnificent views. To be so high clears your mind; to be at least physically above everything has got to be a start. I find that nature is truly a tonic for the mind, the body and the spirit. At night this place is a picture, like a page out of a book of colourful fairy tales. Just magical!

I remember, Uncle Len, how you always dreamed of going to Germany and Switzerland, wanting to experience and share with the people, their country and their lifestyle, and perhaps even indulge with them a little in the occasional stein! It's really much closer than you think.

I find The Swiss are similar to the Germans, but seem more con-servative - gentler and not quite so open. It's in this atmosphere that my thoughts turned to you to-day and wished so very much for you to share and experience this for yourself. Not just this, but something much wider, much broader. The Europeans think and act differently – it's a whole new and different attitude they carry; in short, I believe they know how to *live*. Their mentality is completely different to that of younger countries like Australia and the U.S.

I've had the good fortune to have grown up in Australia, I've lived in the U.S, and have spent time in Japan and to me, these countries reflect a comparatively more materialistic lifestyle where the emphasis is on working to earn more ... to *have* more. But here, there seems to be a greater emphasis on *living,* and I suppose if I've learned nothing else in the year I've been away, I've learned how to relax and enjoy life. No, I'm not gallivanting around having a great time, I'm highly organised because I have to be – probably doing too much at times, but living.

It's been eleven months since I left home ... not that long really, but I've done so much in that time and learned a lot. The French are quite a study! It took me a while to adapt to their abrupt, distant, sometimes cold manner, but that was initially when I had barely any of the French language.

I find to experience a people and to share their lifestyle, you need both the language and the time. I have both now and love living in Paris. It's always been my dream, and now I'm here, living, working, and really sharing the lifestyle. It's more than I ever dreamed. Paris is a city throbbing with an incredibly vibrant energy, totally predictably unpredictable, with a wealth of treasures – culturally, musically, historically and socially – and with the rest of Europe at its doorstep.

One of my favourite holiday haunts is just six hours north of Paris by train and into a completely different lifestyle, language, culture, and landscape ... Holland. I love Amsterdam. I've spent hours sitting over a drink in their little 'brown cafes' listening to their rollicking music, dining in their sometimes boisterous but incredibly friendly restaurants, then walking back to Hotel Schroder (my home away from home), over bridges covering icy canals and brushing snow off my face. The next morning waking up to winter sun, taking a bike ride into their fairy-tale countryside, then regrettably boarding a train through Belgium to Paris, a different and wonderful world again.

Uncle Len, I only planned to stay perhaps one year but the longer I stay, the harder it is to think about going home.

In writing this letter I didn't plan to give you a day by day account of my life and travels, but just in the hope that I might encourage you to come over for a week, a month, a year even! I would love to see you experience a little of Europe and its people. It really is very different to Australia – the way they think, act, live; and live they do. It can become contagious!

I know too that you have a business to consider, but I'm sure if you left for twenty-eight days it would probably still be there when you returned. You would possibly find new and untold business inspirations while you were here to put into action when you returned; like how to operate the business in Dubbo from Europe for a year!

But seriously, I don't think it would be such a drastic step to take for thirty days. All you need is the money, the time and the desire to come, and the funny thing is, you have all three – you really have. My God, you even have a place to stay when you get here – a top guide who knows all the best places in Europe – and I'll even let you out at night! I would just love to see you do something that I know you have always wanted to do.

If you are now doing what you have always wanted to do, in terms of living and working, that's great. If that's fulfilling enough in itself and you have no real desire to do something like this, then I'm as happy for you as you are, as much as I would be if you came over here.

You know Uncle Len, the one thing among many in my life that I treasure and find I must have, keep, and need in all situations and all circumstances, is my freedom and independence to *be* and to *choose*. I'm not an island – to live is to share, whether it be a thought, a word, a deed or a life. But with all that, I believe we must *BE*. Remember the Neil Diamond *Jonathon Livingstone Seagull* soundtrack of the song "Be"– it's beautiful. I believe that to *be* is to *live*, and God knows how hard that can be at times.

It's strange … I think a person could *live* for 150 years and never know what it's like to *be* - and yet another could *be* for only 30 years and *really* know what it's like to *live*. Maybe it's me that's strange, but there *is* a difference. I don't claim to have found it, but I'm very aware of it, and I'm working towards it.

73

I rave on, don't I? I don't write for months and then when I do ...
well, I have so much inside my mind, it's hard to know where to start. I
can say it all in a line, or I can say the same thing on pages upon pages.

I don't believe it's that hard to convince you, or to at least encourage
you to come. I think – no, I *know* – the difficulty is in convincing
yourself. What can I say except that I'm sure when you do decide to
come for however long, you'll wish you had done it before and wonder
why the hell you didn't.

From here we are heading up through Germany, travelling along
the Rhine to Amsterdam, then home to Paris. When Mum leaves, I plan
to steal away for a week by myself just to lie and soak up the winter
sun on Capri, one of the most magnificent islands I have ever seen or
imagined, just to relax before I go back to Paris to do some serious job
hunting. Paris has not escaped the unemployment problems and scarcity
of jobs, so it's essential for me to consider my work opportunities too.
I've made some friends on Capri, and they have invited me to spend
Christmas there.

Capri is almost a night and a day from Paris by train and one hour
by steamer from Naples. Didn't think Heaven was so close, least of all in
Italy. The people there are more Greek than Italian. At one time, before
Julius Caesar, it was a Greek island; later it was sold and populated by
both Italians and Greeks but owned by Italy, as it is today. I'm reading
The Story of San Michelle by Axel Munthe at the moment, and it touches
on Capri's history – a must for you to read when you come.

A few months ago, while working in a French perfumery in Paris,
(pandering to the wealthy French clientele and tourists), I met a couple
from Dubbo and asked them to give you my love. I don't know if they
did. They said they had only been in Dubbo for two years. I don't
remember their names.

One of the most incredible sights I've seen since I've been here is
the excavated city of Pompeii at the foot of Mount Vesuvius. A whole
city over 2000 years old, still standing ... in ruins, but still standing. To
walk through it is a real experience and honour. Pompeii has seen two
major earthquakes in its time and lastly the force that killed the whole

population - the eruption of Vesuvius. And yet, although in ruins, much of the city still stands!

It's uncanny to see the almost tangible strength of a city standing in defiance, in spite of all, and especially Vesuvius, that brought death to the whole population in one afternoon. And yet, above all of this, is the supreme ruler, the real victor, Time itself.

So, when you are contemplating the pros and cons of coming over (for yourself and your business), give thought to Pompeii. Go immediately to the travel agent, book your flights, organise travel documents, pack your bags and board the plane. No doubt in the mad rush and the urgency to get here you will have forgotten to write to me. Not to worry, just call me when you get to the airport – 251 58 79 – and I'll be there in thirty minutes.

It's almost 11 pm, so I'm going to sleep now. Take care with your decision and give it lots of positive, healthy thought.

Love you lots.

While in Zermatt staying at the Hotel Bahnhof, the owner, Frau Paula Biner, referred us to a local doctor there. I remember how openly shocked and surprised he was when Rainey had to assure him, "No, we are not talking about my mother, we are talking about me."

He looked at us in disbelief. Looking at Rainey, his first words were, "No, not you." He seemed confused for a moment and was obviously both surprised and concerned.

He referred us to an eminent Professor of Oncology in Berne.

Rainey and I were desperately hoping that perhaps here she would receive a more encouraging opinion, but it was not to be.

That evening back in our hotel room she wrote the following, which I recently found among her papers. She writes of the afternoon's disappoint-ment, and of her thoughts and feelings during the months she had spent having chemotherapy.

Those four months had a devastating and long-lasting effect on Rainey, and when I read this, even now, I am reduced to tears and overwhelming sadness. I also feel privileged that her words allow me to share her innermost thoughts and feelings, and to marvel at her courage, fortitude and her ability to confront and emerge from such an ordeal with that inner strength still intact. The following is from those pages.

Rainey's thoughts, written in Berne, Switzerland November 1980

I had already decided to write to the better part of myself to-night, even before I had the pleasure of seeing my future or my timeline meet itself.

It's a little like, "Oh! Come in, we were expecting you … sure took a long time. Twenty-seven years you say? Oh well, you're here now …"

They always seem at that moment to close the door in my face … gently, yes, but to see beyond that is always a mystery, and I believe will remain so until the next little rendezvous with Time.

And so it's for this that I choose to please, or should I say, to at least *encourage* fate and destiny in their unfailing success and complete this task, or rather this pleasure, to write. At least I know I'm on the right path as it were … or is there only one path to travel and only one means of getting there?

What to call this? After all, it's not something that can be labelled, only felt, and it's been a whole realm of feeling - hurt, fear, uncertainty, and wonderment on the source of strength, and the most precious of them all, certainty in the face of uncertainty, a quietude born in faith and realised through time in prayer.

A chapter in my life that appeared almost as quickly as it left, guided into and out of my life in a quietly controlled series of events in which I was merely an indispensable prop in a theatre piece – the actors having already been chosen – *au fait* with their parts and places even before the props were made. But without the backdrop, the piece would have no parameters - taken down just as easily as they were put in place. The play is finished, the galleries are empty. There remains the uncertainty for the players … success … failure … or perhaps a non-event? They too must wait for tomorrow's reviews with patience and hope.

Ironically, I leave with the knowledge I would like to have entered with. I think it's called *life*.

I hope one day I may be used to help someone through this initial time; to comfort, to encourage and to share some of myself, to strengthen as I was strengthened.

To enter that chemotherapy arena with expectation means disappointment, or perhaps surprise. I entered with nothing, but I did find there a reality, and in that reality I found in time a quietly profound strength. It is this that I believe was my mainstay, the essence of my comportment during that time.

Yes, David was wonderful. I could never have done without him. Every minute every hour he was there, lovingly and caringly. His presence and his love comforted me more than he will know, but to have coped without my inner strength would have been an impossibility – I know this.

It's for this reason, that I reflect upon that time as a time of being alone – alone with myself and my strength. I still don't know how I found that strength. There have been times and situations where I would have been grateful for even a fraction of it – unhappily never to arrive.

No, I was never lonely, but I was alone.

I cannot begin to describe the effects of those months of chemotherapy, and more, the determination to meet and support it. No, not as a matter of challenge or pride, but purely as a matter of self-preservation – of necessity – of survival.

At times, during that final week, this strength was stretched to a disbelieving point. At these times I dared not question its worth, nor question its roots. To find or to search for more was impossible without reason or energy, and a threat to the little I had left.

These moments for me were intense ... crucial. Hence, in a conscious realm of calm, as delicate as it was intensely strong, I believe was the essence of my strength, or should I say the strength that was so timely and knowingly given me. Almost as if it was given to me but it was for me to find, to cultivate and to retain, whatever the odds.

Yes, there are those who have suffered, who are suffering, and who will suffer infinitely more than I, but I write in praise of something much stronger than ourselves – something that happens so timely and so beautifully into our lives in our time of need. And more; something as great as this gently encourages within us a NEW strength (perhaps almost as great) to house, to hold, and to honour such a treasure.

In December I returned home to Australia. Always our goodbyes were sad, and I hated to leave her so far away. I felt so helpless being on the other side of the world. Why did she have to stay? Was that her destiny? Can we alter our destiny by the choices we make? Should I have begged her to come home with me? I knew she wanted to stay in Paris - needed to stay in Paris. I don't know why, and I don't know if Rainey knew why, but it was what she desperately wanted to do.

I left from Amsterdam, and she returned to Capri for a week before returning to her busy life in Paris. She loved Capri and had always found it relaxing and revitalising, both physically and emotionally.

Letter, 13th December 1980

Dear Mum, Barbie and Jeff,

I'm still unwinding from all the events after you left. I caught the train from Amsterdam to Paris, where I had only six hours to run around organising my life for when I go back in a weeks' time. From there I took the train to Naples, then the ferry to Capri. All in all, a thirty-hour trip.

My arrival in Napoli was an angry one. The train was already an hour late and it looked like I was going to miss the last boat to Capri, so I was fit to kill, maim or injure to get there. My first confrontation was with a stubborn taxi driver. They have to speak English as it's their trade – ripping off the tourists I mean. It went something like this:

"How much to take me to the port?"

"Ten thousand lira."

"Are you crazy?"

"What about five thousand?"

"What about it? I can go over twice the distance for one hundred lire on the bus – forget it!" I can still hear the colourful abuse as he skidded off, and we went our separate ways.

I caught the next bus which was packed. At the first stop, there was an all-in brawl when about twenty rowdy locals tried pushing their way into the exit door without letting anyone out. By this time, the driver was standing on his seat, arms waving, and yelling what may well have been obscenities in a vain attempt to control the masses. All those wanting to alight were yelling, pushing and punching, until finally when those on the outside proved stronger, the driver wisely decided to close the doors regardless of what or whoever was wedged in between. I couldn't believe it. It was incredible. And that was my stop too. I managed to get off two stops later and had to walk all the way back with my heavy bag and find a room for the night.

I stayed at *Pensione Canada* and the owner, Gemma, said to give you her love when I write to you. Or more precisely, "Don-a-forget-a-ta-give-a-ma-love-a ta-ya-mumma."

She remembered you too Barbie, from when we stayed there while we were travelling, and asked how you both were. It's comforting being able to go back to lodgings where you are remembered and welcomed so warmly.

So, I'm pleased to report that Napoli is still alive and well - nothing's changed. I also learned today that Napoli has an airport! Yes! My God, they actually give them pilot licenses to drive around the sky in planes! It must be every driver's dream … no stop lights up there, or maybe it's just a plan to reduce the road havoc down here.

Arrived at the docks in the morning just missing a steamer and had to wait two hours for the next one. One of the crew said if I wanted, I could sit on deck until it sailed. That was really nice, seeing that no one was allowed to board until one hour before departure.

When I finally stepped ashore on Capri, the rush, hustle and general melee that had engulfed me, washed away. It was as if I had stepped into a different time, a different dimension, and the stress of the past forty-eight hours disappeared. You know what I mean … that indefinable feeling of Capri.

Next morning in the hotel, I woke late and rang for breakfast. When I arrived yesterday, the owner showed me to my room. He always shakes my hand now. He thinks I'm okay, even though I told him I got a better offer last time.

"How much is the room?' I asked.

"How- much- a-da-ya-wanna pay?"

Felt like saying, 'Nothing if it's all the same to you,' but I bargained him down to 7,500 lire with breakfast that doubled as lunch. My room has a balcony overlooking the illustrious taxi/bus rank. I can see the *Marina Grande* and up towards Anacapri too.

The few buses on the island constantly move between Capri and Anacapri. A beautiful but hair-raising ride as you might remember, but somewhat challenging for the uninitiated.

Today was very nice. I waited for your call, which came at 10 am, then walking across the town square I literally bumped into Antonietta, the girl you and I met on the steamer. She owns a lovely little boutique which overlooks the ocean and invited me to go with her. I helped her clean the basement to get ready for the summer influx of tourists, and we shared my picnic lunch.

On the way to her shop, we stopped at the church where I watched her go systematically into every little chapel there, put money in a box and light a candle. As quickly as she went in, she was out and into the next one. It's so nice to slip into and observe the lifestyle first hand, rather than just check out all the tourist attractions. Oh yes, Antonietta gave me a beautiful cream pure wool tunic jumper. It has a big cowl neck and buttoned down the sides with lovely caramel coloured wooden buttons – just gorgeous and very smart.

In the afternoon I went for a walk to *Arco Naturale*. This island is so incredibly beautiful and has some of the most amazing, natural rock formations. It is unbelievably relaxing here. I had almost forgotten how serene and peaceful this place is. It's got that pastel, hazy look about it today … pink, blue and grey.

Later I took the bus up to Anacapri to the travel agency. Fifteen minutes and one death-defying trip later, along the edge of precipices dropping vertically down a sheer rock wall to the depths of the ocean, I found myself, once again, on the highest tip of the island. The manager invited me to sit down, and we talked, me about the poster I wanted, and him about why don't I work on Capri for the summer instead of in Paris. He was looking for English-speaking girls to work ex-Capri to Naples, bring over tourists, look after them and sell them excursions. Well, it's an opportunity worth considering… offers like that don't come every day. He said it would be his pleasure to talk over coffee, so I'll meet with him and maybe try to convince him how indispensable I would be to his travel agency. It's an opportunity … if I choose to take it, it's there.

I was waiting for the bus, contemplating the trip down, when I heard an accented voice say, "Hello, would you like a lift down?"

I think I had already climbed onto the back of his motorbike before he had even finished his invitation. My brief, "Thanks, I'd love to!" was drowned by the roar of the bike engine as we sped off towards the little township below. Coming up on the bus, I'd never noticed how tight those hairpin bends were until I had the opportunity to tackle them at speed along the winding road that sits on the edge of the cliff. It was a heart-stopping but wonderful ride. Another friendly face ... another glass of wonderful Caprician wine ... and we were saying our thank yous and goodbyes. I would be sure to see him again sometime.

The travel agency manager had mentioned how elegant I looked when he was offering me that job. I hope he didn't see me screaming down the mountain on the back of that bike, hair streaming, legs sticking out and yelling, "Faster! Faster!"

Tomorrow I must look for my friend Antonio – the tall, dark and handsome Italian who I met when Barbie and I were here. It shouldn't be hard to track him down – I think he operates between the taxi rank and the bar like every honest, hardworking Caprician.

Antonietta has invited me to her place for tea tomorrow, so I'll meet her in the afternoon and go down to the beach (*Marina Piccola*) with her. I also need to visit our friend the pastry man, and Barbie, remember that café called Café Bill with the kangaroo placard outside? The owner is Australian and must have let his imagination run wild trying to think of a name ... obviously couldn't find one, eh? Anyway, he was telling me he used to manage the Captain Cook floating restaurant at Double Bay, and invited me back tomorrow for coffee and a talk ... said I didn't sound the least bit Aussie.

I must sleep now – I'll write more tomorrow.

The second day - rose late this morning and had breakfast in bed – what luxury!

This morning I made a serious effort to find Antonio. Went down to the taxi rank to find that his Dad was driving the taxi because Antonio was sick. It was nice to see him again, even though he bounded straight from his bed apparently against his mother's wishes, I'm sure. So I'll meet him tomorrow afternoon after I see the travel agent and we'll go to the disco in the evening. Antonio wants me to stay until Christmas or the New Year.

Also, this morning I went to visit our friend the pastry man who greeted me like a long-lost cousin. He's very sweet and very Italian. Insisted on giving me one of those lovely, big, round chocolate rum cakes, and said I could choose any chocolate on his shelf. I felt like a little girl let loose in a lolly shop! We had a long talk, and he kissed me goodbye on the hand (the arm's length distance is a good policy), and I emerged, chocolate cake in one hand and chocolate bar in the other. He simply would not let me refuse cake or chocolate and wanted me to come back in the afternoon. His shop is now closer to the town square.

While reading my book this afternoon in the outside café, I met two nice Italian guys, and they came with me to meet Antonietta. We walked down the winding path, the *Via Krupp*, to *Marina Piccola*. It takes about twenty minutes, and the views are truly spectacular. The four of us had a lovely time at the beach and shared lots of laughs.

Walking back this evening, I was mesmerised by the colours of the sunset. Just incredible – from bright pinks to pastel pinks, all reflecting on the water. The colours on this island are inexplicable, especially at sunset, and the place is unbelievably relaxing. I mean if I had done in Paris, all that I've done here in the last two days, I would be a nervous wreck, with buses, cars, people, and 'hurry up and wait' tactics. Here, everything is so laid-back, so relaxed and easy. Here no one seems to worry about anything. Most things just happen, and everyone has time for everyone else, to laugh, to relax, to work, to live … and enjoyably so.

It's so incredible that any one place could have so much beauty and so much opportunity to really *live*. I mean, even if you wanted to play 'let's live in a rat race,' here you couldn't. I don't think I ever want to leave. The first time Barbie and I came here was amazing, and when we went scuba diving in February with those two Navy guys from the U.S.S. Forestall while their ship was anchored in the Bay of Naples, that was wonderful, but the more you experience the actual lifestyle here and the more you become absorbed into it, the more beautiful it all becomes.

Last night Antonietta came by in the evening, and we went for a long walk. The lights, the water, the silence, the talking and laughter coming from the town square made the picture complete, and at times, almost too much to comprehend because it's all so beautiful and so different. Sometimes I thought if I touched those buildings around the town square, they would all fall down like stage props. Yes, I could quite easily become addicted to this place and these people. We are going out again this evening. She isn't here yet, so I think I'll read until she comes.

In this book I'm reading, *The Story of San Michelle* by Axel Munthe, I'm up to the chapter on hypnotism. That one man could have had so many experiences, so much good fortune and adventure, is incredible. That part of his life I'm sure was very rich. Possibly most people have only a fraction of his experience, others perhaps more, but I can't help feeling that he must have been lonely. I promised myself that when I've finished this book, I'll go to the *Villa San Michelle* again while I'm here, this time armed with a richer background and knowledge. That's the only way to visit most places anywhere.

It's the third day now, and Antonietta didn't show last night (must be an inborn trait of the Italians), so I contented myself with finishing the rest of the book which I couldn't put down. It's just amazing ... especially the last few pages. But you must read it.

So much for my early night; it was 2 am, according to the town clock, when I finally turned the last page.

So this morning after I showered and rang for breakfast, Antonio, who was supposed to come at 2 pm, arrived at 10 am! Told me he couldn't wait! Luckily, I was getting ready to go to the Villa San Michelle when he arrived to find me half dressed. He looked at me in my dressing gown – my wet hair, jeans, and no makeup – then came a little closer as if discovering some great secret, and announced, "And look – your hair's growing back! How long will it take to fix yourself?"

"The transformation shouldn't take too long," I replied. "My teeth should be arriving any minute now."

He smiled and said, "At least I won't have to give you any of *my* hair."

"Good thing," I answered, "You can't afford to give any away!"

Ten minutes later I emerged – the new me. So then we went to the *Villa San Michelle* and I gave him a guided, historical tour of the place.

The *Villa* is magnificent – built on the heights of Capri's steep cliffs and commanding spectacular views of the Bay of Naples and Mount Vesuvius. At the top, the panoramic view of Naples to the Gulf of Salerno and the Sorrento Peninsula is truly breathtaking. We had a lovely time. Stopped for coffee several times when Antonio insisted on introducing me as his wife! My God! Then he asked me, "How long have we known each other now – nearly a year?"

"Yes," I said, "but apart from phone calls, I've seen you only twice in that time and we've missed each other on the most planned occasions."

If he's not two hours late (or never to show at all) he's four hours early.

So now I'm fortifying myself with seafood and wine and maybe a coffee, ready for tonight's little romp at the disco up at Anacapri. Did I tell you about the last time we went? We were the last to leave and had the dance floor to ourselves when he insisted on showing me his prowess in the form of a tango. A similar one I've seen enacted by Morticia and her better half on television in *The Munsters*. Nevertheless, we had a really good time.

It's 2:30 pm and we're meeting in half an hour. I might just manage to stagger across to my abode. Italian red is very nice – very, very nice actually. I don't remember the last glass I had. I couldn't drink during my treatment … couldn't handle the taste. The shock to the system must be too much, and now I'm beginning to collapse all over the table. So as soon as I rustle up a little more positive comportment, I'll rise and pay my bill. Then slowly and deliberately I'll walk across the street and upstairs to my digs.

Mum, Antonio was wondering whether you had given any consideration to his proposal of meeting his Caprician friend, with a view to some sort of permanency. I think he was serious! Well, have you?? I asked him if he had a catalogue of potential males, as I might be interested too!

Day four began with a surprise call from you. I was still asleep when you rang – that's why I sounded a little worse for wear. It was a good night at the disco last night with a great group of people. Antonio has some lovely friends. So good to talk to you and Barbie and Jeff, it was what I needed this morning.

As I write, I'm having my lunch in the café. My God – I thought the Italian red was divine and rather heavenly but sherbet, the white is beautifully intoxicating. I wonder if Antonio would mind if I just went home and crashed for a few hours. I'm to meet him again this afternoon – that's OK, he's big and strong, and he can carry me everywhere.

It's quite a tonic just talking to Jeff about anything. He has the uncanny knack of always making me feel as if everything is OK and under control … even if it isn't. Between Jeff's philosophy and this wine, I think I have the happy delusion that all will be okay. I've had to shelve David's last letter for want of my sanity, I can't cope with both, so I choose to relax because I believe I need to and owe it to my body after all it's been through these last four months.

Yes, I have replied, and probably too lengthy as usual. But you know, at times I have to shelve it, both physically and mentally, because I begin not to cope very well … makes me feel like I'm in a confused, cloudy state … sort of dazed. I find it better to wait until I'm in a more together frame of mind to be able to cope with it practically. I find it very difficult.

In Naples on the way here, it wouldn't have taken much for me to have come home instead of Capri. The whole trip, including the six-hour stopover in Paris and the overnight in Naples was truly like walking on or between glass … touch and go to keep above it all … I can't explain.

After a few days here I thought I was beginning to unwind and relax, I really did. I felt slow and steady and fine when I walked into the post office here on Capri. I didn't mind waiting for five minutes … everything was cool. When the lady behind the counter told me how much it was in Italian, I couldn't understand. But she just kept saying it LOUDER and LOUDER in Italian, OVER and OVER. I just cracked … lost my cool and abused her EVEN LOUDER in English … threw money in the tray and slammed it through the window! It was terrible. It was as though I was looking at myself … a strange self. So then I got upset – not with her, but with myself, for getting so angry. It felt like I was someone else … not me. Then a man came up to me and said, "I speak English, can I help you?"

I was normal with him, but My God! I went back there yesterday, and the same man came up to me before I reached the counter. "I'm still here if you want me to help you," he said.

So I try hard now not to make a spectacle of myself. I seem to have little patience lately. Then last night I went for a drive with Antonio. He has a fabulous voice and was singing to this song on the cassette. I asked him to translate the words which he did, and a few minutes later I was welling up in a quiet little flood of tears. Of course, he wanted to know what the matter was (can't take me anywhere).

Then he proceeded to tell me that he doesn't like it when I continually think of David. I told him I wasn't exactly having a high-rolling time of it either, but that I would do my best to blot out those three years somewhere within the next few minutes if he could afford to wait that long. I was so angry … I wanted OUT and was beginning to feel suffocated.

Then, if that wasn't enough, he told me that he had already booked a room for the night, and rallied well with his personal philosophy on why we should spend the night together after I told him I wasn't interested. The best argument was that he doesn't wait very long for a girl who "won't come to the party" and usually just says goodbye. I didn't know whether to laugh or feel sorry for him.

I just said, "If you have *any* intentions of giving me *any* ultimatums, save yourself the trouble and consider it already said."

I hate that kind of pressure and tension, especially with someone I consider a friend. Well, I'm sure we'll both get over it.

Next day now.

What will I do this afternoon? I'll finish this letter after my talk with the travel agent, and if he offers me anything beyond a job … there's something I don't like about him. So as the French say, *"Il fait faire attention"* - be careful.

Last day on Capri.

My premonitions about the travel agent were somewhat intuitively correct. He also offered me a pre-paid ticket to Sicily, would telex my tickets to Paris (plane tickets no less), and we would go together there for one or two weeks, 'for the benefit of good working relations,' quote, unquote. I thought, give me a break! I want a *job* - not an affair! *And* I want my poster. Oddly enough I've decided to pass on the job!

I'll close now as I don't think Capri has a parcel post service for this saga. Tomorrow morning I leave this lovely place behind, until next time.

Back in Napoli now, and after Capri, civilisation is quite an unpleasant shock to the system. I took the new big steamer from Capri back to the mainland, and the captain invited me up to the bridge. Remembering last week's little episode on the bus in Napoli, I opted for a taxi from the port to the rail station. My train leaves in two hours.

Yes, I spent a wonderful week on Capri, did a lot and was sad to leave. While there I was inspired to write the enclosed poem. I hope you like it.

CAPRI

The pastel pink sunsets
The sheer grandeur of the limestone cliffs
The turquoise blue of the water
The refreshing pleasure of listening to a silence
Interrupted only by the gentle melody of the sea
The cry of a bird
The scamper of a cautious animal in the undergrowth
Nothing's changed
The smiles on the faces of the people are still as welcoming
And the Mediterranean sun
Still as soothing
Capri
Crossroads in time where the past is as beautifully alive as the present
Where the stately ruins of Emperor Tiberius' Palace
Still retains its grace and glory
Where the furtive excitement of young children running home
Along the narrow cobblestone streets
Is a precious reminder that
Time is the bearer and the guardian of all things
The Beginning and the End

-Lorraine, December 1980

Chapter 4

Letter, 22nd December 1980

Dear Mum, Barbie and Jeff,

Just a note to say hello and to keep you posted. My week on Capri was wonderful and I feel so relaxed. It's been three days since I arrived back in Paris and I'm staying again at *Montmartrois* behind *Sacré-Coeur*. The landlady gave me a special price for the room.

But the news of the day – I went to Lisa's for dinner the first night I arrived, and Madame Gaba invited me back with open arms. *C'est le française*. What a change of attitude! This lady is one weird case. Throwing me out the last time when she learned I was having chemotherapy, and believing that I was diseased and contagious, explains a lot about Madame Gaba. I know she has asked me to come back only because Lisa now has two nights off and Madame doesn't want to be alone at night; so with me there, Lisa and I would alternate, and Madame would have company every night. But I'll be happy to be there; it's a blessing in disguise not having to pay rent.

Having considered my financial situation and all the things that are necessary to do, like acupuncture treatment every month, finding a deposit for an apartment, an impending visit to the dentist and the melanoma clinic, I had my bags in there before she could change her mind. No really, I have to. It's okay so don't worry, and I'm looking for a job. I move in tomorrow. I'm very relieved, but only plan to be there no longer than eight weeks. With a good job (maybe two) I can save.

I *did* say to Madame that while I didn't understand her change of mind, and if it was a case of personality, then maybe she should keep to her initial decision, because as the French say, "*Nous devons vivre confortablement*" - We all need to live comfortably. I knew she wouldn't change her mind. That's the only reason I said it.

I said to her, "It's your house and your life, but while I'm here it's my life as well," and very nicely, I made her understand that I was not there wholly and solely for *her* benefit, to be at her beck and call, but just for company at night. I just don't want a repeat of my previous time here. She can have very unrealistic expectations of a person.

So, here we are. I plan on staying for a couple of months; by then I'll have a job and a bit of money behind me. Then you won't see me for dust. Since being back in Paris, I've been sleeping early and rising late, taking relaxing baths to repose myself and am feeling much better.

I received my *Carte d'immatriculation* with my social security number, informing me that I'm now an official legal independent worker! I have Jim Wilkes to thank for that, for guiding me so expertly through the maze of legalities and 'illegalities'. He's still in the States, so I'll call him when he returns in January.

I won't go to Capri for the New Year as I need the money for Amsterdam … must ring Antonio and tell him. One day on Capri, he asked me if I would like to meet his mother. I thought why not? That would be nice … until he told me she worked in the post office! Then panic set in at an alarming rate. I knew of two ladies working in that post office, one I had abused up hill and down dale in no uncertain terms, so I was hoping to God it was the other one. On the way, rigor mortis had set in, and I was really scared. I was also hoping that Antonio was having a memory lapse and would soon tell me that his mother worked somewhere else. Fortunately for me, it *was* the other lady, and I'm sure she mistook my jubilant enthusiasm for the pleasure of meeting her.

How I digress! Of course, Madame Gaba reviewed the living conditions again. I didn't tell her about going to Holland for two days and two nights every month for my acupuncture treatment. I don't intend to bargain with my life. I just go, and that's it.

She asked me last night if I had written to you; said that I should, because you would be very happy that I was back with her. At that, Lisa practically choked on her biscuit, and I tried my hardest to remain indifferently composed. For someone who has a mania for germs and disease, and who lives in a beautiful apartment in one of the most salubrious areas of Paris on *Boulevarde Victor Hugo*, she is not very clean. But I'm happy to be here, and it's very convenient.

I'll write a more informative and organised letter when I'm at home with 'the warden' one night this week. Being here with Madame Gaba sometimes feels like I'm in a prison. It's great for my French, though … she doesn't speak English, thank God!

Letter, 3rd January 1980

Dear Mum,

It's Saturday today, and I'm enjoying staying at 'home' and getting myself rested and reorganised. I'm getting back into circulation again and am out almost all the time, so much so that I don't have time to scratch. School resumes January 5th, and then I'll look for work.

I'm out all my free nights, and on our nights at home Lisa and I usually have friends over. Remember Claude, the insurance salesman you met? Well, I rang him to say hello, and forty-five minutes later he was knocking on Madame's door complete with a bottle of champagne. Lisa, her boyfriend Ward, Claude and I talked, champagne'd and coffee'd till 4 am! The next night he took me to dinner at a beautiful restaurant.

Marc is coming to dinner tonight because Madame Gaba wants to have all her beautiful furniture reupholstered, which is what he does.

Recently I met Sébastien, the director of several private schools here in Paris. He invited me around to his office last Sunday. Some office – just gorgeous – and over vodka, pretzels, and Strauss, in front of a big open fire, gave me many contacts and addresses. He explained all about my work papers in relation to the school administration and the French school system.

The worst thing is when they ring; Madame always gets their names mixed up! She calls Marc, Claude and calls Claude, Marc and calls Sébastien something else! I'm sure she makes them up as she goes along. I hate it when the phone rings; I never know who it is because they're all French, and on the phone 'Salute Lorraine' always sounds the same. Then there's always a brief silence while I compose myself to think, *who the hell is this one?*

Anyway, I'm out all my free nights but sometimes … although it's lovely to stroll down the *Champs Élysées* at night after a lovely dinner, take a coffee and have a thoroughly enjoyable evening … sometimes I wish for something deeper, something more meaningful. I want sincere friends, not just admirers.

Frenchmen are incredible. Sometimes I think it's all so superficial, their way of flirting here and there with all different people. Sometimes I just want to stop and relax with someone really sincere … someone who really cares. I mean I have a great time, and I can handle the French, but sometimes I think I can see myself doing this all the time until I'm older because I have my complete freedom to choose. It's safe. I please myself … no complicated involvement. I'm free, and I'm responsible to no one.

I have this fear of giving up my complete freedom, even though I know a better freedom is the choice to share all with another, and there you have twice as much – it doubles and travels and grows infinitely. But the minute I sense that, I back away. Even if I like the guy a lot and have a great time, it suddenly arrives that for no obvious reason I want *out* – I want to get away – I feel suffocated and become agitated. I don't think that's normal. I'm a weird case, but I suppose for the moment it's ok.

Madame Gaba's son has a crush on me, so I let him take me to *Le Café de la Paix* on *Boulevard des Capucines* near the Opera. I've always wanted to go there. It's one of the most chic cafés in Paris. We dined on sumptuous cuisine in the most elegant dining room. Amazing frescoes decorated the walls, and we were surrounded by elaborate but tasteful décor. It was such a romantic atmosphere. I had a lovely time, but he's a playboy-wolf so is ranking low on my list. He wanted to take me to lunch, and was I doing anything next Wednesday? I felt like saying, 'No but I'm bound to find something.'

Antonio rang to wish me a happy New Year. He wants to come to Paris or me to go to Capri. I'll have to start giving out appointment cards soon – mainly to myself.

Lisa and I had a great time on Christmas Eve. Went to church at *Notre Dame* then met friends at a café in *St Germain* where they have live music; then on to the discos, where we danced and partied until the early hours. We had breakfast in another café and got home at 9 am Christmas morning. Took a shower, then went to visit an American friend of Lisa's and spent a lovely day at her house in the country.

For New Year's Eve we had a party with friends here at Madame Gaba's, then went out on the town. I spent part of that evening on the *Champs Élysées* reflecting quietly over the past year … which at times I still don't believe happened in parts, and the New Year was like coming up for a much overdue second breath.

I'm really looking forward to Amsterdam on the 21st for my next acupuncture appointment. I'm on the lookout for two other guys to go out with … one who owns an asparagus plantation, and one who comes from Bulgaria and knows how to make yoghurt! We must keep healthy!

Rainey and I had a constant dialogue via letters and occasionally the telephone. I found some of my letters among her papers.

The following is an extract from my reply to the previous letter:

"I'm glad things seem to be settling down for you now and that you are going out again. It will be better when you have a job and a real interest; then you will be meeting different people too.

It is very natural for you to feel the way you did when you wrote this letter. Everyone feels like that at times – some more than others – so it's normal. Especially for you, because you are so far from home, but try not to get despondent when you feel lonely. One day you WILL meet that sincere person – someone who really cares. Just be patient.

You wrote in your letter, 'Sometimes I think I can see myself doing this my whole life', but that won't happen. You will meet someone who will care as deeply and sincerely for you as you will for them, and there will be no fear of giving up your freedom and no fear of losing your independence – these feelings won't even exist. Instead, you will know the true happiness that brings its own feeling of freedom. Try not to get despondent, love. Just be patient. You will meet that someone, believe me, and while you are waiting, just enjoy life and all it has to offer."

Letter, 20th January 1981

Dear Mum,

As I write I'm en route to Amsterdam for my acupuncture appointment tomorrow, and as there was no train before 6 pm, I thought I'd be smart and find an earlier one which, leave it to me, I did. I found a train leaving Paris at 5 pm which just happened to coincide with the fact that I'd read the timetable backwards, and now I'm here sitting in this carriage on a first-class express train with a cheap *Trans Alpino* ticket. I was in too much of a hurry to catch the train to realise this small detail, which I only discovered when the conductor came through to check the tickets!

Don't seem to be having much success in taking the French railways for a ride these days. But I've since learned not to worry about minor details, like being almost broke after having to pay full fare on this 1st class express train. However, I have bigger problems to sort out like which metro will I sleep in when I get back and what newspaper will I buy to sleep under? And then why not complete the picture with a bottle of red or a bottle of rosé? No – just kidding. I have all very positive, successful things to tell you, which should explain why I've not written of late.

First, I'll blow you away with the good news. Yes, I'm working! After going to many interviews with different language schools, I had several offers. I chose this one, Language Power, and took the course. It's necessary to take their course whether you are a teacher or not to familiarise yourself with their teaching method. I'm now officially employed full-time with Language Power, and I love it.

I'll be teaching English to French businessmen and women in this language school. I'll also go out into the field to different companies teaching groups and individuals. It's great!

Raced around in my lunch hour to-day which was a very welcome experience, seeing I haven't had a job or a lunch hour for eight months, so I revelled in that. Wait till I tell you what I did in the lunch hour … but I'll keep you in suspense for another page.

Well, I must have impressed the director of this language school, that's all I can say. The course to learn their method lasts ten days. On the first day, he called me out of the class to ask if I would mind taking the place of a teacher who would not be available to take his next class at the Fiat Car Company. He picked me out of the whole group, and I have to pat myself on the back because no one over here does. But I couldn't do it because it was for today when I'm travelling to Amsterdam. I'll venture to mention that tomorrow's class at Language Power was cancelled because yours truly can't attend, and the director doesn't want anyone absent.

This language school has ten branches in Paris, and I remember when I was in the early throes of searching for jobs, I had left that place in tears because one of the directors would not accept my independent working papers. They wanted someone salaried. It was exactly the job I wanted, but he wouldn't have me. Then another director in the same school got hold of my phone number (God knows how), and called me. It's for that that I say everything I've achieved here in Paris I've had to fight for and fight damned hard. I'm serious.

I fought that day at the interview; did my homework beforehand by calling Jim Wilkes. He put me through my paces. I learned and practised my lines so that my independent working papers would be accepted. I had an answer for everything. I'm now a graduate in fraud, bluff, charm, and even have a diploma from the 'Jim Wilkes School for Illegal Imports' to prove it! Nothing has been handed to me on a platter here. So instead of celebrating after eight weeks of job-searching, I wiped my brow with relief. It's rewarding in itself.

Actually, these last few months have been spent trying to organise my life. It's been so full-on between living at Madame Gaba's (an exercise in endurance itself) and having to babysit her every second night, spending all day job hunting, writing letters of application, going for interviews and going out too much.

We arrived home one night to Madame's tune of, "You will both have to be out of here in three days because I've decided to move to the country!"

Well, after picking myself up off the floor I boiled inside. I think it's an after-effect of the treatment, because lately, and in the months during the chemo up till now, I get depressed very easily and have little or no patience if hassled. I told her that quite apart from being totally unjust, it was dishonest, as she obviously knew she would be moving several weeks in advance. I said that not only were we *not* going to leave in three days, but that we would be here for at least two more weeks, as that was one of *her* conditions on my arrival. I reminded her that according to her list of conditions, if Lisa or I chose to leave we would need to give *her* two weeks' notice.

Then with everything else, we had the added little bonus of looking for an apartment.

Well, try getting up at 6:30 every morning and getting home at midnight. After that little ultimatum, I reasoned that she didn't need us anymore, so I didn't worry about coming home to babysit and told her nicely that I would be putting all my time and energy into looking for a place to live instead. I didn't *ask* her, I *told* her, civilly. Lisa, I might add, flew off the deep end on hearing her ultimatum and looked at me as if to say, "Don't just stand there – do something!"

I think she expected me to pick Madame up by the ears and toss her out of her bourgeois, fourth floor, society dining-room window … without opening it! But instead, I launched into my little speech. I was there with Lisa for one month this time, and it's been a life-saver in terms of saving money.

Do you know, as fate would have it I found an exquisite studio apartment on the eve of the last night at Madame Gaba's, and two days later I was accepted for the job at Language Power! Whoever is running this show is certainly making me work for what I have, and then comes up with complete surprises at the death knock. I even talked Mr Schroder in Amsterdam into waiting up to let me in at 11 pm tonight for a stay of just one night. It took two phone calls, but I did it. No class, but heaps of style.

Then there's the story of how I obtained my contract and lease of this apartment. I look back on this past month, and it seems all too much to comprehend. I know it's not me who did it. I just come with the show and manage somehow to be in the right place at the right time. Quite frankly I have so much adrenaline flowing now that I have to make myself slow down.

Now it's Movie time. Imagine a little, *très petit* studio apartment on the eighth floor, all painted white with new carpet, two glass French doors opening onto a balcony overlooking the rooftops of Paris, a little park and sky. It has a very quaint wrought iron *ascenseur*, (elevator) just like the ones you see in the old Parisian movies. There's a little hallway entry opening up to a living/bedroom. It has a small kitchen (no, this one's not in a cupboard) and one lovely spacious bathroom, with a separate room for the toilet and bidet. *Très, très mignon, très, très petit, très, très belle.* It's just twenty minutes on the RER express metro to work and five to ten minutes from the city centre. I just love it, and it's *mine!* I even have a contracted lease to prove it! I'm now the leaseholder of this gorgeous little studio on the eighth floor of *223 Rue La Fayette*.

You know in Paris (this is what amazes me) to rent an apartment you need to be earning over four thousand francs per month, have a healthy bank account and all the necessary legal papers. I don't earn *near* that amount per month, I have *no* bank account, and I'm *not* legal. I didn't even have a job at the time I found it. I feel like I've just robbed a bank or won the lottery!

I rang Jim Wilkes and cried, "Help!" He took me through my paces again; I learned my lines and did my homework. I was accepted for the job at Language Power the day *after* I found the apartment, and asked the manager to write a letter regarding my salary. Sammy wrote a letter of guarantor for me. I had to stall the agent for the apartment to give me time to get the letters and my story together.

Jim said, "Go get 'em. You can do it. Be calm, smooth and elegantly confident."

With all of that, I was finally ready for the interview. I dressed up to the nines and had the appointment this morning. With my application for the apartment, I took along the letters and all my false order forms. Told the interviewer I had untold work orders (independent of my salaried position) and anticipated my earnings for this year with my teaching job and my independent work would amount to seventy thousand francs. And sherbet ... I had to do it all in French! Looking back I find it hard to believe that I did it! I walked out of there with my keys and a grin from ear to ear. Beating the system is such a good feeling.

I was mentally exhausted when I left the agency. Raced back to the school to continue the lectures, left early and got sprung on this first-class express to Amsterdam. But that's okay. I figure one good turn deserves another.

I've got my act together now. I've compiled letters of application, curriculum vitae, references, my teaching diploma, and deposited them in all bilingual schools in Paris, ready to be called in the new school year, commencing August.

My carriage is filled with businessmen, seven in all. I'm the only female, and they all watched while I got sprung for my ticket. But I managed to keep my cool. If they ask me where I live in Paris, I could say, "That depends. The benches at *Chateau Rouge* are less crowded on Fridays, but I have a growing preference for *Gare du Nord*. Which metro do you sleep in?"

This train is just incredible. In the restaurant carriage, all these men have dined over wine and a meal. Me? I bought a hotdog with mustard for five francs from some greasy import on the station, then had chewing gum for dessert! Had to give the conductor nearly all my money for the first-class ticket.

Lisa and I are staying with Sammy in between leaving Madame Gaba's and next Thursday when we can move into the apartment.

Now with the chemotherapy over, having my working papers, a good, secure teaching position *and* an apartment, I'm looking for private students to tutor in the evenings. I already have a Japanese businessman for one hour per week, and I've been offered a dealership in Amway Products, but I don't know about that.

This trip to Amsterdam will unwind me a little. I'll take note of all Dr van Buren's advice and follow it religiously. I'll have things written out, and now with the apartment, everything will be much easier.

The train has just pulled into Brussels. I'm so happy that I won't be having any more chemotherapy. I wouldn't be able to do anything like this. If I think about that time, even now I still cry sometimes. Isn't that strange? When I do cry, it's like I'm looking at someone … not me. It seems like someone who looks exactly like me, and I get very upset for that other person … not for me. Like right now as I write, it's me outside myself looking in. I can't explain … but it all seems so incredible that it ever happened.

I wonder now how I did it. It seems even more horrible looking back than it did when I was there, and God knows it was unreal then. So what do they say? Another chapter of your life closed? I hope it stays that way. I never consider myself as having anything like that you know, really I don't. Sherbet, I don't want to make a spectacle of myself here, but you know, I always wonder about that. Did I need it or didn't I need it? Was it really necessary? It's true, I do have more wrinkles, especially around my eyes.

I was sitting in a café the other day with a doctor friend of mine, Carlos, and he told me I had nice hair, "especially all the little ones that are growing on the edge in profusion," he said. And I, in my enthusiasm, replied, "Yes, they're growing back now," without thinking that statements like that invariably need qualification.

He asked me. I told him a little and pushed back the tears that just came up behind and grabbed me. But I'm getting better at that now. It's strange; there are only two people in the whole world who know about that time and how it really was … me and God … and then two more who know a lot: David, because he was here, and I feel you know too, Mum.

Well, I consider myself very fortunate. I'll send you that piece I wrote in Berne when I find it, and when I become a bit more financially secure I want to buy a second-hand typewriter to give breath to my writing, seeing no one (including myself) can decipher my scrawl in those fleeting moments of inspiration.

Recently I was sitting in a cafe when one of my inspirations suddenly surfaced. I had a pen but no paper so I began writing furiously on a paper serviette. Thank goodness for paper serviettes! I filled that one and as I was reaching for another, out of the corner of my eye I became aware of a piece of paper that seemed to be somehow floating in mid-air and coming in my direction … No it wasn't floating. It was being held by the elderly gentlemen at the next table. He placed the paper on my table, rose, politely nodded, smiled and was gone giving me no time to thank him.

We're three hours out of Amsterdam now and about three hours and five minutes out of my bed. I can't believe they cancelled the class tomorrow. I'm really happy at that school. I wouldn't mind a completely free day to collate my life and stop for a while, but now with a job and an apartment, things are looking much calmer. The money you sent was so welcome Mum, thank you so much. It helped me a lot during these last few months.

Nearly all the men from this carriage got off at Brussels. There's one sane one left. I assume he's travelling with me to Amsterdam.

This stop is Roosendaal; nearly there.

Denise is coming back to Paris to work in a travel agency. It'll be so good to see her again. Lisa has a new student, the Director General of one of the banks in Paris. They met to discuss times, place, salary and of course a study timetable. He took her to a restaurant for a 'snack' where they had caviar and sour cream with champagne, smoked salmon, and dessert with dessert wines. I had to knock her on the head when she came home to bring her down to earth. She works part-time (illegally) in a bookshop and has lots of private students. I'm looking for a part-time job too, but it has to be interesting.

Not far out of Amsterdam now. I'd like to order a sunny day, a bicycle to ride through the beautiful Dutch countryside, and a day or so to relax. But there's not enough time this trip. I'm going to have a little snooze now. This month has been very busy with work, contracts, apartment hunting, re-establishing friends, and between all of that – sleeping.

Now it's the next day, and I'm on my way back to Amsterdam from Baarn. Acupuncture was great. They are so thorough, and techniques and attitudes are so completely different to those in Australia. My next appointment is March 6th at 10:30 am, so I'll come up on Thursday after work and spend the weekend at Mr Schroder's for a break. I'll probably need a little holiday by then. I just want to relax, and I'm going to treat myself to a bike ride through the tulips. It's cold here now – there was ice and snow everywhere in Baarn this morning – so beautiful. I'm leaving on the 2 pm train this afternoon; must be at work tomorrow. All my acupuncture appointments from now are on a Friday, so I'll have the weekends here. Amsterdam says to say hello.

PS. Barbie, remember when we took the train into Italy via Pisa, and we were harassed by those Italian boys going to or coming back from the Carnival in Viareggio? Can you believe the carnival is on again? *That was a year ago*! Time goes by too quickly.

Letter, 25th January 1981

Dearest Mum,

Just a short note as I've been so busy. I can't imagine what a hot day is like anymore. I get out of control when I see the sun, let alone when I feel its warmth.

I see less of Marc now, much to his disapproval. He's becoming more and more possessive and domineering. I can't handle that. I see quite a bit of Claude, and at one stage I was going out with six of them, at different times of course. Confusion reigned when they called and Madame Gaba answered the phone. I have some hilarious stories to tell there. It was difficult because I had to be careful with names and dates, but I had a lot of fun. Lisa kept saying, "God, how do you do it? It's an education just watching you work!"

It *was* fun, but it was all a bit … superficial. I liked them all very much, but now they've moved many rungs down the ladder. I'm afraid I don't have much motivation to call any of them because I'd rather spend my time with someone else and yes, he's really special. He is my doctor friend Carlos, and I think all the others may have fallen off the ladder. I'll keep in contact because they're all very nice, but I always feel I'm wasting my time when I'd rather be with someone else. This is definitely not like me to be so involved (but always with reserve) and not feel caged or without my freedom. Anyway just thought I'd tell you. I've known Carlos now for about a month. He's not French, he's Argentinean.

Well, tomorrow I start work officially with Language Power in *La Défense*. I've finished the course, and when I'm not so tired I'll tell you about my acupuncture treatment. It was so good this time. My hair is beginning to grow back at last, and it looks like I'm finally coming together!

I love you.

Letter, 1ˢᵗ February 1981

Dear Barbie and Jeff,

Hello, I think I had a dream about you last night Barbie, but I'm not sure because I woke feeling a closeness to you that I had to remember that I felt, or used to feel if you know what I mean. Of course, I still have it and always will, but you know the lifestyle over here is completely different, and many things you forget – not forget – but you think twice, and then you remember how it feels.

Your sister is now a fully fledged legal member of the French workforce. It's taken a year, no less, but now I have the privilege of running for the metro at the ungodly hour of 6:45 each morning … when you've been unemployed for close to five months, anything before mid-day is ungodly. No, actually I've been working my butt off for a long time now between everything else, trying to get my life organised.

The language school, where I'm now working full time, caters for six languages. As well as teaching intensively at the school, I'll be going out to companies to teach classes of businessmen and women, a completely new experience for me. Anyone over seven years of age, and I have to be retrained. It's challenging, and I love it.

As well as teaching intensively at the school, I'll be going out to companies to teach classes of businessmen and women, a completely new experience for me. Anyone over seven years of age, and I have to be retrained. It's challenging, and I love it.

Anyway as I was saying, I now share with all other Parisians the privilege of being maimed or injured in the mad rush on the metro to and from work.

I arrive home each night with bundles of notes and paperwork to prepare. I don't know how you found time to do it during your year in Brazil, Barbie, but some of the stuff that I'm supposed to teach and explain, I've never heard of. I just speak their language, and I'm expected to analyse and explain it. It's hard, but the course was helpful and I'm improving. I'm really enjoying it and I need the challenge.

Working behind the counter selling perfumes was great, but I was beginning to vegetate. I loved the perfumery. It was special, but to live I need to give – to feel worthwhile and have job satisfaction. My hours at Language Power are good. I work anywhere between 8:15 am and 8:15 pm. I usually work eight or nine hours, five days a week, but tomorrow I'll work only three hours and have the rest of the day free. I'm paid a salary which means, however many hours I work, I get paid the same amount, as long as I get the basic number of hours up. This morning I started at 8:15, worked five hours straight, had a two-hour break, then did another two hours.

It's necessary, if you have to give an intensive three-hour lesson to one man, you must take coffee breaks. So the student, Mr International Businessman, takes you for coffee in a nearby café. It's a policy of the school, to save the teacher's sanity after trying to get a forty-five-year-old director to say, "It's a bus."

"What is it?"

"It's a bus."

"Good."

"What is it?"

He didn't know, so then we learn the expression 'I don't know,' or alternatively, 'Buggered if I know.'

I mean, a little variation helps me retain some semblance of sanity.

In this job, you must be an educationalist, a PR expert and a psychologist as well. Some students are very self-motivated – they *want* to learn.

I learn all sorts of things from my students. I'm now well-informed on the state of the construction industry in Saudi Arabia, as one of my students travels between France and that country. Monsieur Saudi Arabia arrived this morning before 8 am when not even the staff had turned up for work. He's lovely, and I think he likes me, but I can do without that. It takes me all my time to concentrate on my lines, think ahead of myself, correct and structure examples then explain, without being put off by him staring at me, then me getting confused with what to say. He's so funny.

Yesterday for the lesson I was using a slide about a family. Now I'm supposed to introduce it, talk about it and ask him questions according to the slide. It's very structured, very fast, and very concentrated with only time to think about your response. So I'm saying, "You have three children … repeat, please … good. How many children do you have?"

I was looking at the slide because the pace is quite fast, but he wasn't playing. I turned to look at him (this was a one to one situation) and he was just staring fixedly at me. I thought, *Give me a break, I can't cope with more than two things at once.* He still didn't answer my question; instead, he decided he was going to play teacher and still with that fixed gaze said, "*Dites-moi, combine d'enfants avez-vous?*" (Tell me, how many children do you have?)

Well … I then decided it was time for him to buy me that cup of coffee.

Each student I take a break with insists on buying coffee, and at the end of the day I'm shaking, really, so I'm going to have to stick to tea.

The language school has begun to bring out the paper warfare now … fill in this paper, that paper … and they're beginning to complicate my life by demanding all sorts of unnecessary trivia like visas, residence permits, and full-time working papers.

I'm becoming a wizard at beating the system over here, and it's not easy if you know the slightest bit about the French bureaucracy. It's built out of papers, and one day the wind will blow a little too hard, and all the French bureaucrats will be buried alive under their mounds of paperwork and get strangled by their red tape in the mass exodus!

I could write a book and title it, *How to Beat the System in France.* I'm thinking of going for my diploma in illegalities – maybe even open up a school for illegal imports and run courses on how to side-step all the rules and regulations. Jim Wilkes has taught me well. For someone who shouldn't even be here, I have a top job, a lovely apartment, and if you had seen the screening and the paperwork that goes into signing a lease, you would not believe it.

Well, it's after midnight and I must go to sleep. I start at 8:15 am tomorrow which means rising at 6 am. Speaking of work, for two hours over lunch today after a very intensive morning, I vegetated over coffee and began reflecting on the conquests of the morning's lessons. After wading through at length, one grammatical-syntactical explanation, one of my businessmen international gently reminded me of the apparent lack of success I had been having with him by replying to my question, "Is it a metro?" with a very serious "Yes, it's a piano."

I found it very hard to find some correlation there, but some pianos do have wheels, don't they? And having been trained in the positive reinforcement approach with students, I valiantly resisted the urge to scream and cry, "It's a METRO, you bloody idiot!"

He's probably sitting on a piano in some bar with his ticket. I resurrected the simplistic absurdity of the situation at lunch by pondering over D.H. Lawrence's, *Psychoanalysis and the Unconscious* to regain some inkling of sanity and balance. It's very interesting. I'm reading another of his books too. I really like them. Now I must sleep.

It's now February 2nd. I've just spent from 2:30 to 6:30 this afternoon teaching my class and I'm mentally exhausted. The last group left just a few minutes ago, and I'm waiting for the energy and motivation to pick up my books and slide projector and go home. I'll need to unwind in a café on the way.

You know, today was my first experience of walking into a company and teaching. The Director told me on Friday that he chose me to take the place of this company's regular teacher because he thought I was, (quote) 'young and alive.' So, today I was a little apprehensive as he was not at the school to brief me on the four hours I had in front of me. I didn't know where the company was, who I was supposed to see or at what level the students were, nothing. I only had the address and knew I had to be there at 2 pm. So you can imagine my dilemma.

The only preserving factor keeping me from losing it was that I told myself, 'Well here you are – this is what you wanted to do – teach English to people in big companies in Paris, so *go for it* - with or without – whatever.' So, I did!

As I sit here in the conference room of CBS Recording Company, with sounds of Boz Skaggs wafting through the walls and with my first session of company work under my belt, I think I've found that energy to pack away my gear.

It's strange. I wanted this, and I got it. It feels like I've been here before in my dreams … like I've caught up with my future somehow … like I'm actually *living my dream*. Some people spend a lifetime running after goals. At least I feel, in terms of what I've been through job-wise here, that I've caught up with mine …. hmm … interesting.

It's 7 pm, and I'm about to join the throng and brave the metro.

Well, I'm home now and will go to sleep when I finish this letter.

My next little problem will be to open a bank account, because here in France when you are salaried, you can only deposit your cheque through a bank. I'm working on that little problem now. I have a friend here who is the manager of a bank and he said I could open an account, no problem. You need all papers: passport, residence permit and visa, etc., but I've only one small detail stopping me – I don't have anything to put in it as the lease, rent in advance, and agency commission took it all. I'll have to wait – I'll think of something. It's not like in Australia where you can open an account with $5. Here a foreigner must have the foreign currency. Next time I write, no doubt with Jim Wilkes' advice, I will have solved that problem.

As you can see from my letters I've been in hyper administrative mode all month – haven't had much time to 'stop and smell the roses' at all. Between being told to leave Madam Gaba's in three days (we took two weeks), looking for a place to live, attending interviews, finding a job, working full time and going to Amsterdam, I had almost forgotten where I was. One day as the metro was emerging from a tunnel I looked out over the Seine and suddenly thought, *Wow! That's Paris out there … well, hello Paris! Excuse me while I go underground again.*

Now having a studio, a job, and my legal papers almost completely in order, I'm contacting friends again after the massive job/apartment saga. I've also had the telephone connected.

Well, it's now that I must sleep. Maybe in my next letter, I can tell you more relaxing things. At least in the month or six weeks I've been back from Capri I have almost all under control for now, financially and administratively.

So I'll give you both all my love and go to sleep now. Take good care and write soon. I love hearing from you Barbie. Try to write more often pet – really go for it – splurge for a twice every three months job! I love your letters, and in the two months it takes you to write the first one, tie it around your neck or something, so you don't lose it.

To help you get it together:

1. Get pen and paper
2. Write something – anything for God's sake!
3. Finish it
4. Post it

If you follow these steps religiously, I promise that you won't feel any pain.

I love you Barbie.

Chapter 5

Letter, 5th February 1981

Dearest Mum,

I love you. Just to write a quick note that will probably somehow manage to merge into a twenty-five-page epic. But in true form, not being able to resist my insatiable desire to know more about everything, please just note though, that this is only to *know* – nothing else.

Remember me telling you about my good friend Carlos, a doctor at *Hospital Hôtel-Dieu*. One day I told him about my little four months 'interlude' at *Hospital Paul-Brousse*. Of course, he wanted to see all the reports and papers and consequently took them to his hospital to discuss with his Professor, who said that while he tended to agree with Professor McCarthy, he advised getting another opinion. He also said that while Doctor Schwarzenberg is highly respected and famous for his work in France and Europe, he is also known to be very aggressive in his treatments and approach. I can vouch for that in many ways. When Carlos told me this, it was a very strange feeling I had … like … I can't explain.

Carlos made an appointment for me to see one of the top oncologists at *Hôpital Hôtel-Dieu*. I wanted to go just out of curiosity; not with the 'force' I had when I went with you to see the one in Berne (having already decided on my course), but just out of curiosity. I didn't expect them to say what they said. I was surprised. I don't know why, because I know what Dr Schwarzenberg would have said, and they said the same. I can't even remember how to spell his name now. I suppose that's a sign of the times as it were. I never thought I would say that because the whole horrible experience was so intense. You could almost not see out of it. The difference is between knowing and experiencing.

At *Hôpital Hôtel-Dieu*, I was told it was imperative that I take a less potent form of chemotherapy, relatively harmless on its own they said; because in every four months between check-ups, much can happen. Even the slightest thing can start, and…

After that talk with the professor, you know I wanted to cry when I heard her say it was imperative that one special less potent drug, DTIC, was necessary. This is what Doctor Schwarzenberg had said. I'm so confused. I'll write to Professor McCarthy.

I don't know why I'm writing this. I suppose I'm a little scared really. But in all things, there's room for doubt … nothing is ever that sure. The degrees of uncertainty here are all relative to uncertainty itself, where not even the doctors know the answer. So you go for your highest odds.

Well, I think I've done well; I've had the chemotherapy, now I'm having acupuncture. But you know chemotherapy doesn't stop anything else from being created and growing, so it's as if every few years, or time span later, it was as if you had never had it in terms of potential new growth. The fact that I've had four months of chemo was fine for the past, but now … well, it's just that I suppose… I do wonder and you know it's not just yourself that you have to look out for, it's also who you marry and your children. Sherbet! Sometimes that scares me. Maybe I'm being silly, but I don't think so. You have to be realistic and not think pessimistically, but *live* and be discerningly sensible. I'm probably better off than someone in perfect health that's going to be killed in a car accident next week.

Carlos said I must have a *contrôle* done – a checkup – even if I don't have the DTIC, but I suppose I know all there is to know, and I'm being 100% as sure as I can be. He said the best thing I could do, and I must do tonight, was to write to Professor McCarthy myself. Tell him everything, wait for the reply, then decide and stay with one form.

Next day now …

Well, that's life in the fast lane, and at the moment my life is going one hundred miles an hour. Work is keeping me very busy, thankfully. I have many people to go out with and sometimes find dating hard to cope with these days. I thought I was doing okay, but my social life is getting out of control again. Carlos was here the other night when one of my other favourites arrived to visit. Sherbet! I was mentally exhausted by the end of the evening; it was so tense. In the interim Claude rang and Carlos answered the phone! Claude was trying to make a date with me, and they all speak both French *and* English. Shit. After that I thought, *My God it's not worth it.*

You know I have no one to talk to here really, not to make my decisions for me but to air my feelings. I need to vent them. I hated going to the hospital the other day … to smell it … to look at the white efficiency of the staff. I didn't want to know about it and it made me full inside again, like I had to talk. Carlos was good. You know he was my strength during that visit, just like David was when I had the chemo.

After that rendezvous with the doctor, I had to rush back to the school and teach for two hours. My student was just leaving as I was a quarter of an hour late, but the secretary spotted me arriving and dragged him back! I could have done with the break.

One of my students today asked, with that wistful gaze in his eyes, "*Comment voulez-vous dire belle en anglais?*" (How do you say *beautiful* in English?) *Give me a break,* thought I. So I launched into a purposeful, scientific explanation about genders and expressions, after which he wrote in his book in perfect English, 'You are beautiful'and asked with a look that only the French can give, "*Est-ce exact Anglais?*" (Is that correct English?)

So then I thought, *It's time for that coffee break – why me?*

I went again to CBS Company to give a lesson and was setting up the works when I was introduced as *le Professor d' Anglais* - (the English teacher), and one of the guys said, "*Ce n'est pas possible. Pourquoi ne pourrais-je pas trouver je temps de suive ce cours.*" (It's not possible. Why couldn't I find time to take this course?) Frenchmen are unbelievable. Well, I go again to CBS tomorrow.

Remember Sébastien, the private school director who helped me? Well during the big move to the studio apartment, the trip to Amsterdam and job hunting etc., I kept missing his calls. Each time I rang, if he wasn't in a conference, he wasn't available for some other reason, and when he rang me I was out, so he wrote to me c/o American Express with strict instructions to call him. He's special. I didn't look to be getting involved, but I am … with Carlos.

Why me? I keep thinking, give me a break … later, later … but it creeps up on you and grabs you, and it's there before you know it – it's strange. Well, I'll keep you posted. Both you *and* me. I like to tell you things, Mum, because I can really talk to you. I just hope I can have that same relationship with *my* children.

I wrote to Professor McCarthy yesterday. He should receive my letter about 15th February, telling him my situation and asking his advice and for more information. I want to know everything. And I also *want* everything it seems. Tomorrow I'm having lunch with Sébastien, and then later I'm meeting Carlos.

About Carlos, he's Argentinian, a doctor, and I like him very much … too much maybe. He speaks English, French, Spanish and Italian. Well, that's enough for now, I'm very tired, so I'll sleep and finish this tomorrow.

Well, that was yesterday, and I'm at CBS Company again, sitting in the conference room waiting for my students to arrive, with my one-man show ready to roll. I'm here from 2 pm to 6:30 pm and this morning I taught from 8:15 for three hours with a two-hour break between the two classes.

I posted a letter to Barbie so you can read that. She should have it soon. It's a little happier than this one … not that this one is sad, just more serious. One student has just arrived, and I'm waiting for the others.

Now let me tell you about my wage, it's all coming together rather well now. On Jim Wilkes' suggestion, I'm having personal letter-head notepaper printed to make my *note d' honoraires*, telling everyone officially, legally and tastefully how much they owe me. My financial situation is beginning to look much healthier now, and I'll be able to save.

Back again – I've just completed three hours, with one and a half to go. Tonight, I'm going out with Sébastien, the school director. He's the one who explained the educational system and the independent work situation in relation to that, and who gave me a great list of contacts, addresses and tactics. I first met him when I was at the post office one day, ringing Antonio to tell him I couldn't go back to Capri for the New Year. When I went into the phone booth, this man was standing outside. He tapped on the glass to say he would very much like to speak with me after I made my call. He waited for ages till I'd finished, and we exchanged phone numbers. That's the French approach for you!

Madame Gaba thought it was wonderful – me knowing a director and owner of two private schools in Paris. She was so impressed with his title that she would be almost wetting her pants to talk to him. Whenever anyone rang for me she would say, "Oh! Are you the director?" and Lorraine this, and Lorraine that before the poor guy had a chance to ask questions.

"Am I the *what*?" would come the inevitable response.

She was really beginning to put a strain on my relationships. I'd be asked,

"Who's the director anyway?"

Ironically it was sort of a lifesaver staying at Madame Gaba's because I had a naturally accepted excuse for saying, 'No, not tonight thank you,' if I wanted to go out with someone else. When I answered the phone I could never tell who was ringing because they all sounded the same. Once I spent the first three minutes thinking I was talking to someone else. I was becoming quite clever, but it was making me tired. It's easier and less complicated being silly and single, but I want to be with one person who I can be myself with, who understands and accepts me for who I am.

I'm tired. I was out every night -- sometimes all night. Forever I was out – dinner, movies, dancing, coffee, walks, talks – and after a while they all began looking like they were coming off the end of an assembly line and I was bored. I still kept some and let others slide by. I still see Carlos, Sébastien and Claude, but Marc is on his way out – I don't like his chances. I'm spending more and more time with Carlos. I'm just going to have to be more honest with myself and with my entourage, as it were, but I just need to feel that I have that freedom.

Aref, an Iranian friend of ours, is staying here with us until he moves into his own studio in two weeks' time, and when Carlos comes over it's bloody awful because Aref likes me. He's a university student, and Lisa insists on calling him 'our little Iranian hostage.' We laugh a lot with Aref and get on really well together.

Well, my students haven't turned up yet. Sometimes they get bogged down with work, but at least I still get paid for my time.

Just found some more paper. I'm on a money saving binge at the moment. I also have private students: an Economics professor at the Sorbonne and a Japanese guy who works in tourism here.

On Saturdays I work from 9:30 am to 1 pm, then after that the weekend is mine.

I'm seriously thinking of going into business for myself, setting up an audio-visual method and working just five hours a day. I could even have another job and do that part-time. The demand here for English classes is great. I would probably do intensive courses for business men and women and charge twenty-five dollars an hour. They would write it off on their tax anyway. That's my next project, and I will do it!

The Director of Language Power called me into his office today to explain that my pay was late by one week because they had to organise percentages. Apparently, my pay is complicated, being the only independent worker here. He told me he didn't want to lose me; that he was impressed with me from the start and asked how I went about getting my working papers, 'because it's so rare for an Australian to have them.'

Now, having been trained well in the art of the 'tell 'em nothing, take 'em nowhere' technique from the Jim Wilkes School for Wayward Imports, I was very low key and said not very much, as if having working papers was a normal thing. I'm getting quite good at this. I talked my way into an apartment with no money and no job, so that's okay for starters. I felt like saying, "Ask me no questions, and I'll tell you no lies."

Well, this letter is getting longer so I'm going to finish. Tomorrow is Sunday and I'm sleeping in. I love this work.

Lorraine's letter to Professor McCarthy

5th February 1981

Dear Professor McCarthy,

I thank you for your concern and advice resulting in my decision to discontinue the chemotherapy treatment.

Having received four cycles of this therapy, the last of which I received 1st September, I would like now to seek further information and advice from you.

During the course of my inquiries into a subsequent method of control, I find collectively it is the French opinion that a less toxic follow-up in the form of the administration of one drug, D.T.I.C alone is imperative and that the control that I had chosen to accept on your advice, and would still prefer to pursue, would leave too much to chance without chemical support.

It is stressed that unlike the chemotherapy, it wasn't in any way detrimental in terms of long-term side effects, but merely an added precaution.

If it is relatively harmless and independent of the other chemicals, is it then a further hope in terms of positive preventative treatment? This appeal to continue is as urgent as yours is to discontinue. I believe you know my sentiments to follow your advice and to avoid, as far as possible, the toxicity where the necessity to accept the treatment is not particularly evident.

I want only to do what is necessary and in doing so, to give my body the respect that it deserves – especially at this stage. I await your reply and look forward to your advice.

Thanking you.

Sincerely,

Lorraine Walton

Letter, 16th February 1981

Dear Mum and Barbie,

At work again. I thought while I'm waiting for my student, I'd get some paper from reception and write to you.

Arrived at work this morning and picked up my schedule for the day. My first student is a Monsieur Cointy, chairman of Marantz France; they develop and sell high-end audio products. He's also the director of the educational program which includes sending people here to Language Power. On the note attached to his file it said all this, and that through him, we could possibly secure a contract for more students from his company.

I've been working here at Language Power for nearly two weeks now, and the Director insists on throwing businesses and potential contracts my way on a moment's notice. He called me into his office and asked me how much money I needed to live comfortably in Paris. I wasn't sure about the gist of the question and told him I didn't understand what he meant. He said, "Quite frankly I don't want to lose you. You've settled in extremely well and are handling the companies and the students well, and if you were to consider going elsewhere for a higher salary, I would rather pay what they are offering you."

I had made it my business at the first interview to tell him that I *did* have a job but was considering leaving it if this one offered more opportunity; educationally and financially. It's called 'playing your cards right.' How about that!

It's encouraging, though, and you need it. Sometimes some of the students can be very hard to motivate. They're not children, and for me this is an entirely different ball game. As I wrote in my letter to Barbie, 'anyone over seven years, and I've got to be retrained!'

I think Monsieur County has been caught up at his office because he's now one hour late. That's the nice thing about this job; presidents, directors, chairmen etcetera are often late or don't even show up on occasion, but you are paid anyway.

Jim Wilkes has been so incredibly helpful. Because of all his advice and pointing me in the right direction, I am able to earn a good monthly income, *tax-free* because of my *travailleur indépendant* (independent worker status). I'm so happy to be able to use my teacher training over here.

Lisa is going home to California in June, and then I'll have the apartment to myself. It's been great to have her here and to share the expenses. Now I have the chance to save and get my head above water before June. Everything is in my name – phone, lease, etc.

Yesterday Lisa, Aref and I went to *Bois de Boulogne* - the woods outside Paris. It was just a picture! Winter sunshine is magical. The lake was covered in parts with thin layers of ice, so being our crazy selves, we rented a rowboat, took it out onto the lake and rowed for an hour. Aref and I rowed while Lisa navigated. He wasn't content with merely crashing into other boats; he insisted on occasion, on wiping out boat loads of people with these great oars. I kept calling out, "The oars! The oars!"

He was so uncoordinated. Lisa and I thought it was hilarious watching boatloads of people, children and their dogs duck for cover. It was nice just gliding along the water too, with the boat breaking the thin layers of ice.

Oh! On the way home, guess who we saw standing on the footpath outside the Sorbonne? It was incredible. My favourite actor, Omar Sharif! What a wonderful man! He's just so lovely, so natural, so normal and so bloody beautiful!

Well, I keep finding half-written letters that I've started in my infrequent idle hours here at Language Power. I want to put an ad in the paper for a typewriter because I've lots of things to type. So that's my next project when I become a little more financial.

Did I tell you I was thinking of later going into business on my own, teaching English? Not to your every-day Frenchman who thinks it might be fun to learn, but to companies. I would claim my apartment as an office and use an audio program; it's all perfectly legal and expected on a tax return here. I plan on using this method and later will approach companies myself. Don't worry, I'll have it all set up before leaving any permanent job. I have to get my head above water, my social life a little more organised, my legalities and illegalities looking good, and then I'll be there – just you watch.

Before, when Jim Wilkes spoke to me about this, I couldn't see beyond going for the interviews with the Taxation Department and the Department of Social Security. Now it's all becoming clear and I can see strong job prospects ahead. It's just that here your only security is money and freedom, and job satisfaction is important when you're in a situation where you have limited choice and more to fight for.

Amsterdam is looking good for March 6th. I'll spend four days there this time, it'll be so relaxing. I'll catch the 4 pm train and spend Thursday, Friday and Saturday nights and all day Sunday. I'll try to get on the right train this time!

Lisa is going home to California for two weeks, and I've put in my request already – deodorant and music CDs. You know another pleasure of being free of the chemotherapy is having normal or no body odour. My body reeked of that stuff during those four months … it was incredible. Now it feels like I'm living on a totally different level. Now I feel free – free to experience and appreciate the joy of living. Barbie, if you came to Paris now, I could show you a city you've never seen before from the *inside*. I sound like I've only been here for a few days, but Paris is always like that. It feels fresh and new and tingling with life and a magic of its own. When you take a second breath, it feels just like that, no matter how long you've been here.

Monsieur Cointy is not coming – that's good. The Director just came in to make sure the room was comfortable and that I had everything I needed. He told me that even though I'd been here for only two weeks, he had every confidence in me and that I knew as much, if not more than any of the other teachers here. That was nice. He told me I could talk to him at the end of the month and tell him how I was progressing financially. It's a fact that teachers, especially with an independent *Travailler Carte*, are flexible and not contracted. If I were contracted, I'd be permanently working for a fixed employer, but a freelance worker has that legal right to say 'bye-bye.' I'm the only freelancer on the staff here, and because flexibility is the name of my game, I guess he knows this.

Tonight I have my Japanese student from 8:30 to 9:30. I get home at 10 pm which is a long day. I think I'll give my economics lecturer at the Sorbonne a miss. Well, if he wants the lessons I'll take him, but if not I won't mind as I begin not to have much time now on a Saturday. His wife is very sick, and he stopped his lessons to look after her.

Did I tell you Paris had a Metro strike the other day that paralysed the whole city? It was terrible. It took me four hours to get home, from 6 to10 pm! I'll never forget it. The buses (half of them stop after 9 pm anyway), were packed. I spent over an hour waiting with a guy I met at the bus stop; we decided to share a cab as we were going in the same direction. Well, there were no taxies... nothing... and it was freezing – below zero. I then tried one bus stop after another so – wait for it – after three hours and a private little sob, I thought, *Shit! I want to go home and I can't, but by hell, I'm going to be there in twenty minutes!*

Went to the *Châtelet* intersection, donned my most inviting, alluring, beguiling smile, tried to look sophisticated but desperate, and very elegantly put out my thumb. I was going to hitch. I was freezing and so tired.

Yes, they stopped … well, they were already stopped, bumper to bumper, creeping forward at a snail's pace. No one would take me, so now more desperate than ever, I went to another bus stop and waited, in a severe state of depression, motionless, and resigned myself to waiting for buses that were too overcrowded to stop. It was frightful and freezing.

Then about four lanes across the road I caught the eye of a man who found mine. He nodded in the direction he was going. I nodded back (had my hands in my pockets), and it took me three seconds to race across to his car and jump in. It must have looked so funny. I'd been waiting there with the crowd for over an hour and then suddenly I was off like a rocket. My Good Samaritan, my knight in shining armour, dropped me off close to my apartment.

When I got home, I found Lisa very upset. She had received a letter to say that her cousin in the States had been murdered and she was distraught. So now after a long talk, lots of tears and a hot cup of tea we feel a bit better.

Really, there's always something around the corner... one never knows. I suppose after all when your time is up, it's up ... no matter how you go.

I collected all your letters to-day. It was the first time in two weeks that I've been able to go to American Express; no time and too far away outside my hours of work. It took an hour to read them all. Thank you for your advice Mum, especially about the men in my life. It's true what you say isn't it? Now I've met Carlos, who I've become happily involved with and who I feel free with. I'm tired now, and I must sleep.

I love you.

Letter, 22nd February 1981

Dear Mum,

I'm resting quietly today. It's snowing outside as I look through these quaint little french windows. It's been snowing all day, so it's a good time to catch up on all those things that never seem to be done. Had a letter from a friend on Ibiza, a little island similar to Capri, off the coast of Spain. I have to answer it. Carlos has applied to go there to work for a month in the summer and bask in the sun.

Well for once (or should I say twice counting the chemo) I'm not in control of my situation. I told you about Carlos. He's twenty-eight and in June will have his divorce. I just don't want to lose him. He's quite mixed up at the moment. That makes two of us. I can't go into everything here because it makes my mind run wild.

And so, it's like Circumstance has the upper hand, physically and mentally in our relationship all the time. I believe at times that it's Circumstance's private little game against our lives and it makes me so angry. I sometimes think that I have to be quiet and calm because if my mind thinks too much I might lose us and I can't handle that. He bought me a book of beautiful poetry the other day and wrote a message on the first page. So beautiful.

The night you rang I'd been walking by myself, trying to sort out my mind in all this turmoil. I'd decided I needed to be in a quiet space and to look after my mind because I don't want to get hurt. So I wrote a poem where I talk to, and about, Circumstance with the occasional mention to us. But to Circumstance mainly I talk.

When things outside both of you are stronger, sometimes it's a matter of making a peace pact with Circumstance, there at least you have some tranquillity to be and to discern. The other way you just fight angrily and blindly; that way hurts. I find writing through emotions seems to clarify things for me. I was so angry that Circumstance should affect us like this. I guess my feelings at first were outrage and frustration. I suppose it's quite laughable that anyone would try to reason, beg or plead with Circumstance, as if it were an entity in its own right. It's funny how the mind works when it's under pressure or stress. In the end I realise that it's all in vain, not the relationship that Carlos and I have, but the odds we fight against. After all, that's the determining factor apart from our struggle and need for each other.

TO CIRCUMSTANCE

How dare you intrude in affairs
so delicately intense – so tangibly inexplicable -
the very essence of Time and Place itself -
the very essence of your being.
For without her, you too would be
a nonentity without reason or purpose.
I beg you; rise above and out of yourself.
Look! It's a seed;
with light, warmth and time it will germinate
into the very purpose of our being.
We are one – you and I,
so let us share the pleasure, the defeat
all as one entity – as one mission.
Would you not prefer
to share your mission peaceably?
For if you allow us to live ours,
you too will live.
I'm tired - so very tired
of our conflict, our fight, our battle
at every crossroad – at every corner.
And to what end?
I beg you please take the sleep from my eyes.
Let me live.
There is even less reason in your hypnotic disillusion
which cries out at every corner and every crossroad.
It's hard to stay awake,
for in daylight I am,
and in darkness I seem.
I need your strength to be and to see.
We need your strength to be.
You need our lives to exist.

-Lorraine, 1981

Well, that was my little effort tonight on the way to *Sacré-Coeur* to air my problems. I walked by myself for three hours, after which I came home to your lovely well-timed call. I had been crying. *C'est la vie - surtout ici à Paris.* (That's life – especially here in Paris.)

My inspiration for that little number arrived in the Metro, so I got out and sat on a bench with a few other down and outs. They were somewhat better off than me; they at least had wine. I proceeded to write and write because when it comes, I must get it down, otherwise I lose it forever. Pouring my feelings onto paper always did make me feel better; it releases pressures, clears my mind and allows me to see more clearly. Carlos and I both talk about and know the situation … it's hard.

I found the following page of writing among Rainey's papers when I had decided to compile her letters. This was not dated, but I feel it could have been written around this time.

"Someone must have been listening as thoughts of you burned in a candle in Notre Dame one Saturday afternoon while Circumstance whiled away a few idle hours playing with our lives. She is obviously enjoying the experience. And so, having made a peace pact with her there, at least one finds a certain tranquillity to be, and in there a strength to discern, decide or merely ride peaceably amid an intensely uncertain transience.

For without this we fight angrily, blindly, without rhyme or reason, and sadly to no end. And so instead, perhaps I should be writing rather in praise of Circumstance? At least it was she who prompted some semblance of self-preservation and positive comportment.

At this time, I feel I don't have that strength to appreciate, praise, or even respect her untimely entrance... for somewhere I seem to have misplaced a part of myself to a force infinitely stronger than I. It has instead, been replaced by a quietude borne of a need fulfilled. For this, and only this, do I look to her thankfully ... with a certain reservation."

Letter, 27th February 1981

I'm at my company again now. I think lately every time I write to you I'm at Language Power. I've just finished a lesson with a lady who has been taught by everyone in the school during the two months she's been here. She shook my hand as she was leaving and told me she believed I was the best teacher here. That was lovely. The students begin after a while to have their preferences, and of late I've been requested to be the regular teacher for some. They go to the reception desk and say I want him, or I want her, and I notice I'm beginning to get requests. It's good.

If I have a student for three hours straight, I need to take a break so we go to a café for a coffee and a talk. I have coffee at least three times a day during the breaks with my students ... directors, managers, sales staff and businessmen and women. We sometimes speak in French or in English. I look forward to these coffee breaks and understand now, almost everything. Sometimes, when they need to explain something in a different sense, it's there.

This company is good, but the work is very tiring and I find I need my sleep. I'm paid well; over 5,000 francs per month. That's $1,250.00 a month clear take home, or around $300.00 per week. With my social security, I get 1,000 francs per month which I'll put into my bank account and draw it out only for health as I'm not paying into a health fund here. I'm exempt from a certain aspect of 'Valued Added Tax' so I get around 17.6% of my salary every month which would have otherwise been deducted. When Lisa moves out in June, and I take over the studio myself I'll need it and I'll still be okay financially. It's a good chance to save from now until June, and the extra income from my private students certainly helps.

I've just had a most divine-looking Frenchman for a lesson. He was sitting in my room waiting for me, and I didn't know he was there. He speaks English fluently and is on a very advanced chapter. I had already told myself, seeing I wasn't trained as yet by the company for this particular stage, that we would ad lib our way through the lesson of one and a half hours. That's okay, but with gorgeous looking men I find it hard to concentrate on two things at once, especially when I'm bluffing my way through a lesson.

It was one of my best lessons. We talked 'ninety to the dozen.' He completely relaxed me. I sat back and observed and decided I would definitely like to know more about him. He offered me a lift home as *La Défense* is twenty minutes from the city centre - and of course, I had already accepted in my mind before he even asked me. He said he would ask to have me as his teacher next time. He is very studious. Let's hope he is as serious with his women.

Then there's the architect who bought me coffee one Saturday morning during a break in the lesson. We just hit it off right away. He's asked for me for his Saturday class too.

My social life is becoming more and more complicated, and now I get letters from guys who I met last year in Paris who are coming back and want to see me. Jules is French and is studying medicine in Rome. He's in town so I must call him. Claude is still a sweetie. I told you Henri rang the perfumery to find out where I was. You were right, there's no future there; that episode is better left in its place – in the past.

Marc is off the list, and if Carlos doesn't get organised and get his life together soon, I'm going to get tired of waiting. You know, I would give them all the big '*tchao*' for him, but I don't intend to let things overwhelm me and go down like before. I'm playing to win, even though I would rather spend all my time with Carlos.

I had a lovely lunch with Sébastien the other day. I also go out with Aref, the guy who's living with us temporarily. Actually, it takes a lot of energy and tact because they are all more than a nice guy to go out with to me. With each of them, there is a *simpatico*; there is empathy and understanding.

Well, I can't wait to go to Amsterdam in about ten days' time. Looking forward to the appointment and the few days to relax. I owe myself some time off. Will arrive Thursday night and come back Sunday. I'm going to have a lovely relaxing time and opt out totally. If Carlos said he would come, that's different. I even asked him.

I feel like an administration computer this month. Have done all the administrative work, and doing it all when you're illegal is a strain and a worry. Jim Wilkes is really proud of me, and of the way I got the apartment … and you should have been there when I opened a foreign bank account the other day.

I went in and told them I wanted to open an account, and out came these mountains of paperwork that had to be filled in. They wanted to know how often I washed my socks and what I had for breakfast – well almost. I'm getting good at this, but I don't like to do it too often. It's too stressful.

When it came to the lady asking for my passport to verify my date of arrival,

"How long have you been here?" and, "When did you arrive" and, "Show me your *carte de séjour* (residence permit) and all your lovely money." Me, myself and I all had a little panic session. We almost collapsed over the table. Just think, if we'd done that, we'd still be there trying to find our way out of the mound of papers. Anyway, having none of the above, but steeped in my studies of 'How to get everything you want - without having anything you need to achieve same,' we regrouped.

As she was searching through my passport I panicked, and said to myself, 'SELF! DO SOMETHING!' I remembered that I'd made up the arrival date in the passport … the same date that Jim Wilkes and I had made up to coincide with my work permit. This meant I had arrived in Paris October 10th, 1980, which is a load of garbage. I have lots of incriminating evidence in my passport to contradict that, and no entry for October 10th. So, I reached across as casually as I knew how, smiled and offered to find it for her to verify. Flicking through a few pages, I found a blank one, and looking convincingly at her, said, "Ah yes, that's right - October 10th, 1980," and being typically French she couldn't wait to fill out another paper. I think Jim might give me a second diploma after that achievement.

Well, it's always an anticlimax for me when I get a job, a place to live and now a bank account because I sweat it out before and during each ordeal, so feel I deserve it. Also, because the amount of work and homework from Jim, my comportment and composure during the interviews, and my dry-cleaning bills for my trousers, I feel I should have had it ages ago.

I did my tax return and got a good raise in my salary. You know, because I have independent worker status, I'm paid more than most teachers here at Language Power, but I really earn it. I feel like I'm getting down to the nitty-gritty of life now, having received my first electricity and telephone bills.

March is here, and after achieving all of that in the last eight weeks (not bad really), I'm pretty tired. So now is the beginning of another spring; time for nesting and renewal. After Amsterdam this month, I'm going to slow down and start decorating my little studio.

You know, I have an absolutely beautiful, fairy-tale view of Sacré-Coeur from my balcony! At night it looks like something that drifted down from fairyland on a cloud. It's the most beautiful sight I've ever seen at night, and I can't believe I have it from my balcony. Sacré-Coeur is my most favourite place in all of Paris; and to think that because I was running around trying to organise my life in those eight weeks, I only discovered it three weeks after I'd been living here in this apartment. At that stage, I was only spending time at home because I was too tired to do anything else.

Just goes to show you what happens when you 'stop and smell the roses'.

All my love.

Professor McCarthy's reply to Lorraine's letter:

19th February 1981

Dear Miss Walton,

I have your letter of 5th February and note that the French opinion is that "a less toxic follow-up in the form of the administration of DTIC alone is imperative," and once again can only repeat my original opinion. I have no objection if you show this letter to Dr Schwarzenberg.

There is absolutely nothing to be gained by the administration of DTIC in your situation. Your tumour was an early one of good prognosis and there is no indication for any chemotherapy whatsoever. It is a complete waste of time and effort, not to mention money, to initiate or continue adjuvant therapy for early melanoma. Even with the more advanced primary growth, all the recent studies, particularly the international collaborative study of the World Health Organisation Melanoma Group, show no benefit whatsoever for the prophylactic administration of DTIC. This particular study involved patients with much more dangerous tumours than yours, and for them the outcomes were statically insignificant.

We have had extensive experience with melanoma here, having now treated 3,500 patients with the disease. It is highly unlikely that you can find anyone else in the world, and particularly in France, with even a fraction of this experience. We do not now, nor have we in the past, nor will we in the foreseeable future, use adjuvant DTIC or immunotherapy for patients with early melanoma. I would suggest that you pass this message on to your French advisors and if they persist, ask them for the research evidence on which they base the statement that prophylactic DTIC is imperative. Certainly, all the studies in the English language, and I add that the bulk of the studies are in English, do not support this statement and indeed show that there is nothing to be gained by the prophylactic use of any current chemotherapeutic agent, particularly DTIC which has been the most extensively researched.

I do not know what else I can say to convince you of the opinion of myself, this clinic and all other cancer chemotherapists in Australia. We would all advise specifically against the use of DTIC in your situation. Firstly, because it does no good and secondly because it may in a theoretical way, which has also yet to be proven, be deleterious in that it is an immune suppressant. While you are on DTIC your body's immune reactions are depressed and this could be disadvantageous. Again, it has not been shown that the drug is disadvantageous when given in the prophylactic situation, but if one wishes to work on theory, as apparently the French are doing, then the advice would have to be against chemotherapy in early melanoma rather than for it.

I am sorry that you have found yourself in this unfortunate situation. It must be causing you considerable psychological stress to have two conflicting opinions presented to you; however I can only reiterate that our experience here is unrivalled in the world, and if we do not recommend a therapy then it is unlikely that this therapy has any benefit.

Yours sincerely,
W.H. McCarthy
Assoc. Professor of Surgery
Melanoma Unit – Sydney Hospital

Letter, 6th March 1981

Dearest Mum,

Well if ever I needed something since I've been over here in one and a half years, it's Professor's McCarthy's reply to my letter. Writing to him was the best thing I ever did. I remember as Carlos and I walked out of *Hospital Hôtel-Dieu* that day, I was totally confused and concerned because the issue is definitely not black and white. I was very upset and Carlos asked me what I thought because he'd spoken to the doctor afterwards. Well, my mind was so full then. I didn't want to, nor could I talk about it, so I said,

"Let me think about it, there's too much in my head. I'll talk later."

When Professor McCarthy's letter arrived, Carlos read it and he too said to stay with McCarthy. Well, as soon as I read it that was my decision. I still can't work out whether I just needed reassurance or more information, but I suppose if I were at home all would be talked about together. Here it's just me.

I'm in Amsterdam now, this time for three days. I just love it here. Arrived last night, and already I feel relaxed, different and more myself. I look at Paris now and really, it can be a strain living there. I work hard and have had a few big traumas, with the chemo, Carlos and David, and all I need now is to relax. Here I feel like I'm home free.

Doing some shopping for my apartment this afternoon, then tonight I'll go to see that new Neil Diamond movie, *The Jazz Singer*. Tomorrow if it's fine, I might rent a bike or go to the markets. Wow … it's like a little holiday. I absolutely love it here. I worked very hard last month, nine hours teaching per day, so I figure I deserve it.

Lots of love.

Letter, 10th March 1981

Dear Mum,

Amsterdam was wonderful. Didn't get sprung either way on my ticket this time and slept as soon as I arrived on Thursday night. Mr Schroder always waits up for me now. He's really sweet. The next day I had my acupuncture appointment in Baarn. They are incredibly thorough, taking ages to discuss and diagnose. I told him everything I could think of and he treated me for all.

You know, I will never forget one day on the metro soon after I came back from Amsterdam. My periods had been just so irregular; never knew whether they were coming or going – twice a month or not at all – you name it. Then this day it arrived, I think it was six months' worth. I fixed everything then caught the metro to go home. During the trip I noticed a pool of blood on the floor and thought someone had been hurt, so I just moved away because the blood was fresh. Everyone else was looking at it too. I moved and then still next to me another, until I realised I was standing in it each time – drip, drip, drip. My boots and stockings were covered, and I felt very weak and started to shake. I just kept moving around the carriage. It looked like there had been a murder – I'm not kidding. I finally got out and couldn't wait to get home. I went to a toilet, left a trail the whole way, and my boots … sherbet!

Then when I got home, this great clot fell out … huge like a liver. First, I thought it might have been a miscarriage, but when I told Carlos, he said it was a big clot. I was going to go to the gynaecologist but thought more and figured it was the acupuncture treatment because he did give me specific needles to regulate my period. I felt like saying to him the last visit, 'I wanted you to make them regular, not all come at once.' Well, this month was better. Still a lot, and then there's my other problem but I'll explain that other little detail later when I can concentrate more.

It's Saturday now and this morning Aref and I went shopping. I ordered my letter headed notepaper that Jim Wilkes advised me to have; then to the markets where I bought some more plants. My little apartment is looking gorgeous now, complete with hanging plants and flowers. We called in to see Sammy at the markets and the three of us spent a happy hour over coffee in a café, talking and laughing together. Then Aref and I went to buy another plant in a flower shop in *Chateau Rouge* near *Montmartre* where I lived before; then to the market for groceries. We both looked like a travelling sideshow in the metro coming home. Had lunch, and Carlos came over and stayed for a few hours.

Tomorrow I'm going to Carlos' house for lunch, and one of my students has asked me out to a bar and jazz concert Monday night. Another of my students (a scrumptious Frenchman) drives me home after the lesson every Monday night. Sherbet I just remembered ... it's *him* I teach last on Monday and it's the other guy I'm going out with straight after. That's going to take a little organising 'coz I like them both ... hmmm. That's okay, I've had plenty of practice, and until Carlos stops messing around with my life I'm going to enjoy myself, even though I would give anything to be with him all the time.

Then there's also Claude who I go out with. I feel like a little girl in a lolly shop – one day I feel like liquorice, the next day candy and another day – well nothing.

Lately I've been getting home late because of my work, and all I want to do is sleep. Tomorrow morning I'll probably sleep in. I get to sleep in only on Sunday because on Saturday afternoon I'm busy with all the things I can't do during the week.

The other night I had a phone call from an American girl in the same situation as me.

She said, "Jim Wilkes gave me your phone number and suggested I call you to tell me how to open a bank account." Sherbet, I wonder ... perhaps he should promote me and give me a new title. Our business card would read: *Wilkes and Walton: Compatriots in Crime. Get you anything, take you anywhere.*

The next call will probably be, 'Jim Wilkes gave me your phone number and suggested I call. He said you could advise me on how to get an apartment without a job or a penny to your name.' Then maybe after that, I could supply a dossier on how to talk your way back into a salaried teaching position on independent working papers after you've been thrown out the first time by the director of all ten schools in the company.

I recall leaving his office crying that day because it was exactly the job I wanted, and they wouldn't have me. When I was called in again by one of the other directors, I wasn't sure if he knew I was independent or not, so thought I should tell him.

"Why in heaven's name didn't I know before? We only hire salaried" he said.

Then I gathered all the clues I learned from Jim, gave him my spiel and he ended up saying, "I don't know why he didn't hire you then." I spent the next few days sweating it out, hoping I'd get the job. I think they think I'm okay.

It's Monday afternoon 16th March, and I'm back at work in my favourite company – CBS. My class has just finished. They're my favourite group. They love their lesson and always never want to leave. I really enjoy it. It's so *vivant* … so alive. The boss just rang me here and asked me to stay and take the next class, so that's great. I give them a good program. I'd love to work out of companies all the time. I think that when I get established, I'll work only as an independent worker. You earn heaps, and arrange your own hours with the companies. That would really suit me.

This company, CBS, works with many big name recording artists like Julio Iglesias. The last one in Paris was Billy Joel, and when the artists come here on tour, the staff can go to their concerts. My last class just told me they had spoken with their chief and he agreed that I could have tickets for the shows. They've invited me to dinner and to the next show, as long as I speak English with them. If I want to go to any of these shows, I get their discount of 50%, and I can buy tickets for my friends too, at the same discount.

Last night, Sunday, I spent writing reports on some students to send to their respective companies. I feel like I'm doing something worthwhile and love this work. Tomorrow I add another company, Minolta, to my portfolio. The director called me into his office and said he would like me to take the classes there. So, I'm happy about that.

I spent the morning with Carlos at the hospital. For a few weeks now, I've felt that I have something caught in my throat. I had the appointment and was referred straight away for a blood count, then to x-ray and then to an ear, nose and throat specialist. It took four hours, and Carlos was with me the whole time. He told them I was his fiancé, so I didn't have to pay. I go back on Friday when they'll take a biopsy of my throat. It's very sore – not just a typical sore throat.

While we were there, Carlos showed Professor McCarthy's letter to the two specialists, and they both agreed that the chemotherapy treatment I was given was far too radical for me. You know, these days I still feel the effects … no energy, I get tired easily and can't concentrate for very long. Sometimes at work in the afternoon I feel myself drifting. It's a very strange feeling. I'm awake, eyes open, and suddenly I 'switch off.' It's like my mind snaps, and I'm out – literally out – and I never know I've gone until I come back with a jolt and feel my body again. It's like a blackout. I never know for how long, but I judge by how much my students have read, and I always come back to where I passed out to hear them reading, and say, "No … that's not correct." When it is … in fact they've read a whole page!

I can't hold it, and sometimes I fear it. It usually happens in the afternoon, but never before has it happened like this. I feel my mental concentration is weak. I told the acupuncturist, who said that the chemotherapy drugs I'd been given have left my blood without energy and proper content, and the blood can't serve my brain under high concentration so the brain just literally collapses. He said it's 'cerebral amnesia' and he can treat it. He gave me treatment on my last visit, but it still happens almost every day in the afternoon.

I must have my sleep – I have never felt this feeble – my body tells me many things. Today when I had the blood test, and she pressed the needle in, I felt sick to my stomach and could smell again in my mind the chemotherapy! I was surprised and found myself feeling like I did during that time. My God, when I look back, I can't believe just how I was able to divorce myself from the situation and had the strength to endure all that. Whatever they did to me then, I could cope with mentally, and today I automatically did the same thing, but I felt ill as the needle went in.

Carlos was lovely this morning at the hospital; he stayed with me, and we talked the whole time. Lately, I find I don't have the strength to hold on to him, but I do because I want to. But I must be almost uninvolved, so much so that I wish sometimes he wouldn't ring me so often because it hurts too much, and I find myself being so distant. I have to be. Today he said, "I'm with you. Please give me time and space for the moment."

His wife is giving him hell; I'm sure she must be a little crazy. Well, there's a lot happening there that I don't want to go into here.

Carlos is going home to Argentina in June for two months then coming back here to do a two-year course in plastic surgery. I hope he gets himself together (and us) in that time.

Yesterday Aref and I went to the zoo again. It was so nice to be out with a different focus. The animals and their antics are such a good tonic. We had a lovely time, and in the last two weeks I've come home to dinner cooked, everything done and all I need to do is sit down. I'm told to go and have a bath and relax. He has helped me with things like shopping and keeping the place neat and tidy while I'm at work.

Lisa arrived home from the States this morning, and now we are three again. I spent a wonderfully relaxing two weeks in the apartment with Aref while she was away; we got on so well, so naturally. Carlos wanted to come to stay with me during those two weeks. I was angry when he said that. I said, "No. I can't love you for two weeks knowing you're going back up on your mountain after and keeping your distance. Only when you're ready in yourself, not just for two weeks. I'm here for you but…"

Anyway, Aref didn't have his new accommodation available and was still living here, so it fitted in.

In two weeks David will be here, and I'm going to ask the acupuncturist for some treatment to help me cope with the talk and the decision

I must make. Already I feel weak just thinking about it. My God, to read his letters he really does love me. I told my friend Jean-Pierre about David. He said, "But Lorraine if it is finished, it is over, and you must say this. If it is not, then you must work together, but do what you have to do."

My head hurts at the thought of it. I go home to Aref and I feel so much better. Talking with him is like a weight lifted, and a few times I've just cried about everything … the situation with Carlos, my heavy workload, David coming, and here at home being not so private. I'm fine now, but you must cry occasionally.

One night a few weeks ago I was feeling very full with stress and couldn't handle the prospect of going home so went to *Sacré-Coeur* for about three hours. Got home about 11 pm and Lisa told me Carlos had been calling every ten minutes, asking,

"Where is she? She should be home!"

That was the night you rang, and I felt better after that. I did a lot of soul searching while I was at *Sacré-Coeur,* and decided to mentally give Carlos time and space, which I know he needs, but to keep myself sane through it.

Consequently, before I knew it, I was going out with my entourage again. I think I did it all unconsciously and now I play very carefully because I need to keep above it all. I don't like to get upset; it's not good for me - especially now that I need to be careful. My body and mind keep reminding me.

Now I'm going home, to see Lisa and catch up on all the news of USA, and to sleep.

I wonder what Luke's parents think these days – I wonder if they ever understood our situation or if *I* ever will. It's sort of an unfinished mystery, the way he died, sort of unreal, but very bizarre nevertheless, like a movie.

I don't cry about it anymore, I haven't for a long time. Instead, I can think about it calmly, look gently at the good and the bad and be wise to the difference now. I don't mix those feelings anymore, confusedly like I did before; it's like they've mellowed and become clearer in time, like something that's definitely passed. I have thoughts that want to cry through on occasion, but that depends on my mood. It *was* a time though, wasn't it? You can't put anything like that into words. Like the seasons, it passes, never totally. It just quietly fades, but still always there.

Yesterday was the first day of spring, and I feel in my heart that I begin again, leaving lots of things behind, either buried or dormant.

Rainey first met Luke while she was living in The United States as a Rotary Exchange Student in 1972. On subsequent visits to The United States over the following years, a strong relationship developed between them, a long-distance romance ensued for four years until he was tragically killed in a road accident.

On hearing about his death, Rainey and I flew to the States; she needed to see and talk with his parents. Our families had become very close. We were told very little about the circumstances of Luke's death. It seemed to be something they specifically didn't want to talk about. It seemed to be shrouded in mystery. There was veiled mention that at the time of the accident Luke was delivering important government documents and that the accident may have been deliberate. I had the feeling they knew more.

I remember we left feeling devastated and confused, and for Rainey there was no closure – no feeling of knowing. It remained a mystery and there were too many unanswered questions. Nothing was resolved for her.

Long buried emotions were surfacing. There was so much going on in her life in Paris at this point, and it was easy reading between the lines, to realise she was feeling alone and vulnerable despite being surrounded by people. Going out so much and burning the candle at both ends might have been her way of taking her mind off her confused emotions, her relationship with Carlos and her uncertain health issues.

Hurry up and come over again Mum, but after June when Lisa goes. You will love the apartment. It's just a little piece of heaven on the eighth floor: old, but fresh and white, with glass panelled French doors opening onto a balcony. You will see *Sacré-Coeur* from my balcony, and at night it's a truly magnificent sight.

This apartment is almost too good to be true. I feel it's a part of me. I found it, I fought for it, I sweated and worried over it, and it's exactly what I would have wanted if someone had given me a wish!

Chapter 6

Excerpt from my letter to Rainey regarding the blackouts, March 1981

This morning when I got to work I rang Professor McCarthy. I wanted to know more about the blackouts you are having, so I asked him and read to him the part of your letter describing how it happens.

He explained it was a condition known as petit mal – a form of epilepsy – a physiological condition where the brain cannot cope with the pressures it's under, and the subconscious takes over for that time in an attempt to ease the conscious.

His explanation fits in well with what you have told me – how stress affects you.

One of the first things he said was it is imperative that you have plenty of sleep, as it is during sleep that the rebuilding process takes place.

He said that if this is what is happening (the blackouts), there is too much emotional build-up and that it must be eased. He also said, "Why don't you bring her home where she can get the care and moral support she needs from family and a sympathetic medical advisor who will sit and talk with her? One who can help her sort out and cope with the emotional build-up which is a very real and normal part of the problem."

He went on to say that not only had you to deal with the emotional trauma of the chemotherapy, alone and so far away from all moral support, but also that you had been subjected to the distress of having two conflicting opinions presented to you. He said it's obvious that it's all becoming too much for the brain to handle.

He does make sense and what he says is true. And then I thought of all the other problems and emotional stress that you are trying to cope with that he is unaware of. All that in addition to what he believes is the sole reason for the blackouts. Rainey, love, there has to be a limit to all this, and I think the limit has been reached.

Letter, 30th March 1981

Dear Mum,

Talk about a dirty stop-out. I've been having a lovely time, but I'm not used to checking in and saying, "I won't be home tonight." I should have but didn't. I just like to do things without having to explain my movements.

I spent yesterday, Sunday, with my friend, Jean-Pierre. We had a seafood lunch with his two lovely children, aged ten and five years. He's divorced and sees them every second weekend. During the evening he received a phone call telling him that his mother had passed away. It was unexpected and quite a shock. The evening was so busy with phone calls, and it was very late … too late for him to drive me home, so I stayed. Jean-Pierre drove me to work this morning.

Then this afternoon Aref came to Language Power to see if I was okay. Lisa told me he'd been up half the night worrying. I had coffee with him between lessons.

"Your business is your business," he said, "even though you know how I feel – but please call next time, I was worried sick."

The sooner I have my apartment on my own, the better. Lisa is to be moving out soon as they were the original arrangements. I just like to do things without having to check in with anybody. I can't handle people keeping tabs on my life. Aref is okay, but still, I *did* leave home early Sunday morning and came back Monday night. Try having an entourage of six when there are only seven days in a week, and you're living with one. Sometimes I wonder about me.

I spend lots of time with Aref – we are getting very close. A few nights ago, we went to a café for wine and cheese. It was all very nice. When we came back, Carlos, Claude, Sebastian and Jean-Pierre (who is getting a little too serious) all phoned within the hour, and Aref answered every call. He didn't say anything, but I could tell he was thinking. I know he likes me.

Tonight I'm going to dinner with Frederique, one of my students from CBS, and another teacher from Language Power. It will be fun.

Next day now…

Back again. Last night we had a fantastic time on our girls' night out. We went first to a jazz club for drinks then finally to a seafood restaurant at around 11 pm, where we talked and laughed over dinner. Later we went for a drink in another cafe then to visit Frederique's friend George, who is living in a little studio in one of those narrow back streets in *St Michelle*. The studio is owned by one of his friends – an artist – and George is living there for two weeks while he's away. The artist's little studio is just incredible. The four of us drank coffee and talked until the early hours. I got home at 4 am, and Aref was still awake and smoking like a chimney.

I have to stop now as I have a report to write for CBS; their contract with Language Power finished yesterday. I'm going to lunch again with Frederique next week, and she's going to give me some records.

Well, must write that report.

Back again.

I have another company now. Van Cleef & Arpels The other day the director of Language Power called me into his office. He told me he was thinking of going into business himself … starting up his own language school and working primarily with companies. He asked me if I would consider joining him as a partner! After I had recovered from the shock, we talked a lot about it, and he asked if I would at least consider it. He's been the director here for eight years and knows the ropes backwards. He's already had offers of offices and such and is planning his move for September if all goes well. Said it would entail a lot of P.R work to find clients. He's serious and really wants me to join him. I would love it, but I have to think of job security.

I talked to Carlos, and he said that if by any chance it didn't work, I'd be out in the cold; but if successful, I'd have a hell of a lot more freedom, more income, and more holidays and would work exclusively in companies! It's exactly what I was going to do myself in about a year or so. I'll wait to see what happens at this school. Tell me what you think, and I'll talk to Jim about it.

The director here at Language Power told me about a contract being offered in the north of France in *Rouen*. They wanted a teacher for two weeks to travel up on the train, teach for four hours in a company, have lunch with them and be paid as if you taught for eight hours here. He wanted me to go and suggested this to the other directors, but there's another teacher who's been here longer than I have who wanted the contract, so he got it. That would have been fun. Next time maybe. There are always more opportunities on the horizon.

I met another very nice student here on Saturday morning (I work one Saturday per month for three hours). He arrived and announced that he hadn't woken up yet and fifteen minutes later said,

"Why don't we go for coffee?"

Well, after two coffees in a café (good job eh?) and after I dropped the slide projector on his head and hit him with my ruler, he stirred a little, then for the next three hours we talked philosophy – in French – just wonderful. No work was done, and afterwards he invited me for a drink but I already had plans, so he said,

"Well, the next Saturday we work together, keep it free and we will have lunch in Paris."

My student, Monsieur Saudi Arabia, who drives me home every Monday night (because I teach him last,) returns on Monday from his business trip to Egypt. He's your Pierre Cardin/Cartier type, but really very nice.

Well, I must stop now and finish writing my report. Oh, and then there is this other guy I teach at Minolta Camera Company who drove me home the other day. We had a good talk, and he invited me to play tennis and to dinner. This Job is ideal for meeting people, but I choose who I go out with. More often than not I say, 'No, thank you.'

I think I need a social secretary! Pretty soon I'll do my little number *comme d'habitude* (as usual) and opt out completely.

I've done pretty well though. In eight weeks I found an apartment, a job, opened a bank account, an insurance policy and gathered up all my contacts again – very diplomatically of course. Now I'm circulating too much and don't have enough time to myself.

Next weekend I go again to Amsterdam, April 9th to 12th. I'll meet David there – he arrives in London April 5th. I'm going to ask the acupuncturist for calming needles.

Well, I must stop now and finish this report. Love you.

Back again. So, that's the business and social life taken care of.

When Aref and I went to the zoo the other day we had such fun, and it was so relaxing. I love it there. He told me I was just like a little girl and gave me a big hug. That's how I felt. We were just like two teenagers, so I said, "I'm a little girl? Now when are you going to buy me an ice-cream and take me to see the monkeys?"

On the way home in a café, I tried desperately to resurrect some semblance of grace by ordering wine and camembert. We laughed a lot and had a great time, then I blew it when we got to the bus stop and discovered I had left my *Carte Orange* (bus/metro ticket) in the café, so he sat me on the seat and ran back to get it. On the way home we bought tulips and daffodils for the apartment. He cooked a scrumptious dinner, and we floated off on the music. That was when we had the apartment to ourselves when Lisa was in the States.

I have to ring Jim again to get my illegal life in order and up to date with my residence permit, tax reply and visa situation. I also want to discuss with him the business proposition. The director of Language Power wants to change his status to an independent worker so that he can start his own business ... how to explain that little number? So far I've successfully avoided any detailed explanation of how I obtained my working papers, so will have to have more advice from Jim. I know a very nice Australian girl here from Brisbane. She said she could never have come to Paris knowing no one and nothing from scratch. She's been living in London for twelve months and got tired of it. I told her it took me just twelve days to work that little number out!

I think now I'll adjourn to a café, take a coffee and finish my report.

It's now 6th April

David arrived in London yesterday and called me from there. He's coming over on Thursday and we'll spend four days in Amsterdam before he goes to back to London for meetings. He'll be there until early next month then flies back to Australia. This week I've had to put everyone out of the picture both mentally and physically. Well, I hope everything will be all right. I was upset last night about the prospect, so I had a long talk to Aref, and it was just like talking to you. He's so good to talk to. I'm going up to *Sacré-Coeur* tonight, and he won't let me come home on the metro alone, so will meet me there at 11 pm.

The following few postcards were the only correspondence we received from Rainey during David's visit. He was on a working trip and they spent several weekends during that time travelling together.

18th April 1981

Dearest Mum,

David and I are in Monaco now having coffee at Gracie's. She wasn't home, so we're sitting on the doorstep until she gets here! We've walked around the palace grounds, it's just incredible. A long time ago the palace and the little village immediately below was all there was of Monaco, and it's all still here; winding cobblestone streets … just gorgeous. We are having a lovely relaxing time; staying in Nice and going to visit Cannes tomorrow.

24ᵗʰ April 1981

Do you like this card? It's the same as the beautiful poster of Cannes I had in my little room at Montmartre. It's raining so we've spent most of the afternoon in this café watching the passing parade. The film festival is due to start soon, and there is an atmosphere of anticipation and building excitement. If it's fine tomorrow we'll take a long walk along the *Boulevarde de la Croisette*. Cannes is so lovely. I'm flying back to Paris on the 26ᵗʰ.

26ᵗʰ April 1981

I'm sitting in Nice airport at the bar sipping on orange juice while waiting for my flight. Quite frankly it's going to take more than an orange juice to get me back down to earth. David and I had a truly fantastic time here … just incredible. Late spring on the Riviera is so beautiful. I'll be on my way back to Paris at 8 pm.

The following newspaper article was enclosed with Rainey's next letter dated May 4th.

YOUNG AMERICANS LOSE A FRIEND

Near press time we learned that Jim Wilkes, one of the original co-founders of the Institute of Artistic and Cultural Perception, is presumed to have died in a fire in the early hours of Wednesday, April 15ᵗʰ.

He had spent the previous night out with friends, going from the Front Page to Mother Earth's, to the Top Banana, to

Le Dreher. He left his friends about 2:15 am to return home; it was between 3 am and 6 am that the fire took place. Positive identification of Mr Wilkes was being withheld pending a check of dental records; as of press time, the fire was still considered as being of unknown origin.

Mr Wilkes, 37, had been an active member of the Franco-American community in Paris for many years. Originally working with the U.S. Embassy here, he went on to become involved in numerous activities. He helped found the IACP, gave it its name, and served as Director General for the first three years of its existence; he managed the Top Banana for a while; he was a kind of all-purpose legal advisor to Americans of all persuasions, for he knew French law to the letter and, it seemed, could always lead someone who needed help, through the complicated maze of law and red tape.

Everyone seemed to know Jim. He was always around; whether at home or making the rounds of the bars and clubs where he knew he'd see people – his clients, his partners, his friends.

Above all, Jim Wilkes was someone who was there for people in need, providing advice, friendship, and crucial support, whether emotional, financial, or creative. Artists, musicians, anyone with a dream in Paris could come to Jim and benefit from his encouragement, energy and know-how. He was one of those unique people who help define the scenery they are in, who fill a role and meet needs no one else would or could. His passing leaves a real void in the American community in Paris. His friends – and he had many – agree that things won't be the same here without him.

Burial is tentatively planned for the American Legion Cemetery here, pending positive identification.

Letter, 4th May 1981

Lorraine Walton
Professeur Indépendant d'Anglais

223, rue La Fayette
75010 Paris

205.91.19

Dear Mum,

I thought you might like a sample of my printed writing paper. Jim told me I should have it.

I'm including in this letter a piece from one of the newspapers here. Oh my God, I still don't believe this! You know I owe my status, my apartment and a lot of my confidence in settling here, both legally and practically, to Jim. God, what a loss to his family and to everyone he shared his life with here. He was buried here last Saturday, 2nd May. It was a quiet and very feeling ceremony. Randy Garrett read the eulogy, and Jim's parents were presented with the American flag which draped his coffin.

I still can't believe it. I feel a great loss and terribly sad and confused when I realise he's gone. Jim was so alive – so vibrant. It's incredible when someone like that dies; you just feel that it didn't happen, that somehow, it's a mistake. That's how I felt when I was told after returning from Nice. But I'm sure God has reasons for things like this, even before we are born. Heaven will be a richer place now. He's probably already set himself up trying to admit the 'ring-ins' from you-know-where. He probably already has St. Peter twisted round his little finger.

Jim was such a beautiful person – I only wish I could have known him a little more deeply. He was also a musician, played many instruments and set up some nice bars here in Paris. He was a veritable source of energy and inspiration; gave his advice, his time, and himself to all who knew and sought him. God, what a loss - and so young! I will visit his place in the cemetery. I still can't believe he's gone. I just can't believe it.

149

When I placed the rose on Jim's coffin, I had the same feeling I'd had at Luke's grave. Jim wasn't there. He had already gone to wherever he is now. Maybe he was lingering there, but I believe, and felt so strongly that he had already reached his calling and it was certainly not there in that cemetery.

He will be forever remembered above my love for Paris, not only for all he did for me but for the beautiful person he was.

I wrote the following few lines for Jim, although I think I can write something softer - quieter and more gentle. I was upset, confused and shocked when I first heard, so it's probably a little too harsh.

For Jim.
Death lurked between every page,
Sneering,
Longing for the morning of Time's decree.

I'm in Amsterdam now and the weather over the past few days here has been so beautiful. The countryside is a picture. David and I visited *Keukenhof*, the famous flower fields, acres and acres of flower gardens; just a mass of colour. Tulips, daffodils, and hyacinths in a multitude of colours and patterns, as far as the eye could see. The tulips were the size of a man's hand … just incredible. We lazed over coffee in the sun, taking in the beautiful landscape, the lakes, swans and gardens. It was so very relaxing and peaceful. I thought of Jim and still can't believe he's gone. His funeral was four days ago. I still can't believe it.

Letter, 7th May 1981

Dearest Mum,

It was so good to talk to you on the phone the other day. I'm going to do something special for you on Mothers' Day pet. Just think, it was on Mothers' Day the year I was born, and now my birthday will be on Mothers' Day again. It's the third time only in my life so far. I love you.

I hope my student – I was just going to say, 'I hope my student doesn't come,' when she poked her head around the door and said *'Je suis toute encore.'* Good thing I can understand the lingo! That translates to 'I'm by myself again' which means she can't take her lesson. Most of my students cancelled today, so I had most of the day free.

One of my students is also a friend, so after his lesson we spent two hours over coffee and lunch, and then he drove me back to this company where I have two more students this afternoon.

I like to be quiet in the evenings of late, although I'm going out to dinner next week - shock of shocks. I used to have 'em double booked and forget their names into the bargain! It's better this way; at least I keep my sanity. Tonight, I'll finish the book I'm reading, *They're a Weird Mob*. You should get a copy. It's so funny and so true, much better than the movie.

You would be proud of me; I'm eating vegetables, taking my vitamins and sleeping early. I've had the place to myself since David went to Munich for a few days, and Lisa has been away in the country.

Love you lots.

Letter, 14th May 1981

Hello Mum,

At the moment, I'm sitting in the foyer on the 24th floor of one of the skyscrapers in *La Défense*, waiting to give a lesson to two men from a company on this floor. *La Défense* is literally a forest of towers overlooking the Seine. After the lesson I'll meet Lisa and her friend Ward in *Café Cluny* on *Boulevard Saint-Michel*; we'll have coffee, then go to the museum across the road. I have to give another lesson from 5 to 6:30 pm then will meet up with them again.

I'll ring you, Barbie, and David from a 'you know what' phone, and that will be my day. It was great to talk to you and Barbie on my birthday.

Now May 19th and its lunch time at work. As I write, I'm sitting in the square near where I work in *La Défense*. From here looking straight ahead down *Avenue Charles de Gaulle*, I can see the *Arc de Triomphe* at the far end of the avenue. It's a gorgeous day and I'm going to have a little soak in the sun before going into the Minolta Camera Company to give my lesson, where they fall all over each other to drive me home in the evening. I always accept; it beats the metro rush.

It's lovely spring weather now, and here in the square there are fountains and trees and people everywhere. *La Défense* is the very modern business district of Paris. Do you remember looking out from Lisa's and my bedroom window one night at Madam Gaba's and seeing those tall skyscraper buildings all lit up? Well, that's where I work.

Next day now and I'll be teaching at Tupperware Company today; I'm already fifteen minutes late, so maybe they think I'm not coming. It's a gorgeous day here. I miss the sun so much and love days like today.

One of my friends gave me a bottle of red wine for my birthday, so we invited Aref over for dinner. We sat out on the balcony with wine and cheese and talked for hours. It was a lovely night, and *Sacré-Coeur* looked beautiful lit up in the distance. This morning, all last night and all today I've had a headache. But we had a lovely evening. I go to Amsterdam tomorrow afternoon ... can't wait.

Today I had four hours off, so met one of my students for coffee and we sat in a café in the sun for about an hour then went to his place to listen to music. He lives in the middle of a gorgeous park, and his house is full of plants, flowers and antiques. He's almost an antique himself – he's thirty-six! I asked him for some tablets for my headache, and he told me, "You must fight the bad with the bad."

I had two glasses of champagne, and it's a bloody good thing my students haven't turned up! Don't know whether I could have handled the pace.

Home now and I feel very relaxed. Aref is bringing dinner tonight, so I can have a little sleep before he comes. I'm working in three different companies now; two and three times a week in each, and they all pay my travelling expenses. I've made some good friends there too.

I've just finished reading another French novel. I understand well now, and my speaking is always improving. If my students don't understand something, I can explain our crazy language to them in French now. It's important, especially for beginners.

I'm learning about the broken public phones here and know how to 'work' them. Last Friday night I went out to a phone at 2 am because I wanted to talk to you and to David in Cannes, but the bloody thing wouldn't work, so I cried instead. I did so want to talk to you. It was just so very frustrating.

My birthday flowers are just gorgeous. I love them and you and Barbie.

Letter, 21st May 1981

In Amsterdam now and I had an excellent treatment today – over an hour – so well thought out. I wish you could be here to see it. It was great, and I slept soundly at 8 pm last night. Dr Van Burien always has his assistant who is just as involved as he is. After the treatment, his assistant invited me to join him for lunch at a seafood restaurant in Baarn. We had a great time. He was so interesting to talk to. At one stage he looked at me across the table, squeezed my hand and said, "You're going to make it; you're on your way," and 'Little Miss Can't Take Her Anywhere' started to cry.

After lunch, he took me to where I needed to buy all the things Dr Van Burien said I must have, and I received a lengthy lecture about the importance of diet. My God, they'll have to exhibit me soon as a specimen of perfect health. This guy is a physiotherapist, chiropractor, acupuncturist and physical education teacher and believe me, he is a specimen of perfect health himself. On the way to do my shopping, he stopped at a flower stand and asked something in Dutch. The man gave him a long stemmed red rose and refused to take the money saying, in English, "No, I can't take the money. I can see what's happened to you."

How embarrassing! We walked the streets with the wheat germ, the muesli, and the red rose. Arriving back to Mr Schroder's, he greeted us with a grin from ear to ear.

"Hey Lady, you had a good day!" then walked away laughing. I'm sure he hasn't managed to figure me out yet.

Later, Aref rang the hotel to see how I was and to ask what I wanted for dinner when I came back, and then David rang. The next morning while chatting to Mr Schroder I told him I was going to meet a guy for a drink and as I was leaving he looked at me, shook his head and laughed (he always laughs).

"Hey Lady, I don't know how you do it – you've got a lot of friends eh?" Chuckle, chuckle, chuckle.

It's now the next day and I'm having a lovely time in Amsterdam, very relaxing. I always feel quite different when I come here … more myself. The pace in Paris is so fast; sometimes I forget what day it is and the weeks go by so quickly. This time I forgot to book a room.

Language Power was going to close, as most of the teachers have been on strike for the last two months for higher pay. All of my students were advising me to look for another job, and I was feeling tired already, just at the thought of going through all that again. Never a dull moment here that's for sure. Well, they got their pay raise and better hours. The strike didn't affect me, as being independent I'm paid twice as much as anyone here. When the strike was in full swing I took over a lot of the companies in addition to my own. I was working outside of the school most of the time, and one by one, the teachers who were on strike and whose company I had taken over for the duration of the strike, came to me and said,

"Don't try too hard there Lorraine, I want my company back."

"Well, I can only promise what I do in my own companies," I said, "and that, by the way, is my best."

I was very angry, and now the Director wants me to keep all four companies and not give them back because he says I'm a better teacher!

"Don't worry," he said, "I make the decisions here. Companies are more fun, pay more money and have lots more advantages."

He's really looking after me because he still would like me to join him as a business partner when he gets established. As I said, there's never a dull moment here.

Well, where was I? Oh yes, I forgot to book a room at Mr Schroder's with all that going on. The morning I was leaving, Aref said something about a hotel, and I panicked. "My God – where will I stay?"

I phoned around and everything was full ... even Mr Schroder's. At 9 pm, even if the hotels are open they won't wait up. It's too late!

"Calm down," said Aref, "you'll be all right – I know you will organise it, you always do. I really admire that in you. You always fight and come up with a good solution."

With that little bit of encouragement, I spoke sanely to all the hoteliers; I found a hotel for the first night and booked into Mr Schroder's for the last two. Aref winked, smiled and said nothing.

I shopped today, went for a walk, organised somebody's European trip through five countries over breakfast at the hotel, and for a repose, I found a bar with excellent music and sipped a martini for one and a half hours. I can be a very anti-social creature sometimes. I enjoy my own company immensely.

Letter, 30th May 1981

Dearest Mum,

I feel like Miss Suburbia in Paris at the moment. Having just finished my washing, the balcony is looking like the local wash sheds and the day is gorgeous. But in the Paris sun you must look to at least three days to dry clothes, so we have knickers, woollies, trousers, etc., all dancing gaily in the breeze.

Today I cleaned house, relined the kitchen cupboards, vacuumed, cleaned the bathroom, the windows and the French doors. Now I can see through them, and guess what? As well as being able to see *Sacré-Coeur* from my balcony, I discovered you can see the *Eiffel Tower* through the bathroom window if you stretch up and around! After cleaning, I had a long relaxing bath, sipping a martini and listening to my music. Afterwards, I finished reading my book on the balcony in the sun.

The other day when I came home from Amsterdam, Aref was there to meet me at the station. While I was on the train, he had let himself in and prepared dinner.

Last night he rang and asked if I would like to go with him to his friend's house. I hadn't met Iranians before, but they would have to be the warmest and most sensitive people I've ever met. We had dinner, listened to music, danced, and played cards. One of the guys spoke a little English, so we used French, English and Iranian.

Lisa has been away for almost three weeks now, and this place has been like a little haven. I know you'll just adore it. Everyone says it's gorgeous; it's so *petite* but spacious and so mystical, light and white. It's on the eighth floor – the top – so you can see everything, including the lady across the way, who walks around in her apartment with nothing on all morning. Finally, she decides to put on her knickers, then later in the day, her bra. Hang on, the music has finished.

Last night my dreams were all in French, and I woke thinking of what I had to do in French. I've just finished reading a French novel – 300 odd pages. Never thought I would arrive at that, but now when I read French, it's normal. Occasionally, if I'm aware that I'm reading the French text in English in my head, I stop and revert back but I never know when I've changed until after. I find now, because of the sense of the language, that it's easier to read, realise and understand in French. I feel I could do some translation work now. I read with ease the French magazines, and sometimes translate business letters for my students.

Remember how hard I used to work at French in high school? It's paid off because I find now that it all suddenly falls into place. The language doesn't sound romantically foreign to me anymore. Sometimes on the Metro, I pretend I can't understand when I hear people's conversations, just to try and recapture that romantic idea of listening to a foreign language, but it just sounds like words now.

The other night I went to a restaurant for dinner with one of my students, and we spoke French most of the evening. Sometimes he would say something in French, and I would answer in English, then we would continue in French or vice versa. He told me I spoke and understood well and that he adored my accent when I spoke French. I find now I lack many English words outside the regular vocabulary that most people have because I don't use them and so have forgotten them.

Carlos rang this afternoon to say he was going home to Argentina on Tuesday for a month. We don't see each other these days. It's a long story that I don't think I will ever understand. I hold my distance now and can't believe all that has passed ... and now this. He's coming around tomorrow to get his watch that he left here. It's been nearly three months since we've seen each other; it's going to be very strange and I don't know how I'll react.

Well, that's all water under the bridge now. Never thought I would say that about Carlos. Isn't life strange? I know I still hold a certain distance inside me, not to think or reason it out but sometimes ours is not to reason why. I don't know what else to say there. We are still good friends. He calls me occasionally and we talk at length on the phone, but for some reason known only to him he gave me the 'Big A.'

Next day now...

The other night when I came home, I was tired and didn't feel like cooking, least of all eating, when the doorbell rang. First of all, I saw food, and then behind it, I saw Aref.

"I hope you are hungry," he said.

"No, I've eaten; I've just had some cheese."

"That's not enough, you can eat this too."

157

"I can't eat."

"You will eat a little," he said, and proceeded to cook.

He brought it out on the balcony as it was a lovely evening, but I didn't feel like eating. He said,

"I know what you eat for breakfast, and you don't eat much lunch. Now eat." and I was presented with a plate.

"Eat the vegetables first," he added.

I couldn't believe it. "Who are you – my friend or my mother?"

"Do I have to *feed* you too?" he responded.

So, I had to eat a little. Then I climbed up and sat on the balcony wall to get a better view of *Sacré-Coeur*. I figured that would make the veggies go down easier. Then, "*Mon Dieu Lorraine! Qu'est-ce que tu fais là haut?*" (My God, Lorraine! What are you doing sitting there?)

I was on the ledge of the balcony wall, and we were on the eighth floor. I was careful, but Aref was throwing a tantrum.

"I'm eating my vegetables if that's still okay with you."

"You can't sit there, you'll fall. Get down!"

"I won't fall, I always sit here." He was just flabbergasted.

"Please move and promise me you won't *ever* sit there again."

"Okay, I'll move."

"No … promise me!"

I promised in the middle of a mouthful of cabbage. I thought it was quite funny, but he was so upset and serious. Then we talked, and in the middle of the conversation he said, "You know when I get married, whether it is tomorrow, next week or next year, I want to marry someone exactly like you, with your character and your qualities."

Then he expanded on that for ages … talked for so long, and finished by giving me a kiss on the forehead. I looked at him in anticipation, and he said, "What is it? What are you waiting for like that?"

"A proposal of course," I replied.

Before he had time to react, I dived into the kitchen to make the coffee. He looked through the window from the balcony and said, "Will you be my fiancée?"

I couldn't resist. I said, "Look make up your mind, what do you want to be - my mother or my fiancée? My mother is the only one allowed to make me eat my vegetables, and even *she* doesn't tell me where to sit when I eat them. No, I don't think so."

We both laughed. We had a lovely evening. He is such good company, and we get on so well together.

I'm going to have an early night, relax and read. I don't get blackouts anymore – only if I have a late night, or get over-tired, then I can feel myself losing it and can't hold on to it. But I'm careful now.

The weather is so nice now. Tomorrow I'll go to see Sammy; he rang to say he had a letter for me and that we must have *un petit verre* (a small drink) together. Denise has moved out of Sammy's place and they have separated. It's very sad. Sammy is strictly Jewish and Denise was not accepted by his family. She is devastated. I think they both are.

One of my students has invited me to play tennis, another to go windsurfing, and another to go scuba diving, yet another has invited Lisa and me down to Bordeaux near the beach and the forests for the weekend. I go out regularly with Frederique, one of the girls I used to teach at CBS who has become a good friend. The contract there has finished but I still see her. We usually go out to dinner with another professor and a girl from the Tupperware Company who likes Amsterdam too. She has suggested we drive up in her car for the weekend. That would be fun.

I've been asked by one of my students if I would coach her daughter for the Baccalaureate (higher school certificate), but I don't think I have the time. I still have my Japanese student, and another man at Minolta Camera Company wants private lessons and is prepared to pay heaps, but time is the problem. Mainly I do company work now and have lots of regular students at Language Power who ask if they can have me for their teacher.

It's 9 pm, and I'll take repose now and listen to some music. Tomorrow I want to go for a picnic in the park if it's sunny. Another of my students asked me to go dancing last week, but I just wanted to be quiet – maybe next week. I have a nice lifestyle – lots to do, many opportunities, many friends, and some select close friends – and I can be by myself too when I need to be. Think I'll play *Jonathan Livingstone Seagull* now; it's lovely to listen to and you can just float on the music.

Last night the lounge room electric bulb broke, so we lit a candle for the dinner table. I wasn't watching how close I was to the flame, and my sleeve caught fire. I screamed. I was so shocked and couldn't move for fear. All I could see were the flames, and I can remember them getting bigger and bigger. My jumper was nylon so it was twice as bad.

Aref dived across and grabbed my arm with his hand, which is burnt, and we both have horrible blisters. He grabbed the butter and smothered my arm and his hand with it. It's hard to tell who the victim is, him or me. His hand is covered in blisters and I've got horrible welts all over my arm, and only one sleeve left in my lovely jumper.

On that delightful note, I'll close. I figure if I can get this letter into the envelope now, it'll have a good chance of being posted on Monday.

All my love always.

Postcard, 4th June 1981

Just a quick note on this postcard which shows where I work in *La Défense*. It's about forty-five minutes on the metro from where I live, and I worked today in the building I've marked with a cross. *La Défense* is a completely new area, exceptionally modern, with every convenience, and now in summer the whole area is draped in trees and flowers. I give class lessons in some of these buildings.

They often have jazz concerts and entertainment in the plaza, and I walk by here every day to go to work.

Have to hurry this coffee down because another teacher and I are meeting Frederique for dinner.

Love you.

Letter, 11th June 1981

Dear Mum,

I'm sitting here in the open air at *La Défense* again. It's beautiful in the sun. Just bought a croissant to eat and a big woolly German Shepherd came up, and the bugger grabbed it off the seat, so I fed it. Figured if he didn't eat that, he'd eat me.

My view from here looking straight down *Boulevard Charles De Gaulle* is the *Arc de Triomphe*, and the sun is exquisite. I love the sun - and you Mum.

I worked this morning from 11:15 till 2:15 pm and start again at Minolta at 5 till 6:30 pm.

Went to pay my electricity bill and you wouldn't believe it; in one week the rent, electricity, telephone, and my quarterly work tax payment are all due, plus the portable colour television I've rented arrives on Friday. Getting quite bourgeois now, are we not, and it's even nice to know I can afford it all.

I'm going to the movies tonight with Aref. We had a competition the other day; he won and the prize was a shout to the movies ... winner's choice.

It's so beautiful sitting here in the sun. Acupuncture again on Friday 26th in Amsterdam. I'll arrive on Thursday 25th at 10 pm, and this time I'll remember to book. Bloody dog ... hope he chokes on my croissant.

I have three private students now, including the fifteen-year-old girl who I am coaching for her Baccalaureate. Yes, I accepted the challenge. Her parents, who are Japanese, recently invited me to dinner, the night they had two Australian businessmen as guests. Oh, and another man at Minolta France wants lessons. With all, I charge heaps because my time is valuable and I do a good job. I get two thousand francs ($500) per month just for the private lessons, so it's good. I can squeeze most between my idle hours and still have heaps of free time.

I'm so glad you loved your Mother's Day flowers, but I wish they had arrived on time for you. My birthday flowers are still beautiful and thriving. The pot plant was a lovely idea. Did I say thank you for my birthday parcel? I just adore the trousers which I'm always wearing and the gorgeous jumper. Thank you Pet!

On Monday night, five of us went to an Iranian restaurant for dinner (which was Aref's choice). After dessert, or probably between sips of wine, he stood up, looked at Lisa and me and said, "Okay, pick a hostage."

"We don't have to. We've got you, remember?" Lisa said.

We had a great night – I'll tell you about it later. I should go into Minolta now and start my lesson.

Inside now waiting for my student. I had a lovely time sitting in the plaza in the sun … still dirty on that dog, though. What I wanted to tell you was about the restaurant a few nights ago when I made a real spectacle of myself.

I don't remember much about the evening except that the wine, the aperitifs, and the vodka were awfully good, and I forgot that my system was not what it used to be. Lately, and especially since my last acupuncture treatment, I've felt almost normal so I did drink a lot, and it hit me suddenly. Before the chemotherapy I could hold it, but these days everything just grabs me and takes over. It felt just like it did during the chemotherapy – dizzy and really nauseous and I knew if I started throwing up, that mentally it would be like a re-run of last year. I just can't begin to tell you how hard I fought to keep from being sick.

I asked Aref to take me to the bathroom where I kept hearing myself say over and over, in French, "*Non, c'est assez – son assez.*" (No, it's enough - it's enough.)

Oh, it was horrible. I spent the next hour sitting outside, and he told me later that I just kept repeating in French, "No more, no more – last year was enough – I can't, I can't."

God, I remember most things. I can remember *thinking* that, but not *saying* it. Aref spent all his time with me except when they called him inside to play the music. I didn't want to move. I just wanted to breathe fresh air. And you know … no, you don't … David does, though. I used to have too much inside me during the treatment and used to breathe out heavily all the time, and found myself doing the same then.

Well, I slept that night, woke up with the same headache and was sick the next day. No doubt about the old willpower. I couldn't handle it the night before at the restaurant. It was horrible both mentally and physically. I stayed home from work and Aref came over at lunchtime with a bunch of roses from his house and cooked something for me to eat.

The lady whose house he lives in had said to him, "Bring Lorraine over here and I'll look after her." How nice of her. She's just gorgeous.

Now I realise how fragile my system is, even when I feel well. Sherbet, what a bastard of a treatment that was. But I still can't help feeling that it must have been meant for me to have because I figure you only go through something like that if you have to or are meant to.

I'm good now, though … getting better all the time.

Letter, 14th June 1981

Dear Mum,

Actually the main purpose of this letter, besides to say hello and to tell you that I love you, is to ask if you would renew and send my Australian driver's license so I can apply for another international license here. It's coming into summer now – very hot today 25° C– too hot to be outside for a long time. Some of my friends have cars and have proposed that we take a weekend and drive out of Paris into the country, to *Mont St Michelle* or the *Val de Loire* (Loire Valley) to see all the castles, and we would share the driving. Sounds great! I'll need my licence, so could you write and tell me what I need to send you, to have it renewed.

I feel so much better now because I sleep more, take my vitamins, 'eat' all Dr Van Bruin's advice, and have great working hours with endless time off.

I've rented a colour television and pay $40 per month which is good for Paris. You wouldn't believe what I had to go through to rent it. They want to see your passport, ID card, last three salary receipts, electricity bill, last rent receipt, how much money you have in the bank, plus the bank's name and address. They also wanted my social security number (which I don't have), but I made up a story that it was in the process of being re-regularised, and they believed me. Then when the TV is arrives at your door, you are almost buried alive under the mounds of paperwork they make you complete. It's unreal, but I know to expect it now.

This weekend I'm spending at Aref's house in the country, one hour from Paris on the metro and ten minutes from my work at *La Défense*. This morning we walked the dogs in the woods for an hour. Last week we had a picnic there. It's gorgeous. We have just spent an hour watering the garden, the dogs and ourselves. We were drenched but had so much fun. Aref is in the kitchen at the moment preparing lunch. I've made a salad and we'll eat in the courtyard. It's lovely here and we are surrounded by trees, plants and flowers. Lunchtime; back soon.

The elderly couple who own this lovely, two-story, old-style stone mansion will go on vacation soon for three weeks and she said to me, "Lorraine, you are welcome to move here for that time, and you can use the whole house while we are gone," So how about that?

This mansion is set beside lovely woods on the outskirts of Paris; Aref loves it here. Today we walked the dogs, talked, and laughed, sat in the sun, listened to music and prepared lunch which we've just finished. The Monsieur who owns the house gave us a bottle of wine, and Madame gave us a big bowl of cherries. She's the lady who had told Aref to bring me home so she could take care of me when I was sick.

I just finished the washing up, and Aref is making the tea. I'm well looked after here, that's for sure.

I can't wait to go to Amsterdam again next week. While there I'll replenish my stocks of muesli, five-grain cereal and yoghurt, and you can exhibit me when I come home as a specimen of perfect health.

Aref just asked me what I was writing. He doesn't speak English, just his native language and French. He just sat down beside me and said, "Say hello to your Mum for me," so, hello from Aref.

Next day now …

Barbie, Suzie is coming to Paris to spend a week with me. I haven't seen her since we travelled with her and Kathy in Germany and Austria. That was such a good time, wasn't it? She arrives tomorrow. Apparently, she finished her studies in Scotland, so has more time to herself now. Must call Lisa to see if Suzie has called so that I know which train to meet. It will be lovely to see her again. Also, must remember to pay the electricity bill. Otherwise we three girls will be cold, hungry, and all in the dark like mushrooms.

It's now 10:45 pm. I work tomorrow at Language Power from 9:45 am until 6 pm. I have three students for one-and-a-half hours each, then I go to the Tupperware Company for one-and-a-half hours, and finish up with a private student for two hours.

Love you. I must sleep now. See you soon.

Letter, 16th June 1981

Dear Mum,

It's a good thing I got up when I did, as I wanted to spend a leisurely morning before starting work at 11:15 but instead, it was go, go, go, and the phone rang nonstop. There were calls from Suzie, my Japanese student, Language Power, some friends, and Lisa's father. Then the postman delivered your parcel, and the concierge lady who looks after the apartments came to check the heating. So by the time I tidied up, washed up from last night, ate breakfast, showered, ironed, opened my parcel, read the letters, and went downstairs to pay the rent, it was time to go. After all that I actually got to work ahead of time.

My Japanese student called at 8 am to confirm his lesson time tonight, but he wouldn't change to an earlier time. Suzie arrives tonight at 6 pm, and I wanted to finish early. But that's okay; I'm going to hit him with a rise in my fees tonight.

I can't wait to see Suzie. Lisa will meet her at the station and take her to dinner in *Saint-Michelle*. Then Denise, Aref and I will meet them for coffee in a nearby café after I finish work. This café has live music and is a lot of fun. Tomorrow I start work at mid-day, so Suzie and I will do something in the morning and after work too.

Last night I watched the colour TV for the first time, a fascinating medical documentary on sclerosis. They send people to the Dead Sea to relax and take natural treatments there, including acupuncture. They showed different conditions and treatments, and I cried when I saw people in the hospital having chemotherapy. It's like … I can't explain … but it's because of that that I know the events of last year are still inside me, mentally and emotionally. I don't think of it often, but when I see things like that I just cry.

I feel 100% better than I did twelve months ago. I can't believe the change. I've slowed down too and am more careful. I can't drink wine now – found that out the other night at the restaurant. I'm going to limit myself to just one glass now, so don't worry when you read my last letter. It's okay now. Most of that was pure fear of nausea and of being sick like last year.

I could understand everything in the documentary and in the movie too. It's good for the language which was the primary motivation for renting the TV. You will love my apartment. On June 25th, Lisa is going back to the States for the summer, so then I'll have it all to myself.

The weather is improving now – lovely, fresh sunny days – just gorgeous. Paris is enchanting at night; it seems to come alive with a new energy when the whole city is illuminated. No wonder it's called 'The City of Light.' It's a magical time to wander along the banks of the *Seine*, enjoy the long, warm evenings and watch the lights reflecting from the boats that travel up and down the river, throwing stars and shadows on the water.

But Paris is soon to become inundated with American tourists wearing bright red t-shirts and thongs (they spend the first week in the metro trying to find a way out), and the Japanese tourists who can hardly move because of all the cameras they carry, at least three each you know.

They tell their mate to stand stock still like a board, six inches in front of the *Arc de Triomphe* without smiling; hold up the traffic while trying to work out which camera to use and when they decide to use all three, the subject finally cracks a smile and it's all over and time to go home. Then they go into *Eden Perfumery*, buy the most expensive bottle of perfume, a Cardin bag, a St. Laurent scarf, and a Cartier lighter. When they get home, they flash their photos of the *Arc de Triomphe* and their wares and say they've seen Paris. I shouldn't generalise, nor be so cynical, but sometimes it's difficult not to be.

Now I'm at the Minolta Camera Company again, and it's here that I've had a request for private English lessons. I'm going to track that down today.

You know Aref is younger than I am, nearly five years in fact, and the other day when he was talking about marriage, he said that he thought there was too much difference in our ages! After I got over the shock I said, "Just a minute, I don't remember asking to marry you!"

"I know Lorraine, but if we were the same age or if you were younger, I would ask you to be my fiancée for a few years."

"Hey, wait a minute," I said, and went into my big spiel about age difference and spirit and we talked for the longest time. The next day he told me he had thought about what I said, and gave me a speech that was the same as what I was saying yesterday! So, I'm expecting a proposal any day now!

Back again. I've just finished my private lesson with the Japanese student. Told him my new fee and he said he'd think about it. I felt like saying, 'There's nothing to think about on your part, Fred, it's yes or no.'

Well, it's now the next day and I'm waiting for my class at the Tupperware Company.

We had a great night last night. Lisa met Suzie at the train station. She had no idea who Suzie was, so she made a sign in bold letters that read SUZIE DREW, and paraded up and down the platform holding it high above her head. They had dinner at a sidewalk cafe near my work, and while I was waiting for my Japanese student to arrive, I ran there to say, "Hi! Bye!" and, "I'll see you after my lesson."

Denise, Aref and I joined them about 10 pm. We went to a fantastic café with live music in *Saint-Michelle* and had a wonderful evening. Suzie kept saying to me, "This is wonderful. I'm so glad I came. I can see why you love it; it really suits you."

We left the café about 3 am, and on the way to the taxi, Aref found a public phone that worked (he fixes them to work without having to insert money). Suzie and I called Australia; it was lovely talking with you and Barbie. Aref and Lisa called the US, and Denise called her mum in London. Suzie was funny. "I can't believe the things you do," she kept saying, "You are really *living,* and you do such outrageous things – I don't believe it!" We had such a great night.

Next day now and I have to work until 6 pm. Lisa's not working today, so she'll occupy Suzie all day. I'm meeting them at home at 7 pm. Tonight we will go walking in Paris: *Champs Élysées, Saint-Michelle, Notre Dame*, and *Saint-Germaine.* We'll have dinner at *Saint-Michelle*, and I'll be free to show Suzie the sights tomorrow. Lisa's going to the opera with a friend from the US tomorrow night, and after that, we'll all meet at a jazz club. Then Friday we'll do things during the day with Aref, Lisa, Frederique and two friends of Lisa's. In the evening we'll all meet for dinner up at *Montmartre.*

I went to the hairdresser last week, and Vivienne said to say hello to you and Barbie. She said my hair needed a complete nourishing treatment which she gave me. I was there for two hours and she only charged me for the cut. It looks lovely at last, all the same length, and so soft and healthy.

Letter, 26th June 1981

Hello, Pets. Amsterdam says to say hello. So do Mr Schroder and Herta. She doesn't bark at me anymore; I'm beginning to look like part of the furniture now. The train on Thursday night was an hour late, but Mr S was still waiting up for me at 11:30 pm. What a pet!

Can't wait to come home and see you. I'm inquiring about return airfares from Amsterdam to Sydney. If I fly from Paris, they tell me it will cost $2000!

I had a great treatment today. I'm back at Mr Schroder's now, sitting on my bed. It's 7 pm, and I'm going to sleep in a minute. I don't know what Dr Van Buren's acupuncture does to me, but every time now I fall asleep in the train from Baarn to Amsterdam. If the train didn't jolt to a halt I'd probably end up in Germany somewhere.

It's still raining here. Six days into summer and the weather thinks we are still in winter. After Amsterdam next month when I get back to Paris, I'll be staying at Aref's house. The people who own the little stone mansion are going on holidays, so I'm there for the month of July. They must think I'm okay.

Mum, you know Aref shared the apartment with Lisa and me for three months, and before that, I knew him (through Lisa) for two months. Always I thought of him as a special person – a true friend. My feeling for him was always close, and during the time he was with us Lisa and I grew to know and respect him.

For me, it was always a feeling deeper than friendship – for Lisa, a real friend.

You know, usually with men, and very early in a relationship, I feel for them very strongly and sometimes write about it, then with time, sadly, for some reason my feelings fade a little but still remain close at heart.

With Aref, it was five months before I really began to feel for him deeply. This particular evening he had invited me to his friend's place to play cards, and it was while I was watching him play, it suddenly hit me. The next day I was moved to write what I felt the evening before. Beautiful people and beautiful things compel me always to write.

"I think I started to love him last night, or perhaps I began to know him.

He was, last night, not at all a physical entity, but a sensuous mélange of quietly subtle intangibilities – too beautiful to decipher or comprehend. There I remained to sit merely as an observer, almost as if I was stealing time, unnoticed, uninvited, as if seeing him for the first time.

The newness of this moment captured me and rendered me a mere observer to something – or rather someone, strangely beautiful, and it suddenly hit me more intensely than I thought possible, especially after such a long time."

-Lorraine, May '81

Letter, 11th July 1981

Dearest Mum,

I'm having the most relaxing three weeks. Aref and I are looking after this lovely, lovely house and the animals: two dogs and a cat. It's so very peaceful here, I don't ever want to leave. Maybe Monsieur and Madame might lose their way or forget to come back.

Lisa is in California and will be there for two months, then when she returns I'll be in Australia for Barbie's wedding. After I come back to Paris, Lisa will choose another apartment with another friend, and from then the place will be mine. So that will be just fine when you come over.

At the moment Aref and I are watching TV. Occasionally I get a handful of peanuts, and every now and again he wants to know what I'm writing, and to say hello to you. He is really beautiful.

I can say now that I understand most things on television. I follow with ease; it's so natural, and I'm not even aware that it's in another language. Last night we watched a variety program from Brazil and thought of Barbie all the time.

Yesterday at 6:55 am the rugby match between France and Australia was on television. I set the alarm but turned it off unconsciously so didn't get to see it. We saw a bit of it on the news. I bet it was fantastic. I kept telling everyone that France didn't have a chance; I don't even know why they bothered to go and play. I kept thinking of Keith Holman too, Mum, watching some of those clever passes and fine runs, but I'm sure if he were playing he would have run rings around everyone on the field.

Tomorrow I begin lessons with a new private student, a company director. We met the other day to discuss price, time and place, and I told him he could come here to this house for the first week. We had drinks and he took me to the Club Mediterranean for dinner. It was a Caribbean night with candles, coloured lanterns, fantastic food and a live band playing rumba, cha-cha and samba all night.

This director used to be a ballroom dancer, so I was in my element. It brought back great memories of my ballroom dancing days. I had a wonderful time and arrived home at midnight after telling Aref that I would be home early. I kept ringing him to say, "I'll be there ... I'll be there."

I had a fantastic time dancing but would much prefer to be with Aref. You should see him move when he dances – Aref, I mean. Incredible!

Now let me tell you about my eventful day last Wednesday. I worked in the centre of the city in the *Tour Montparnasse*, that very tall building near *Saint-Michelle*. My second student was a lawyer and the mayor of a town just outside Paris. He's an advisor to the present government, a novelist and poet. We didn't do much work! Instead, we talked philosophy, books and poetry and he even recounted some of his wonderful stories and poems to me in French. I was in heaven ... completely wrapped up in the conversation. He said he would give me some copies and scripts to read, so I made an appointment with him next week to pick them up. It's so good to talk deeply with people like that.

Then in the early afternoon, I had to work in a company with one of my Language Power students. That's where I met their director who asked me for private lessons. This company has a contract with Language Power for English tuition, so it's not ethical for me to take him as a private student. Even so, I thought I'd mention it to my boss, and he said, "I won't tell anyone if you don't," which is good as I need the money for my ticket home.

Later that afternoon, while I was waiting in the conference room at Language Power for my next student, I ran downstairs to buy a newspaper to look for a part-time job. Found one: a professional photographer was advertising for a debutant model!

Well now, I thought, *sherbet, I should call him ... hell, why not? I've lost a lot of weight, my hair is nice, and I sparkle!*

"How tall are you?" he asked on the phone.

I told him I had worked in Australia as a part-time model (unprofessionally), for clothes and hairstyles, and he said he would like to meet and talk with me. I made a rendezvous with him for the following day at a café near my work. When I hung up the receiver I thought, *Oh my God, what have I done?* I was really nervous but that evening when I went with my new director/student to the Club Med, I relaxed and forgot about the next day's rendezvous for a few hours.

Up early the next morning, I took ages to get ready. It worked, because when I emerged as the new me, Aref said, "You look beautiful!"

I did look okay in my black slacks, a soft feminine white blouse and black leather jacket. On the way, I bought a pair of tweezers to make some semblance of my eyebrows, *et voila!* I went to the café.

Hang on, I want to watch this movie. Love you.

Back again. It's Bastille Day today, July 14th, France's national holiday.

Back to the appointment. I arrived right on the dot of 11 o'clock. He had said I would recognise him by his beard, and that he would have a camera sitting on the table. He wasn't there. Just as I walked out of the ladies' room I saw him. "*Voila!*" He said – he knew it was me.

We talked a lot. He told me it was hard to find beautiful, tall women in France. "You *are* beautiful," he said, "and I am sure we will have success working together. "

He's a professional photographer and begins his sessions either at the end of July or after I come back in September. Can you believe it? Well, it's a start. I know I can do it, given half a chance.

Actually, he's an artistic industrial photographer and showed me some of his work. He seemed a very nice person – not a hustler. That's what I was wary of. Aref met him too, told me I had to be careful and insisted on being in the café to check him out from a distance, which he did. Towards the end of our discussion, Aref came over, kissed me, then shook his hand, and introduced himself. Later he gave me a character analysis of him and said, "He seems very genuine, *and* he has good taste. You look beautiful today."

So I have my first session when I come back from Australia in September after Barbie's wedding. I knew if I could bluff my way into getting an appointment I'd be okay.

He wanted professional models but can't afford their price as yet, so he is starting with debutants – I'm not even that. I have a foggy rec- ollection of walking down the catwalk in the civic centre in Dubbo one night, sporting a hairdo which I didn't like and thinking, *Jesus, if I don't make one of those swivel turns here I'll fall off the end of the bloody catwalk.* Luckily, I made the turn in time. No, I didn't recount this experience to him in any detail.

My new director/student comes tonight for his first lesson. Hope he brings his money with him, although he must have spent squillions on me the other night at the Club Med. God, all these Frenchmen are the same: married with children and looking, looking, looking. It's incredible. They must have very unhappy lives – or is it just the French way of life?

This week I have to see that lawyer for the copies of his stories, also see Frederique to arrange a night out with her.

Back again.

The couple who live here are due back this week, so after the weekend I'll move back to my place. Aref is taking a bath at the moment, so I ran downstairs between my modelling experience and married men to wash his back.

I did the washing this morning, and the backyard looks like a rumble with clothes hanging everywhere. There are no clotheslines here.

The French surprise me. These people have a cleaning lady who does all the washing, ironing, cleaning etcetera. She washes blankets, clothes, everything, and hangs them to dry in the bathroom downstairs. The clothes take a week to dry there and end up smelling horrible. She washed Aref's clothes last week and hung them to dry inside. Talk about the smell! I won't let her do mine. I do them myself and hang them outside. This morning I re-washed all Aref's 'clean' clothes by hand … couldn't handle him wearing them smelling like that.

They had the Grand Parade down the *Champs Élysées* this morning (the Army, not the dirty clothes). Bastille Day is very impressive with all the celebrations in the city. They do things on a grand scale on France's national day. The *Champs Élysées* is transformed; it's decorated with flags and lined with thousands of people. There is a spectacular military parade, many marching bands, uniformed contingents representing the French Foreign Legion, Army, Navy and Air Force, etc., and a massive display of tanks and armoured vehicles. Nine fighter jets swoop low along the length of the avenue, trailing behind long colourful streams of red, white and blue vapour. It's truly spectacular, and the whole atmosphere is amazing.

Staying here for the past three weeks (a month almost) has been a real haven for me, away from all derangements – telephones, noise and people – and so perfect with Aref. It's lovely here, and I feel like I'm hiding in luxury. We've been waking up late morning about 11 am, sleep in 'til midday and have a leisurely breakfast in the sun on the patio. I've had since Friday off because of the public holidays.

Now I'm waiting for my student to arrive, 7 pm I think. The cat is sitting on my knee 'cos I've just played with her for twenty minutes. We completely turned the lounge room and living room upside down.

It's now Sunday 19th July, and the couple who live here arrived home last night. Madam brought me gifts from her holiday in the south of France: a lovely grey silk blouse and a pendant. She is so sweet.

Thank you for the vitamins you sent Mum – they came just in time. Everyone at work now is saying how healthy I look. I don't think I was well when I first started working, because really after five months of not working then going head-first into long intensive hours of teaching (which may have resulted in the blackouts), it was all too much. But now I'm more relaxed and feel ten years younger.

Today I was telling Aref that now I know what it feels like to be very old. Last year during the chemotherapy treatment I felt like an old lady, and now honest to God, I feel as though time has turned back and I'm a little girl by comparison. I feel younger, lighter and more alive. Even compared to about three months ago when I first started working I still felt older. I'm sure it's the acupuncture and the diet, and I've slowed down a lot too. Before that, I was out every night – it was like a compulsion. Even if I didn't want to go, I went. Now I feel more normal, more myself.

Tomorrow I'm going to the perfumery to see Denise before work, so I'm going to try to be at the 'free' phone at 8 am to call you (it's at the pharmacy nearby). That will be 4 pm your time. I'm trying to think of details to tell you, but it's better to take half an hour on the phone tomorrow if the pharmacy near the opera is open.

I've learned and now understand so much about the French mentality, and more interestingly, I can compare it now with other na-tionalities. Maybe I'll write something about that when I have more time to myself. I want to write more seriously.

Here is my little present to you, a treasure I found in a book that means you are the only person in the whole world who I can share it with.

175

The Mother is everything
She is our consolation in
Sorrow, our hope in misery,
And our strength in weakness.
She is the source of love,
Mercy, sympathy, and
Forgiveness.

-Kahlil Gibran

To my Mother, my help and
My inspiration, the one who
has had faith in me always
and who has stood by me in
brightest day, and darkest night.
To my only sweetheart,
My Mother.

-Octavus Roy Cohen

And *this* … my favourite, for both you and for Barbie:

The best and most beautiful things in the world
Cannot be seen or even touched.
They must be felt with the heart.

-Helen Keller

With all my love to you Mum, always and ever.

Letter, 1st August 1981

It's Barbie's birthday today! This morning I spoke to her on the phone and to you and Jeff. It was lovely to talk to her. I'm bringing her birthday gift home with me.

It's Saturday today and I'll be sleeping in Bombay on Monday night. I'll probably collapse in Sydney on Tuesday, so you'll probably see me before you get this letter. I have a list of things I want to do when I get home, that is literally as long as my arm.

I'll be missing the Julio Iglesias concert here in Paris, but I can get free tickets for whoever is playing in Sydney at the moment.

I'm glad I've got money to come home to in Australia – that's a relief.

My flight ticket was 1,475 Dutch guilders. With the dollar exchange it's very good ($550), but of course, we paid for it in the poor old French franc!

This letter and I will probably arrive on the same day because I'm going back to Paris for a few days, then return to Amsterdam for two days before departure, and I have some stopovers on the flight too.

Can't wait to see you all!

Letter, 9th August 1981

Dear Mum,

I'll be home before you get this letter, but thought I would share a little Indian elegance with you in the form of the Centaur Hotel stationery. It's very nice.

My room here in Bombay overlooks one of the swimming pools, but I've had a better offer: an invitation to the beach from the most handsome waiter when I arrived. They don't waste any time here. And he asked me out tonight, but I have too much respect for my health and not enough for anonymous men, even if they are gorgeous-looking.

Also, Jim would be proud of me. I managed to have my room, my transport and all my meals here, *free*! It's all in the knowing how to book flights, transfers and stopovers. I swear he's watching over me. I've learned so much from him.

I can't believe the intense poverty here in India. It's a lifestyle that people are born into, and it's very sad to see.

I sleep here tonight. Going sight-seeing for a few hours tomorrow, then to the airport, and fifteen hours later I'll be home. What a trip! I feel like I've been travelling forever – Paris, Amsterdam, Geneva, Rome, New Delhi, Bombay and then home – all in short stages with some night stopovers. I'll probably get to Sydney and wonder where the hell I'm going next.

Can't wait to see you!

It was wonderful to see Rainey when she arrived home in Sydney. It was an exciting and busy time over the following few weeks, catching up with family and friends and last-minute preparations for Barb's wedding. Most of the arrangements were in place; the only thing remaining was to select a bridesmaid dress for Lorraine. The three of us being together was wonderful, but the time passed all too quickly.

Barbie's wedding day was perfect. She looked beautiful and so very happy.

Several days after the wedding Rainey and I returned to Paris.

Chapter 7

This time in Paris was much less eventful for us than the last, thankfully. Rainey's studio apartment was just as she had described; small but so lovely and it suited her perfectly. I was able to reconnect with many of her friends who I had met on my last visit, and others for the first time including Marcel, a young man whom I liked immediately.

Rainey and I settled into a comfortable routine and I was able to live and experience the Parisian lifestyle. This was good as it gave me a greater understanding of her life and her love of Paris. Most days I would leave with her in the morning and spend the day exploring while she was at work. We would meet for lunch and depending on her routine for the day, we would visit museums, galleries, or stroll in the beautiful gardens around the city. We would stop for coffee at sidewalk cafés and, as the season grew colder, we would find a cosy nook inside, reminiscing while watching the passing parade.

We took short trips outside Paris to Versailles and Chartres, and spent time in Holland. While there we explored Volendam and the fairy-tale village of Geithoorn. The time passed all too quickly, and it seemed in no time, I was boarding a plane to return home.

Letter, 30th November 1981

Dear Mum,

I've been as busy as ever since you left. Sherbet, what a night that was! We always seem to have some sort of minor catastrophe at airports whenever you leave. You manage somehow to make grand exits, and I hate goodbyes – all that hassle about your ticket at the airport check-in. I really didn't think you would make the flight. They left it to the very last minute to give you the okay to board. Oh, the joys of concessional travel.

When I left you on the elevator, I expected you to be coming back down the next one to tell me you had missed the flight. Well, the longer I waited, the more I thought you would be back any minute. Then I heard your voice, *"Rainey!"* and saw you waving to me from upstairs. I thought, *Sherbet! Mum is playing goodbyes from every level.*

Well after a while I left, very upset. I always am after our goodbyes. Caught a bus straight away and we were travelling along the highway when suddenly we had a collision with a little Renault car. I couldn't believe what I saw. It spun around like a child's toy and slammed into a telephone pole. And you know, that bus driver saw it and didn't even attempt to swerve or slow down to avoid it. He ploughed right into it. God – I thought I was seeing things. He just sat in his seat.

We passengers told him to open the doors so we could get out and see how the driver was. She was in shock of course, didn't know if she was Arthur or Martha. We talked to her and were able to calm her, but the bus driver just watched, still sitting in the driver's seat. Fifteen minutes later he emerged and told her that it was her fault. Eventually, the ambulance, police and fire truck arrived. No compassion, this bus driver, he walked around with a grin on his face the whole time. I was stunned. Then he bragged to his replacement driver over the intercom, "Had little accident – pushed a Renault off the road – it's a write-off." Unbelievable!

Had a coffee with Lisa when I got home, then woke up the next morning wondering firstly where the hell I was, then when I got that one sorted out it took me even longer to work out where you were. Not real quick in the mornings.

Next day now; I'm at CBS and have just finished my lesson with the director.

Ran into my old students on my way out and they want me to start again with them. I hope Mr Harrison, Director of Harrison Linguistics, gets their contract. If this director is pleased with me, he might renew with Harrison and I'd get the job. Mr Harrison rang tonight and said he might have some work for me at his school. It's right near the opera.

Had another call from a voice that said in broken English, "My name is Nicolas. Monsieur Donella told me you are my new tutor."

Mr Donella is the councelor at the American school. I start with this young man next week, two hours per week, and will charge ninety francs per hour. He lives with his parents near the Eiffel Tower. That's another student from the American school. I'm supervising the American College entrance exam this Saturday, and I get paid for it.

Went to dinner with Marcel on *Rue Mouffetard* in the Latin Quarter, the same street as the Spanish guitar place he took us to when you were here. Marcel is somewhat of a connoisseur himself, and loves fine foods as you know. Yesterday he went into the National Service for a month to play soldiers, and in January will start at the *Ecole Militaire* here in Paris as an interpreter. He speaks five languages.

I've had the phone off the hook so I don't know what's happening in the outside world, but as soon as I plugged it into the wall to make a call, Carlos rang to say, "When can I come to see you?"

He announced his wife still loves him and is coming over from Argentina to try again with him. He wants us all to go out in a cosy little threesome! God only knows where his mind is at.

I haven't heard from Aref for such a long time. He seems to have disappeared from my life except for a mysterious phone call from someone who said I knew them, and wanted to talk to me, but wouldn't give their name. "Well, there is no point in talking to you then," I said, and hung up.

I was angry. It might have been one of Aref's friends. I have too much to do in work and organisation to run around after someone who wants to play childish games.

The bolster you made for my lounge looks lovely Mum, and I'll take the cushion material to the sewing lady when I get time. She said to say hello to you, and asked if you got off all right. *Well*, I thought, *if all right means relative to your other major exits, then I guess it was all right.*

We are having wonderful weather here for ducks and fishes.

Lots of love.

Letter, 7th December 1981

My work is finally getting organised – I could end up making my fortune over here. I taught at the Fiat Company this morning. No one there has scored full marks for their dictation yet, thank God. Then I went out to the American School to find out about the young seventeen-year-old German student who I will start tutoring in written expression on Wednesday. I missed seeing his teacher and will call her tonight. I talked to the counsellor Monsieur Donella, who keeps sending me new students and asking, "How many more can you take?"

I told him about 'Mr Rich Egyptian' who baulked at paying ninety francs an hour, and who wanted to make a deal of ninety francs for one and a half hours! Monsieur Donella almost fell off his chair when I told him because these people are dripping in money. I had said to him on the phone, politely but firmly, "I am offering a professional service for which I have never had to negotiate over a price. My price is ninety francs per hour and if you need more time to think about it, please do, but call me, as I need to schedule other students into my timetable."

I was listening to myself speaking to this guy and couldn't help chuckling. I can imagine him going to the doctors, 'Twenty dollars! … How about ten?'

He probably thinks he's still in a bazaar in Egypt. I'm still awaiting his decision, but not losing any sleep over it.

Monsieur Donella told me about another possibility. Kodak France is conducting an ongoing English intensive course. Business men and women from all over France come to their company to learn English, and I know if they have a teaching vacancy they will accept me. He said it's very well paid. At Language Power, I get fifty-six francs per hour which is not a lot. I don't see why I should break my back there when I can do it by myself, but I'm assured of a job there so I'd like to keep it on. Then when all the other extras decide to suspend me for a while between courses and school holidays I would always have a regular job; so I have to think of that. I do like working at Language Power.

This month has been devoted to work and seeking out more possibilities that give me the most money and more free time. I have another hour before I start the next class. I might go and see if I can buy a good diary. My memory is a bit like a sieve these days – I have to write everything down.

Oh yes, Monsieur Donella complimented me yesterday. He said that I look so healthy and alive and with so much energy, the picture of health, he said. So I asked, "Can I please have that in writing, so I can send it to my mother?"

Really Mum, I *feel* healthy too -- not so worn out as at the beginning of the year. Any day now I expect to change into a Brussels sprout or a carrot. I go into the vegetable shop, and all the Brussels sprouts and carrots smile and wave and carry on. I just pretend I don't see them.

Love you lots.

Letter, 11ᵗʰ December 1981

At the moment I am sitting in complete silence at the American School, supervising a group of eighteen students for their college entrance exam. I thought this was only supervision, but it's everything: roll-call, distribution of tests, books full of instructions to be read and explained, and time interval calls.

It's a bit like the good old days when I taught at Rosehill School. It's great to think that I have all that study behind me now. There are three one-hour long tests. These exams are so easy but complicated by the fact that these kids are not as academically-oriented as we are at home, so they seem to find it hard to write creatively.

There's one guy up the back who reminds me of myself. He's a bit paranoid because he hasn't finished his essay and when I called half time (sounds like a football match), I think he almost peed in his pants. I get paid for this!

Denise is in England at the moment. I got a classic postcard from her yesterday, so funny. I'll try and draw it on the back of the envelope. It's hilarious.

Ten minutes to go before the end of this English exam, then we have a sanity break. Don't know how much longer I can handle the silence. Think I might just let out a high-pitched scream, but they would probably all pee in their pants if I did that, and I'd be left to clean up the mess. Talking about peeing in pants … if these last few minutes don't go quickly…

On my break now, waiting to catch up with Lisa. She's supervising in the next room.

I had a phone call from another seventeen-year-old student from this school and start with him next week, twice a week. So now I have two students from the American School – one for two hours per week and the other for three hours per week. One is the son of the guy from the Egyptian embassy who was quibbling about my fee, but I stick to my price now as it is very reasonable.

When I saw the mansion they live in by the Seine – glass walls and an apartment you could not see the end of – I was kicking myself for not charging more. The father even said that if I had any problem getting to their little castle in the sky, he would send an embassy car to pick me up. Thought I, Here's a go, here he is, sitting in the lap of luxury while quibbling about a little money that's going towards the education of his son, (who they seem to think is God's gift to mankind) and the week before, there was I, tossing up between getting my coat out of the dry cleaners or buying half a kilo of Brussels sprouts – but onto bigger and better things.

The other day I came home on the RER with one of the American teachers from this school. He was telling me about his apartment, how he had no furniture but a fantastic view of Paris, and how he eats off the floor with newspaper as a tablecloth even when he has friends over. I told him how I'd come up in the world since I'd arrived here, how I was streets ahead of him because after some deliberation, I too had invested in a paper tablecloth that you can easily *wash* forty times before it disintegrates.

Such is life in 'Gay Paree,' bright lights, sparkles, movement, excitement, and paper tablecloths that fold and unfold themselves and wash out, stand up and lie down by themselves, living in fear of that dreaded fortieth wash.

Oh, just for the record, I bought the Brussels sprouts. I just couldn't decide whether to be warm but hungry or cold and fed. Don't tell anyone. I don't want to disillusion them about life here. Actually, I eat well, very sensibly. It's essential.

One of my students drove me and another guy home from work at 8:15 pm the other night, so we ate together at a lovely Japanese counter supper place near the Opera. That was fun.

Now I only spend three days a week with Language Power at *La Défense*. The other two days I'm outside teaching in the companies and also at the American School. Some of those private students come to my apartment for their lesson. This travelling one hour or even three-quarters of an hour to get to each person has got to go, except of course if they want to send a chauffeur driven embassy car to pick me up and take me home, then I would probably consider their offer.

This month has been rather work-oriented. How about *completely* work-oriented? Yes, when I look at my bed, as I've done for the past week, still in the same state as when I get up each morning except for the quilt being pulled up, you could say all my time has been taken up with work. It's okay because I fall into it when I get home! On the days I work at Language Power my hours are from 10:30 am till 7:30 pm, with breaks in between of course, but still I get home at 8:30 pm, and considering it gets dark at 5 pm, it's a long day.

Now having given you the latest history on work, the weather (which would be great if you were a duck), and having concentrated my efforts this month on broadening my work portfolio, it seems I'm totally incapable of directing my thoughts to anything outside of the same. Here's Lisa. Back later.

Another exam now. This group is doing a mixture of tests: English, Maths, French and History. It's a shame that achievement tests here are limited to multiple-choice questions. Expression and creativity don't get much of a look in. At home, all subjects except for maths were essay-oriented, even if it was writing an essay on fats, carbohydrates and proteins. That's expression, but here it's (a) (b) (c) or (d) except for maths, science and language, which are precise.

What will I do this afternoon? I think I'll go window shopping, then go to the *Galleries Lafayette* and take a book to read upstairs in their cafeteria. I got up at the uncivilised hour of 6 am to get here by 8:30 this morning, as this school is just outside Paris. Lisa is in the next room with another class. We had a 'natter' in the break – haven't seen her for a week – we don't even bump into each other in the bakery or the lift, so we caught up today. She's going home to California around December 20th for Christmas and New Year, and then she'll leave Paris for good at the end of next summer.

I'm home now. Aref called the other day. I almost fell off the lounge, not having seen or heard from him for ages. I just don't respect people who won't get off their backsides to do something to help themselves. He rang to say sorry for not getting in touch. It doesn't make it any better or make me any less hurt and angry.

I just don't get it. I know he has a lot of problems and I feel for him, but I think sometimes he believes he's the *only* one with problems.

Admittedly I would hate to lose my country to religious fanatics, and to know that if I went home, I couldn't study or even get out; and not to have much money … but that's all the more reason to try and improve your situation.

Well, I should finish here otherwise this letter will be too heavy to post.

Love you lots.

Letter, 14th December 1981

Monday today and I'm at Fiat Company again waiting for my first class – 'the dreaded seven.' Last night I scanned my preparation sentences and couldn't see any double meanings in them, but no doubt they'll be able to find some. I make all their dictations hard enough now, so no one gets full marks. Don't think I could handle the pace if that happened

This morning before 8 am I had a phone call from a very cultured, Australian voice asking to speak to Miss Lorraine Walton. At first, I thought it might be the Australian telephone exchange wanting to abuse me for never having the phone plugged into the wall. But no, it was the Australian Embassy here in Paris!

I thought, *My God he's going to read me the last rites!* It could only mean my deportation order … how degrading! At least it could have come from a rude Frenchman sitting behind his little desk somewhere in the midst of the French bureaucracy, doing only what he's paid to do. But no, it was much worse than that. This embassy man wanted me to tutor his son for his final two years of high school in maths and algebra!

Now having taught only kindergarten, I had attained the scholastic heights of counting to twenty with beads and shells, so of course, we had to decline the offer. I think this counsellor at the American school is spreading my name around all of Paris.

I've been teaching my new student, Nicholas, for several weeks now, and it has become another adventure into the realm of parental paranoia. Nicholas is the seventeen-year-old son of an American diplomat. His mother is a French socialite who has the English vocabulary of an Outer

Mongolian muskrat. Considering she can't even speak Outer Mongolian, she has almost as many problems as her son.

So having just returned from a skiing trip to Switzerland, Nicolas is sporting a monstrous cold and looks even worse, which is why his mother has put a lid on his going out at night. In jest, I suggested he steal into his mother's makeup bag to remedy the situation. I said, "If I saw what *I* looked like under my makeup, I probably wouldn't let myself out either."

Not having realised he had taken my kindly advice to heart completely and literally, his mother found him in the bathroom, putting seductive touches of rouge with a hint of powder under his blue eyes.

She had an actual case of irreversible paranoia on the spot at seeing her only son quietly turning into a cute little fruit in such serious delight in front of the mirror. He, trying to save the situation and the sanity of his *très bourgeois* mama, told her it was *my* idea!

After that little episode I'm not sure whether I still have a job at their beautiful apartment in the shadow of the *tour Effiel*, but being a firm believer in the philosophy that one door leads to another gives me an idea for added versatility. I could place an ad in the local paper:

MOTHERS, FATHERS, ALL!
One competent, many-talented, *professeur d'anglaise* can elevate your
son's grades, and turn them into little queens in three easy lessons.

I'm actually more versatile than you thought I was. Not half as versatile as me mate Nicholas though!

Well, I have a few more classes before I finish today, and Mr Harrison called to say he had more work for me, come January.

Letter, 17th December 1981

Dear Mum,

Here is my little once a month epic on my pilgrimage to the north.

I'm on the train to Amsterdam again for my acupuncture treatment tomorrow. You should see the countryside; it's completely white with a blue-grey sky and as we pass by villages, they are lit with a lovely blue haze. This gorgeous scenery is so very relaxing – you'd love it. I've been on the train for over an hour now and have been talking with a very nice, elderly French lady. A few minutes ago I nodded off and had this dream that couldn't get itself organised because it was in both languages.

Marcel has almost finished his month of military training before he begins work in Paris as an interpreter. On Saturday he'll come up to Amsterdam for the weekend. He said to say hello to you.

No, I haven't seen hide or hair of Maxwell. He must be away. I'll give him your regards when I see him next.

I'm a bit tired now, so I think I'll have a bit of a rest. Might just check my eyelids out for cracks!

It's now a few days later, December 21st, and I'm waiting for my students at Fiat. Work is pretty sparse at Christmas time with everyone taking holidays.

I spent a rather wonderful weekend in Amsterdam with Marcel. He came up on Saturday morning and I met him at the train station. He spent most of the weekend skating. Everyone was out skating on the canals – everyone. The landscape was magical; everything was white, white, white, pale pink and grey … so beautiful.

In Volendam, the bay where all the boats are moored was frozen, and the sea beyond was frozen in waves. Marcel skated there and in Amsterdam. He is beauty on ice … a fantastic skater. If we hadn't been so pressed for time he would have skated on the canals along the side of the road. I've never seen Amsterdam's winter countryside so wonderful.

On Friday in Amsterdam, I went to the photo shop to collect my prints, bought two plants at the markets and went to acupuncture. Had a good treatment, and then went to the post office where I called a guy in Paris to say *bon voyage* as he is going to Hong Kong. I really like this guy, a student who I've been working with for quite some time now. He's a journalist. I liked him from the first day I met him. He's studying Chinese philosophy. So I called and he was ever so happy that I did. I know, because he's a bit shy! A shy Frenchman you ask? I almost fell off my chair too. Well I know that can work too when he gets back; he is so very, very lovely.

But I'm also involved with Marcel at the moment. He is beautiful too, and because I can't choose, I opt for both. It's impossible to do that. I'll have to start defining my relationships I think, but it's hard. I find it very comfortable and very beautiful to be involved with two people at the same time, and it's bloody difficult at times, but I just find it hard to choose one at the expense of the other. Each time I'm with one, it's like no one else exists. I think it's made simpler and easier to do, as I never give anyone my all – I always hold something back. I feel that people sort of own little bits of me, not all, and no one person owns all. 'How to expand the company and reduce the risk factor?' So at the moment, that's my big problem.

The other night was pure disaster. My apartment has everything I ever wanted, except a hole in the floor that opens up to let me disappear from traumatic situations that I always manage to get myself into.

I told you Marcel and I spent the weekend in Amsterdam. He's been staying at my place when he gets time off from his military service, and sometimes during the week he gets a lift to come and see me, and goes back early the next morning.

Aref called the other day, and after such a long time he decided to meet me at the bloody station on my return to Paris from Amsterdam. I didn't expect it.

Arriving in Paris with Marcel, I breathed a sigh of relief as Aref wasn't at the *Gare du Nord* train station. But when I surfaced out of my *Louis Blanc* metro station, *voila,* there he was!

Marcel had gone to his place to pick up his belongings for the barracks, and I was to wait for him at home. He would arrive in an hour. Aref came up to the apartment, and then David rang from Australia. I was also tired and felt sick from the train trip. I told David I had to go and to call back later. I had to talk to Aref. I told him I had a friend coming, didn't define the relationship though. I didn't *ask* him to leave, I *expected* him to leave, but he didn't. Then while I was talking to him,

David rang again and while I was talking to him on the phone, Marcel arrived and Aref answered the door. Marcel looked totally bewildered and asked, "Do you want me to leave? What is going on?" (I had previously told him about Aref.)

So, I'm talking to David on the phone, in a complete flap by this stage, trying to put some semblance of sanity into a situation that was too far gone anyway. Marcel asked me again if he should leave. "No, Aref is going soon," I replied, "He usually meets me at the station – it's okay."

But Aref had no intention of leaving and at that stage, short of telling him in front of Marcel to please leave, I just wanted to grow wings and fly away. Really, you could not even imagine. Well, we just stood there. I couldn't do anything. I have never seen anyone (except myself) turn white and shake as Marcel did. Aref was completely calm, like it was he who lived there and Marcel and I were the visitors. Finally, I don't know what made Aref leave but he did, after telling me in front of Marcel, that the last train had left and that it was too far to go home, but that perhaps he could go to a friend's house.

When he left, Marcel asked me to explain the situation and asked where did he (Marcel) fit into all this? He asked nicely, not demanding because he was very upset. He asked me why Aref intended to stay. Oh, it was awful. And that's not all. I really like Marcel, but I know when this other guy comes back from Hong Kong I'll be going out with him too.

Anyway Marcel said I should take time to decide what I want, to define each relationship, tell the other person, and stop trying to be nice to everyone because it serves no good purpose. You end up being manipulated and confused, hurting yourself and other people.

I know he's right, but I just have this thing about being tied to one person. I want the closeness, the trust and the honesty that goes with sharing with one, but I want my freedom to explore as well. I guess it's the same story that happened with David over again. He wanted complete control of me, but Marcel is different – he *does* give me space, but that space is not for gallivanting with other people if you know what I mean.

Anyway, it seems I want to have my cake, and eat it too, and finally, I don't know what I really want. Then when I decide that I want someone close, I feel closed in. Marcel told me I'm like a beautiful bird, that when it flies (in thought and action) it's difficult to bring back. He said, "I want to give you that space but hope you come back by yourself."

I still don't believe what happened that night. After Aref left, it was like a nightmare that never actually happened. This is not the way I want to live, even though I choose the people I'm with, not being willing to give them my all but giving the person a little of my confidence, with reservation.

In the end it's all a big fake. You spend half your time putting this one off with an excuse to see the other and vice versa, and then the honesty disappears and you've got nothing.

I don't know. It's not a situation where you have fun and just enjoy going out with everyone lightly. If it were that, it would be no big deal but it's not like that, it's deep and involved. It's like I have two serious relationships that I want to cultivate and you can't do that – at least I haven't succeeded at it. It's not right … possibly not from a moralistic point of view, but definitely from a practical point of view. It's impossible to keep a serious relationship going along with another. Okay, one serious relationship and a 'light' one or several light ones, but not two serious ones, and that's what I have. (Sounds a bit like home-decorating or buying cakes … or maybe I'm just more French than I realised.)

Aref doesn't come into the equation. It's this other guy that I'm looking forward to getting to know – I just feel it. So it's going to be a problem. You end up losing everyone, so I don't know. I suppose ultimately, I'm like every sane, sensible person. I want one person, but until I make up my mind, I want my freedom. I guess that's what I have to tell Marcel, even though he may not want to share me; I certainly wouldn't like to share someone I liked. There's more chance of telling him gently and keeping him than saying nothing and losing a trust, being hurt and ending.

Anyway, you can tell me what you think. I don't appear to be getting much sense out of myself. Marcel said the most important thing is to be true to yourself, after that everything falls into place. I suppose when I finally work out what I want, I'll let myself know.

'Self.'

'What?'

'Let's decide on an aggressively definite course of action.'

'Great – I'm with you.'

'What did you decide?'

'I decided on a positive perhaps. And what about you?"

'Fantastic! We're on our way – at least we agree on the basics – I got a definite maybe, a bunch of nails and a saw to cut a hole in my apartment floor that drops directly into the metro for a quick getaway in the case of unforeseen emergencies.'

So much for a positive course of action. Making choices and decisions just isn't my forte, I've decided. My most positive decision since I've been here is that I've decided that I can't make decisions.

Anyway, where does Christmas fit into all this? Marcel had invited me down to Toulon on the Riviera to spend Christmas with him and his mother, but in all this mess I don't know what he expects from me. I want to be a bit less tied down; I want it all without the ropes, so I don't know. I'm so lucky to have a mother I can talk to like this.

Maxwell wrote me a letter with an infallible plan to meet in Amsterdam between 25th December and the 1st January. I'm considering it. He's great, and I treasure his friendship.

Well, I've just finished a lesson with one of my regular students – at least *he* thinks I'm okay. Work is good and I have a lot of students here at Language Power. Mr Harrison (Director of Harrison Linguistics) sent me a nice Christmas card and wrote 'Hoping to work together more and more in the New Year.' I have two more private students now and more in the New Year when school starts again.

Letter, 31ˢᵗ December 1981

It's now after Christmas, and two weeks after my last trip to Amsterdam. Mr Schroder was his usual hospitable, jovial self. I think he believes I'm a bit of a rogue, 'bringing all me mates,' and I think he gets embarrassed when he asks if I want a double or single room. I've been going up there by myself for so long now he thinks I'm an angel. It was funny to see Mr Schroder's reaction when I arrived with Marcel, and when Aref or David rang, Mr Schroder's face looked as though it might crack if he lost control. He always says, "It's for you, lady."

I usually ask, "French or English?"

And his reply is, "This one's French," or, "This one's English."

It was wonderful to talk to you and Barbie on the phone at Christmas and to receive the gorgeous white sheepskin rug. It's so perfect, and I love the beautiful handbag; I'll guard it with my life, and my legs think it's still Christmas in these stockings. You wrapped everything so beautifully. Thank you, Mum. I hope you had a good Christmas.

Lisa and I will probably hit the town on New Year's Eve with dinner and dancing. Just had one hour off between lessons, so did my veggie shopping at *La Défense* complex; carrots, spinach, Brussels sprouts, bananas, mandarins and grapefruit. One more student, then I'll be home by 8 pm. Didn't work much today — taught at CBS, had coffee with Frederique, received your parcel with the beautiful white sheepskin rug (thank you Pet, I love it so much), saw Mr Harrison who has more work for me, and now I'm at La Défense.

So tonight I'm going to celebrate this beautiful rug by spring cleaning the apartment.

I had a wonderful Christmas with Marcel, his mother and his grandmother in Toulon on the French Riviera. We went down Thursday afternoon, Christmas Eve; it takes eight hours by train. Most of Southern

France is flooded because of the freak weather, which is very warm at the moment in the middle of winter, melting all the heavy snowfalls on the mountains. The water has been gushing down for over a month now, and the situation is becoming quite serious. I'm sure God wishes he'd given the French webbed feet.

Anyway, Christmas in Toulon was lovely. We stayed two nights with Marcel's mum. I did so enjoy talking with her. She has been on kidney dialysis for the longest time in French medical history – fourteen years – and it's taken a heavy toll on her. She has blood transfusions every three days; she's an amazing lady and I could relate exactly to her feelings because of my chemotherapy. I could completely understand her situation, where I believe Marcel doesn't. Neither would anyone else who has never experienced the feelings that go with such a treatment. His grandmother is a doll, quite a character, and would give anyone a run for their money.

The way the French celebrate Christmas can be summed up in two words: they gourmandise! And how! I had never really been introduced to food until I came to France. I mean that! The French know how to prepare, eat and appreciate food. To them, it's an art to be savoured delicately.

Christmas dinner is a most elaborate meal that the French eat traditionally at 11 pm on Christmas Eve, as well as opening their gifts at that time. On Christmas Day everyone is so tired, they sleep while the children play with the toys they received the night before.

Our menu consisted of wine, cold smoked salmon with buttered rye bread and foie gras, wine, pheasant with the most amazing stuffing – full of flavour, fried potatoes, green vegetables and rich sauces, wine, cheeses, cake, chocolates, nougat and coffee.

I think that was just the preliminary, because the next day was Christmas when we adjourned to Marcel's grandmother's house for another dinner. More wine flowed, together with lobster, fried prawns, baked chicken, fried potato balls and a 1959 vintage wine; cheese with buttered rye bread, more vintage wines, *Bûche de Noël* (a traditional

French chocolate Christmas cake), dried fruits, chocolates, coffee and mints. The mind boggles. The food was fantastic, but I still believe you can't beat an Aussie Chrissie dinner.

Have to stop now to get ready for my next lesson near the Opera. My student there is a young, gay guy. He's so funny – I have to pinch myself to stay in control and to stop falling off my chair in fits of laughter. When he makes a mistake he puts his hand over his mouth, says 'Oooh,' and then giggles. It's all too much for me late at night when I'm relaxed. He is so nice, like a little boy, and with a lovely smile.

Anyway, now for the monthly report on my love life, which always seems to render more problems than it's worth and usually ends up with me telling everyone where to get off and to leave me alone for just enough time to gather another little entourage.

Carlos is back with the news that his ex-wife, who came to Paris to try again because she said she still loves him, has evidently decided that she doesn't after all, so my phone is running hot with, "When can I see you?"

Aref is wondering why I'm not seeing him, and Marcel is wondering who the hell Carlos is. André, who is the student I like and with whom I've been out to dinner, returns today from Hong Kong, where he has just spent Christmas with his son, his ex-wife and her husband. On his return he will have the privilege of complicating matters even more. Oh, and another minor complication, Marcel is head over heels in love with me. Really. I'm not kidding, and me? Well I'm head over heels in love with my apartment. It's like whenever anyone knocks on my door, I turn paranoid and have these wild, horrifying thoughts, like, "Shit! What if they sit on my lovely lounge or walk on my beautiful white sheepskin rug?"

But seriously, the apartment *does* look beautiful. In Amsterdam, I bought a dreamy *Pollyanna* lamp made of glass with prisms falling all the way around, and when the sunlight captures the prisms, it comes to life. It's just so gorgeous. I have it sitting on top of another wonderful creation for a plant stand, which I bought at a flea market. It's made of old gold wrought iron filigree work.

My class at Fiat Company, 'the dreaded seven' (all male), have triumphantly conquered three short stories – very simple and very nice. Being a teacher at heart, I objectively suggested, for purposes of optimum motivational responses, that if they had any preference of subject to let me know, and the next book would try to follow their ideas. The decision was unanimous and took less than a few seconds. "*Playboy* in English!" was the enthusiastic response.

Then mutters of, "Yes definitely in English," and another, "I'm sure we'll learn a lot, especially if we practise in our own time."

At this point, I'm swallowing my laughter that kept coming up in little burps. The students were having a wonderful time thinking all their Christmases had come at once; except the one up the back in his navy Dior suit and Yves Saint Laurent tie, who announced that he usually finds commercial colloquial English very difficult to follow. Someone chimed in with, "Don't worry Victor, it's got plenty of pictures ... you won't get lost."

My God what a riot of a lesson!

Oh yes, my guitar work is improving. I'm going to take more lessons if I can find a good teacher, a little more time and a lot of money.

Back again. That was a few days ago now. I was sick yesterday and threw up most of the day. I had a shower to see if I would feel better but I had to cancel CBS, Language Power and my private student. I slept all day between bouts of throwing up, but I'm fine today.

My student should be knocking on my door any minute. He's a seventeen-year-old German boy from the American School, and I'm helping him compose his English essays.

The 'Egyptian money wonders' rang me after a month's silence to say they *do* want English lessons for their son twice a week. Now I have three private students spread over four hours per week at ninety francs. That's $260 per month, exactly my rent, which is nice and that's not counting work from Language Power or Harrison Linguistics.

Today was the first day back to work after New Year, and I asked my students at Fiat (the dreaded seven) what were their New Year's resolutions. They replied with some sobering thoughts, like 'stop smoking, stop drinking,' etc. I told them mine was to work less and earn more, and they thought that was actually funny, but 'very sensible.' I'm serious and told them so.

So my projects for this year are to firstly, render my life in terms of work, leisure and relaxation; to work enjoyably for a minimum amount of time for the most amount of money. Funnily enough because of the nature of my job at Language Power, I can realise it there more effectively. Secondly, to come to terms with myself – to at least have a free heart and in time, give someone else as free a heart. I don't want to live like this anymore – I can't – so I must define, or at least *re*define all my relationships and stay with one person. So *voilà*! There are my New Year's resolutions. We're going to have a drastic change and hopefully, in doing so improve the lives of others to make it a little more supportable.

I guess what I really want to do is know myself … know what I really want and be honest with myself. I mean practically and actually honest with myself. In part, the catalyst for this change of heart is André, my mystery man who has just returned from Hong Kong. He is special.

Must go now. My stomach is still a bit squeamish, so I'm going home early and sleeping tonight.

Hi, again Pet. Your letter I received today was encouraging. It reminded me of Jim's words … 'Go get 'em!' I've got so much on my plate at the moment, but I can do with some better job offers. I want to keep Language Power in the balance because it's a secure job, whereas the others are only temporary.

The boys at Fiat this morning concernedly suggested that if I had any problem in French, they would bring in the French version of *Playboy*! Yes, I'm sure!

Tomorrow I work in that tall sky-scraper at Montparnasse, and then at *La Défense*. In the evening my friend André is taking me out to dinner. He called me from Hong Kong to wish me a happy New Year. Then on Friday, I'll go to dinner with the girls. I was to have taught André the day I was sick and had to cancel the lesson, so he rang that night to ask how I was and to talk. He asked me out to dinner Saturday night! He's very nice – not at all a 'wolf.' He's been burned few times in relationships I think, so I suppose that's why. He's gorgeous-looking too, and taller than I am. Don't I rave on, but it does mean that I can wear my new, high-heeled black suede shoes!

On Saturday Carlos is coming around for lunch, I feel with proposals to start our relationship again. I hope not, because that's definitely not happening. Marcel is away for two weeks at Fontainebleau Military College but rings every other night. I wish my student would hurry because it's nearly 5 pm.

What else can I tell you? Monsieur Donnella had spoken to me about another company, Kodak, that has ongoing English courses all year and they pay well, so I'll just trot out there and see them. Mr Harrison is giving me another company also, so I'll have two companies from Mr Harrison, Language Power students, three private students, plus I'm sure I can get Kodak, which would be great.

I just received my tax bill for the TV, just for the privilege of having one. They put a tax on everything here. I received a letter from Maxwell wishing me a happy Christmas. He sends his regards to you as do Marcel, Denise and the sewing lady.

I'm going out to dinner with André - not half excited about it, only told you five times already, or haven't you heard? I'm going to dinner with...

Love you lots.

Letter, 9th January 1982

Well, here I am again. You called me the other morning and we talked. Thanks for all your advice Mum. David called today, and we talked for two hours. It was interesting because he has thought further and thinks that he won't come over again for his sake and mine. So that's one relief over. I was still in bed after 11 am talking with David and having gone out to dinner and a movie with André last night, I was already tired. After I had put the phone down, I had one hour to shower, tidy up and do the shopping because Carlos is coming to lunch at 1 pm. I'm just waiting for him now. He's late, which is considerate given my current circumstances.

I had a call from André earlier, "I've been trying to reach you for a while. What are you doing this afternoon and would you like to go out tonight?" Yes, I would.

Then Marcel called, and I sloshed out of the shower to tell him, yes, I would visit him at the Barracks on Sunday. He wanted to know why did I sound so tired when the day had only just begun. Thought I, *shopping, cleaning, long difficult conversations from Australia; it's better you don't know everything. You're already complicating my life enough without the extra complication of you knowing what's going on, which would be difficult, considering sometimes I don't even know myself.* But I know one thing, I'm having a hell of a lot of fun trying to find out.

Carlos is never late. Maybe he thinks it's tomorrow. Wish he'd hurry ... my schedule is tight. André is ringing at 5 pm to ask what time to pick me up. I'm seriously thinking of fazing everyone out of my life for André; it's just too complicated otherwise. Carlos wants to live with me, Marcel I'm sure would like to marry me, and André, well, he's not saying, but he's coming up to Amsterdam with me next month. I'll leave on Thursday, and he'll come up after work on Friday night. Mr Schroder will surely be impressed, especially if David, Aref and Marcel decide to call. Aref and I are just good friends now.

André is about twenty-nine – very nice, gentle, down to earth, but dignified and *literally* 'tall, dark and handsome.' I was trying to think of another way to say it because that sounds so stereotypical, but he is just that. He's not at all pushy, which is unusual for a Frenchman. He's even a bit shy and reserved, but confident. He speaks a little English with difficulty, so we speak in French all the time. He is one of my students at Language Power and has been since May. He's a photographer and journalist but has recently switched to the commercial, administrative side of the same business. I really like André. I can't imagine what

Mr Schroder is going to think when he joins me in Amsterdam next month.

My little apartment is looking lovely; it sparkles. I've never invited André up to my apartment, he's always dropped me off. I'm sure he would come up for a drink if I asked him, but he'll come this evening as he's picking me up to go out for dinner.

Carlos is now one hour late and I'm hungry. He'd better get his act together and call me because he only has until 4:30.

For lunch (which is looking more appetising every minute because I'm getting hungrier) we have a martini with – I think he's here … no – savoury biscuits, salami, black olives, rosé, a parsley omelette with rye bread, strawberry and prune cream dessert, cheese with a hard toasted biscuit, fruit, coffee and mints. At least that's what I'll be having if he doesn't come. I've been listening to some great jazz music this morning on my cassette player.

Well, that's four pages on today and its only 2 pm.

I've just added another private student to the fold. The councellor at the American school keeps ringing to ask, "Can you take any more?" I rang him yesterday to say I couldn't supervise the upcoming exam as I would be away.

"Okay, but would you like to have lunch with me after the next exam?" was his response.

Actually, I could even consider adding him to my little entourage if he's always as far thinking as two months' notice for a dinner date. I couldn't go wrong with him. But knowing my luck, everyone would turn up at the same restaurant!

No, really, I'm looking at just one person. I can't believe I was completely ready to commit to Carlos three months ago. I was such a mess after we broke up. I told all my admirers to hang in there for him, and look, he's one hour late for lunch, and all I can think about is my stomach. If you had told me this back in March … life's funny, isn't it? I hope the same thing doesn't happen with André.

I'll call Carlos if he hasn't arrived by 2:30, and tell him to take a rain check. I could have been with André today but then this was my decision, and we have to live with our decisions. But I know one thing, if I don't eat soon I'm not going to live much longer. If Carlos thinks he can arrive at 2:30 without a phone call … I'm going to call him. He's obviously forgotten, which is strange considering he invited himself; it was a choice between his place and mine. I always feel safer on home ground.

Lisa is back from the States. She had a good time there. It's been snowing here, very cold and the balcony is covered in snow; it's so pretty. You will love the balcony and the apartment. I'm very happy here.

Still waiting. My director student at CBS is going to Puerto Rico for two weeks and then to the Festival of Records in Cannes, so I'll start teaching him again in February. I'm going out with Frederique and the old gang sometime this week. Everyone is bringing their boyfriends, but I can't decide who to take. You think I'm kidding? Well, I've got news for you and it's all bad. I usually like to go by myself. Last time someone asked me, "Don't you have a boyfriend to bring?"

Frederique turned to me and said, "You just couldn't decide who the hell to bring, could you?" I told Marcel I'd take him next time because both he and Frederique were born in Algeria.

Well, now it's a few hours later. I called Carlos, but he wasn't answering, then I called Lisa and asked her up for lunch. She's sharing a flat downstairs with Adrianna, one of the girls from the perfumery. She had a hangover after her night out with Ward and says she's very much in love with him. We had lunch and a talk, and then Carlos rang at 4 pm. Said he slept and didn't even apologise!

Well, there you go. I ran around this morning like I don't know what. My God! I don't believe it. He said he could come over now, so I told him it's not convenient, I'm going out, and tomorrow I'm busy.

It's now Monday. After Carlos didn't turn up, André called for me around 7 pm, and we went to dinner at his friends' house. They are a married couple with three lovely children. We had a beautiful evening, left around 1 am, and I stayed at André's place.

Next morning we woke about 10 am to a snow-covered Paris. It was beautiful to watch it fall. André couldn't get the key in the door lock of the car, as everything was frozen. The most amazing were the long icicles on the frozen trees, grass and plants. When I washed my hair, he was downstairs scraping the ice off the windows of the car and yelled up to me on the fourth floor, "Make sure you dry your hair well, or you'll end up looking like these trees down here!"

André drove me home around 11 am and I went out to visit Marcel at the barracks. He (Marcel) had written the most beautiful piece of poetry for me. He just rang actually and is coming around tomorrow.

On Wednesday Marcel and I, Lisa and Ward, Frederique, Denise and Carol are all going to meet after work in a café on the *Champs Élysées* and then to a restaurant for dinner on *Île Saint-Louis*.

I went to see the Kodak Company again today. It's looking good, and I have an appointment to see them tomorrow. I'm sure if they have a vacancy they can use me.

Oh, another thought about your holidays; come over in May because everyone wants to take me out for my birthday and I've decided to spend it with you on Capri instead! We will buy for each of us a Eurail pass for a month. We'll go to Amsterdam and then to Capri for ten days, and the rest of the time just relax in Paris. So come early May. Besides, it gets too busy in June and July. The month of May would be good.

André just called. God, I really like him … hence the scribbling on the side of your letter. I melt and go weak at the knees when I talk to him and draw indecipherable squiggles on your letter which I should have finished twelve pages ago. You'll meet him when you come over. I can't wait to see you.

Letter, 19th January 1982

Dearest Mum,

Love you lots. All your letters always come at the right time. Whenever I need advice, a letter seems to arrive and out of the blue you give me lots of support. Like yesterday when a letter arrived, and you said I was very normal with a healthy attitude to life. I was beginning to think I was not, with my love life in such chaos. I seem to get myself into situations that are difficult to get out of.

Marcel is lovely, but he likes me too much and is understandably upset because I told him about André. I find for some strange reason that whenever it comes to guys, I never seem to have much feeling for them when I do something that hurts them. It's like, they probably deserve it anyway, and it's different because they're just men, and the world probably owes them a hard knock. That always seems to justify it for me, I suppose because of all the negative experiences I've had in my life from all of them, bar none.

I know it's not good for me to feel like that in the long run. You don't trust, and you hurt them easily, without much feeling. With me, it's always, *so what … it probably served them right. They are just men.* I know I have a great deal of compassion and feeling, but I can also be the other way.

On thinking about her life, up to this time in Paris, I know of some experiences during her formative years and later, where trust was abused leaving her vulnerable, hurt and disillusioned. Over the years I believe she subconsciously developed a guard, armour to protect herself, even though she was a person who truly loved the people in her life, and who needed to feel loved.

My God, I really like André my photographer friend, heaps, squillions. He is special, so warm, and so wonderful. I would like to marry someone like him – exactly like him. I feel so good with him. He is beautiful. How many men do I say that about? A lot, but this is different. He is on my level totally, and I suppose he's the one (at least the first one) I have ever been able to look up to if you know what I mean. Others have been young and with a lot of maturing to do.

I sometimes I get a little scared that I'm shutting the world out in my little ivory tower on the eighth floor. I can fend for myself, I don't need people too much. With everyone so far it's like, 'Quick, come here but not too close, except when I want you to be, then get out of my life for a while and let me breathe.'

I began to think I was dangerous to myself, and I've never been like that, that I always needed an entourage I mean. I've had a lot of pressure, so much so that sometimes I feel just tired out and empty. It makes me feel old, tired and confused. My fault though, especially with David, when I know that relationship would never have worked. But I find it hard to let go, even when I have a clear mind. And when I don't, it's confusing and I become unsure of myself when I know that what I'm thinking and feeling is right. But I put myself in situations that ultimately bring me emotional stress because I'm not strong enough to control them and be harder and more definite than I should be.

I feel I have to be careful about stress. It makes me feel old and tired out sometimes, and I look in the mirror and look older than I should, especially around the eyes. Sometimes I feel I'm trapping myself, not feeling free at heart, but I know it's me that must learn to be harder for my own benefit. It's for that that I decided even though I have a few hang-ups and relationships on *my* terms, I really think I'm pretty normal, especially when I'm with someone like André. He makes me feel like myself … the real me. I'm beginning to trust him. I don't feel threatened because he gives me space naturally. We are very well together.

I think I've been with the men I have been with because I always like to be in control. I feel … superior to them, for want of a better word, and always have. It puts me in the position of driver, when, where, how, and completely on my terms. When I want their undivided attention it's automatic and natural, but when I want them to disappear they do because they don't have a choice – but that's where the difficulties start.

I seem to turn my feelings off and on like a tap, but then I suppose that's because I haven't met the right one. On the way to meeting him I have this habit of choosing people that I like but people I can manage, but I truly feel for them too. (It's probably my genuine, soft, intrinsic, 'Mother Nature' side that makes it more automatic for me to get attached, and for them to think all their Christmases have come at once.)

I was just getting my thoughts organised like this yesterday, and I said to Marcel, "I know I have a few hang-ups and even if *you* don't, if you give yourself enough negative experience in situations that you probably shouldn't be in, you can't help believing it anyway. I know I have hang-ups … I can see where they've come from, how I react and what I should do to change them. It's very logical. I can't be that far gone."

He responded by saying, "You know, the most intelligent people in the world are neurotic. They understand it completely, but can't do anything about it."

I didn't need that. Then your letter came that said I was normal. Well, thought I, *Mum is always right...* But seriously, all things considered I don't think I have that many hang-ups. It's just that I put myself in situations that I really don't want to be in, and it all begins again.

André is special, so at this difficult stage, I have to re-define my relationship with Marcel, who cried when I told him what the situation was. He was just amazing. I knew he was sensitive but, my God, he turned white and shook like I don't know what. I know he is not strong emotionally; I don't need that. He confuses me sometimes and weighs a little heavy at times. I just told him I need time to myself. He knows about André.

Marcel tells me on the one hand that he'll give me time and space; he understands I don't want to be tied down. He said he will try to be understanding and patient and relax his hold on the relationship but yesterday when I said no, when I told him I couldn't see him that was difficult. He just flew off the deep end and became totally disorientated and didn't know what to do next. It's so difficult, because I know I'm hurting him, but to do this, to break up with him, I have to emotionally detach from my own feelings, which I suppose means I appear very cold and heartless.

I tried to be gentle, but gentle or not it doesn't matter when you're dealing with a feeling as strong as his. Marcel makes himself too vulnerable, projects himself into the relationship and lives on expectation. I know he does feel a lot for me, but one must always keep abreast of the relationship, not in front of it or behind it. At least there, you have a real perspective.

I would like to soften up a lot. You think I'm soft, but I'm not really. I always like to have control so I can see where it's going or at least where *I'm* going. But I suppose to have control means that you are trying to balance something for yourself, whereas if it were already beautifully balanced (the idealist in me) you wouldn't feel the need to do that. I feel like this with André, he gives me time and space; he lets me be myself and doesn't push. I think he is just as wary as I am. He is the most beautiful man, inside and out, that I have ever met.

I have *never* in my life given myself totally to a person. I have always held back, trusting to a point, making sure I don't feel too much and when I do it's hard to let go and feel – really feel – so I end up supplementing it with a sense of control. I don't want to do that with André, I would like to just relax into the relationship. It's not healthy and not being honest with myself either. Admittedly the reason I haven't before is because I've never been totally convinced of a person. I never realised how good it is to be with someone you can look up to and not feel like a mother, but a real woman. I don't believe I know yet what it must be like really. I don't think I have ever been in love either … I mean *really* in love.

There are so many different kinds of love aren't there? The kind I'm looking for, between a man and a woman, I haven't found yet. Just now, the way I feel with André gives me the impression that it has to be something like this amazing feeling of well-being (that's not really enough to describe it, but it has to be something like this). I suppose if I spent more time feeling and less time analysing and not compromising myself, I would understand it a lot better and faster.

Anyway, that's my situation. I think it's a wonderful thing to be able to speak about these things honestly and openly, one's mistakes, faults and defeats and just exactly the way one is, and even more wonderful when you can do that with your mother. Usually, when you think about it, mothers are the last to know. I hope my children will be able to talk to me the way I share things with you. You're like a friend just as much as you are a mother. You have the strength of character to hold fast to your ideals and principles whatever they are, and impart them to those you love with respect and diplomacy which I think must be very difficult for a mother.

In May I will be twenty-nine! Shit … ye gods! I don't feel that age. Sometimes I feel like a little girl, and other times I feel very old, but generally I don't even feel my age. When I'm having a normal time of it all, I don't feel any particular age. I just feel alive and living which is the way it should be.

I'm going to work from noon to 6 pm today, and then I have my Egyptian student. It's funny; never in my wildest dreams would I have thought of Paris as home. I mean I'm no longer 'awesome-eyed and bubbles' about Paris. I love it in a more mellow way. It's my home for however long that I feel here is my home – not as strongly as Australia of course – but in every fashion, my home.

I had a call early this morning from a mother who wants me to work with her son. So altogether my private tuition totally covers my rent. Next week I have an interview with Kodak France. If I get that, it will be the very first contract I've made independently with a company! Language Power gave me another company yesterday. Harrison is giving me another company as well as CBS. If all goes according to plan, I'll be working with Fiat, CBS, Kodak, Minolta, Language Power, Harrison Linguistics (they have a petroleum company coming into the fold that will be mine), and four private students – we are finally on our way!

It's now several weeks later, and I would like to footnote this letter and bring everything up to date.

Marcel is fine. He sends his regards to you, and we are now classically just friends. On Monday we are going to see an Aussie movie. I think he's trying to make me homesick so he can console me and come back into my life.

I'm with André now. No entourage. There is just André, and it's rather wonderful.

Work is going from good to better. Spring is almost here. You'll soon be coming. My little apartment is looking wonderful, and I'm on my way to relaxing in Amsterdam where I'll meet André tomorrow night. I love you Mum.

P.S. We have all new letterboxes downstairs with our names individually and beautifully printed on them. My box is B44. The B is for box, or in French, *boîte.* So it's:

Lorraine Walton

B 44

223 Rue La Fayette,

Paris France

Lorraine's graduation from Teacher's College in 1975

Posing with our dog, Sarita

Rainey's cat, Doopy. Though not mentioned in this book, Doopy was her much adored pet in Australia.

Doopy would follow her everywhere. Rainey certainly missed her while she was away.

Lorraine in her classroom with some of the children 1977

Hotel Schroder on Haarlemmerdijk 48B, Amsterdam City

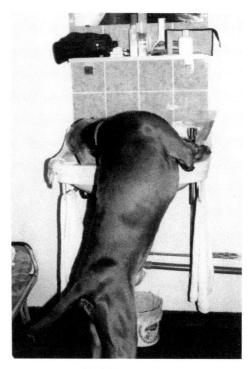

Mr Schroder's dog, Herta, drinking from the basin in the girl's room. January 1980

First trip to Paris. January 1980

Scuba diving off Capri. February 1980

The girls in St Mark's Square Venice. March 1980

Lorraine (right) and Barbara (left) with two Australian friends in Germany.

Amsterdam March 1980.

Barbie arrives home March 1980

Bois de Bolougne Paris 1980

This photo taken on Capri. Possibly November 1980

Lunch break in the square outside Language Power, La Défense.

I took this photo of Rainey walking in a Paris flower market.

Lorraine outside the Fiat Building. This was one of the companies where she taught English.

These were taken on the balcony of her studio apartment on the 8th floor, 223 Rue Lafayette, Paris.

The inseperable three; Lorraine, Barbara and yours truly on Barbie's wedding day.

Boarding a canal boat with Maxwell in Amsterdam.

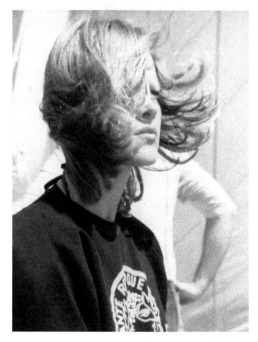

The following photos were taken while sailing on Arcachon Bay August 1982

Home from hospital after surgery. Lorraine in a pensive mood on Christmas morning 1982.

At home in Sydney, mid 1983. These are two of the photos taken for the newspaper article written by Karen Allison, which was published late August of that year.

Rainey with her good friend, Joan, who she met at Hippocrates Health Clinic in San Diego, August 1983.

Yours truly with Lorraine in her Goofy cap at Totality House. November 1983

This photo of Rainey was taken during one of her admissions to San Diego University Hospital.

Chapter 8

Letter, 21st January 1982

Dear Mum,

Another Amsterdam epic, but I deliberately took only three pages from my box of paper to limit my ravings. I'll just try to write smaller. I've been on the train for nearly an hour, and as we move closer to the north, there's more and more snow on the ground. I'm sure it will be cold in Amsterdam. It's just as cold in this train right now – no heating.

André is coming up to Amsterdam tomorrow night. We went to a Walt Disney movie last night (a late showing), and before that he took me to a beautiful, luxurious seafood restaurant decorated in early, almost gaudy and lavish 19th century décor. He picked me up from the train station at 8.30 pm as I had been working in a company way outside of Paris (one hour away) then he stayed at my place and went to work from there this morning. I worked at the American School today – cancelled my students at Language Power because I got a better offer at the American School. That's the beauty of being independent, but I don't do that very often.

When we arrived home after the movies last night, there was another big bunch of flowers on my doorstep with a lovely card from Marcel. André said, "Are you sure you're not going out with a florist?"

Don't think he was too impressed. Actually, it's not even funny because when I translate it into English, it loses all its impact; it's sort of like an inference, but he doesn't say anything else.

I like André a lot. He's twenty-nine (seems older to me), is very mature and a real gentleman. I know he misses his son terribly. Tristan is five years old and lives in Hong Kong with his mother and her new husband who is attached to the French Embassy there. Tristan comes to Paris for school holidays, and André goes to Hong Kong about four times a year.

He asked me when I was taking my holidays this summer. If we go together, we might go to Portugal or Spain in August. He is really beautiful, Mum. You'll meet him when you come over, and I just know you will like him. I've said that before haven't I? I can walk in my high heels and only come up to his shoulder. Sherbet, that in itself is worth something! I'm just thinking of Mr Schroder; I'm sure he's expecting to see Marcel again like last month.

I can't wait till you come over again, Mum. We are definitely going to Amsterdam and to Capri, whatever we do or don't do. Come over in May … I can't wait to see you! For Capri, I'll book a room ahead and take a week from work with a weekend either side … eleven days! I think that would be perfect.

Now Monday at work, January 25th

Well, Amsterdam was wonderful. André and I had a great time. I met him at the train station on Friday night. Haven't quite worked out Mr Schroder's impression yet, but I think it must be very confusing for him. I did my tour guide act at breakfast, and because I was with André, it was as though I was doing it for the first time.

We walked along the streets to the antique market where André bought a beautiful Japanese sketch, and to the Van Gogh museum where we had a great talk about the paintings. Then exploring the city, café sitting, tram riding, exploring more of the city, lunching in a little brown café, then to a loud music filled café, dinner in a Dutch restaurant, and on to a wonderfully sophisticated jazz piano bar.

Sunday we spent in Volendam where everything was iced over. There we had a luxurious seafood meal in a restaurant overlooking the bay, and then literally raced to the train, just catching it in time. It was a wonderful weekend, and we laughed a lot together.

Arriving in Paris, we went to eat at McDonald's then came home to my place where we talked for ages. He stayed, of course, telling me about his travels. He's the kind of person who revels in the 'nitty gritty' of people, travel and life.

Next morning just as André and I were leaving to go to work, Maxwell called. He's in town with his parents, and I'll meet them at the Opera for lunch. I have private students from 5 to 8 pm, then we'll go out to dinner with his family. Looking forward to that as I haven't seen Maxwell for some time.

André couldn't believe it when I said I'd never eaten snails or frog's legs, so this week he is taking me to a restaurant to introduce me to them. I was a bit out of my depth when he said, "It's really not the season for snails at the moment, and April is the best time for the frog's legs!"

I wasn't sure about eating snails or frog's legs. I didn't think either frogs or the snails cared very much about the time of year – a bit like rabbits – wherever and whenever. It appears they have a bit more style than rabbits. We'll see.

Well, I'm going to pack up now and if I'm lucky might catch American Express before they close so I can change my Dutch money before meeting Maxwell.

André embarrasses me. He won't let me pay for anything – just wouldn't hear of it the whole weekend in Amsterdam and all week in Paris, so I fixed up the accommodation bill before he arrived, that way he couldn't say anything. In Amsterdam, he was lost in terms of language as he's not yet able to speak English well, though he understands a little, so we always speak in French. He is so funny. You know, now when I listen, I'm not conscious of it being another language. I still am when I speak though.

Write and tell me what date in May you will be coming because I want to book our accommodation in Capri.

Can't wait to see you.

The following letter was neither finished nor sent. I found it some years ago in a basket of papers, and is part of this current timeline.

Letter, February 1982

Dear Mum,

I haven't seen my place for the past three days; actually since Friday. Now I'm at work at Fiat. I spent the weekend at André's. We had a lovely time. Saw two movies, coffee'd in beautiful cafes and talked. He has the most wonderful collection of music at his place. We played baseball in the park near his house with the couple we had dinner with and their children.

I think I'm falling in love with him. It's so beautifully natural, but I'm just taking things as they come, very slowly. I know he is too.

He drove me to Fiat this morning on his way to work. Yesterday we walked around the lake in the woods outside Paris. It's so beautiful there. Remember, you and I did the same thing when you were here.

Marcel called Fiat and left a message for me to call him at the *École Militaire*. He's trying to track me down. He's obviously been trying to find me on the weekend.

André will come to Amsterdam with me again next month. I can't wait 'til you come, Mum. That's a good idea to go to Greece. One of my students is giving me an address of a place to stay so hurry up and send me the dates.

It's good not to be confused. I feel so normal when I'm with André. I was beginning to think I should go to see a therapist. I was really starting to think I was crazy. That's Europe I suppose.

I feel so much better about David. He hasn't called me for a long time. That's not like him, so I guess he's resigning himself to the fact … well, I'm a little confused, but I must talk to him. I believe I know where

I stand now. Either way, it's time. Life is too short for indecision and turmoil. It's just a matter of living it now and being strong. In the past, just as I've made a decision to end the relationship with David, he calls. The last time he did I threw up after the call because my stomach was in such a state. Once, after his phone call, I even forgot to go to work.

Anyway, I say to myself, 'Self, get a hold of yourself. There's no reason for such indecision and complexity when already your life is one-third over.'

I have successfully bitten all my nails down to the quick in anticipation of something. I think David will be in England soon and he might call me. I need to see him and talk to him face-to-face. I'm tired of telephone calls that last hours. I don't feel free. Inside I feel bound and tied, and not myself, and sometimes that feels incredibly destructive. I want to let it all out and break things. It builds up, and in the end makes you old and tired.

I'm going to make an appointment with the special clinic for my three to four-month checkup with the doctor that Professor McCarthy referred me to. I should do it soon as I think there will be a long wait. I'm sure everything will be all right; I hope so anyway. At least I know I'm in someone's hands who thinks the same as Professor McCarthy.

Letter, 19th March 1982

Dear Mum and Barbie,

'A letter! – Oh, My God! She must have gone to Amsterdam!'
Another trip … and another making a spectacle of myself. I was day dreaming as usual, my head in the clouds and a million miles away. Arriving in Amsterdam, I took the bus from the station to the bus stop at the back of Mr Schroder's and remembered only about two yards before my stop that I had to get off. I pushed the button, and the driver slammed the brake pedal through the firewall. As I was the only one aware of the impending catastrophe and everyone else was taken unawares, they all ended up sitting in the driver's seat with the

driver who was not impressed. With the majority up front and a few remnants sliding along the aisle, I was feeling rather conspicuous near the door. Not for long though … I slinked out anonymously to incomprehensible four-letter words. It looked as though everyone was having a little orgy in the driver's seat.

At breakfast this morning, I met two girls from Australia and made a two-month itinerary for them. Think I'd make a good travel consultant. I've also planned their three-day stay in Amsterdam. They are having a lovely time. Tonight the three of us are going to the gay restaurant at No. 114 down the road, and I'm writing this while waiting for them.

I wish they'd hurry, I'm hungry. I can hear them drying their hair, so with me as a reference, that means they should be ready any hour now. They want to go to the red-light area too, but I don't think I have that kind of energy. I'll just take them and then as it's on my way to the post office I'll call André and then go home to bed. It's Saturday tomorrow so I'll sleep in, have a late breakfast, wander out about eleven, do some shopping, walk along the canals and relax over coffee. The weather here is lovely now. I had my acupuncture treatment today. It was great – my health has improved so much.

Last Sunday, André and I went to the International Agriculture Show, and as he had clients on different stands (he does their publicity), we visited them and at each stop they brought out a bottle of champagne – rather wonderful. We went upstairs to the gormandizing salon – the French really know how to present food – then to the most delicious oyster display. Huge things, they were. We had a dozen (they were shucking them on the spot) and chased them down with white wine.

Then on to see the animal display. The rabbits had me in hysterics. They looked like, well not like rabbits, but rather like something between a cat and a basset hound, with a body almost as big. They had the most amazing designs of fur. André said of one, "*Tiens, c'était croisée avec une moquette.*" (Here, this one's been crossed with a carpet.)

Have to go - the girls are ready now – back later.

It's Saturday now and dinner last night at the gay restaurant was a riot. These girls are lovely, both from Melbourne. They remind me of Barbie (lucky girls), and will stay with me in Paris if they catch me at home.

The gay restaurant was packed, as usual. It's been remodelled after it was damaged by fire last year. It looks great. The same three still run it: the fat man, the gorgeous blond male singer/waiter and their chinchilla cat. When we arrived, the blond waiter saw us and began carrying on with his hilarious antics; I don't know where he gets his energy. Then he sashayed through the restaurant, found us a table, turned, held both arms high in the air and yelled at the top of his voice, "Would the three lovely virgins come this way?"

We made the disastrous mistake of responding just as quickly to his call, and everyone was killing themselves laughing. I said to the girls that the least we could have done was look behind us before careering down the aisle to our table. Toward the end of the night he kept calling me 'beauty' whenever he came to our table. Well, I'll be serious, I could fall for this tall gay blond with a hell of a body and a sexy voice. And you should see him move … my God.

He was singing this romantic song and towards the end of it he came and sang to me, bent down, held me and gave me a wonderful long kiss, so tender. (Well I *do* know him a little after my numerous visits to the restaurant.) I'm sure André will be impressed when I tell him I melted when my favourite 'fruit' held me in his arms and kissed me to the loud claps and encouragement from all the patrons.

That's OK. I'll just say, 'Don't worry. If *I* scored with him, imagine how *you'd* do!'

From there we went to the red-light area, and the girls were very surprised to see the ladies of the night sitting in the shop-front windows. It's safer for them there than standing out on the street, and warmer too. Then on to Barbie's and my favourite brown café where there was a riotous party in full swing, just after me asking the girls, "What about a nice quiet coffee?"

The music was fantastic. Several guys joined us and dutifully bought us drinks all night. Before that, we had coffee and when I got up to regulate the bill, a handsome-looking Dutchman grabbed me and waltzed me all around the café to their bouncy Dutch music and to claps and shouts from the patrons. The girls embarrassed me by taking photos and then everyone started to dance and sing. What a great night! We left at 2 am, and Mr Schroder woke me at 9:30 this morning.

I don't remember going down to breakfast, but I do recall the confusion at the breakfast table for a split second when I didn't know which language to speak. I had French sitting next to me, English the other side, and we had been immersed in Dutch since Thursday. I was embarrassed yesterday when I was working out the itinerary for these girls. I had to keep searching for the English words – even simple ones. They kept staring at me, and I was forced to explain that, yes, I do have a reasonable command of my native language if only the words would surface. So I ended up explaining something in a roundabout way, with French structure.

My dreams are more often in French now, and furthermore, they are in incredible colours! The movies we see are mostly in French, and sometimes an English one subtitled. No, my dreams are not subtitled – yet.

I can't decide whether to go home this afternoon or tomorrow morning. I want to go to the antique market, and to an exhibition of publicity posters through the years. In Europe, these are so interesting and artistic. Then I'll go to the stereo shop, pretend I want to buy a record and listen to it on the headphones. I also want to go to de Bijenkorf Department Store to buy some Easter cards in English. I can't find any in Paris. Tonight the girls and I will go to a Dutch pancake restaurant on the *Prinsengracht* near the Anne Frank house.

So I guess that has decided it. I'm leaving tomorrow morning, Sunday at 11 am and will arrive in Paris at 5 pm.

I always become paranoid about ten minutes out of Paris, because as you may or may not know, I've had a somewhat elitist fan club in Paris of the masculine variety, who invariably manage to find out when I'm going on my monthly pilgrimage to the north.

It has also been known for me to take a chosen member of this club to Amsterdam and on my return, have yet another member meet me as a surprise … and hell, what a surprise that is. To complicate matters even more, it has also been known to have two meet me while I have one in tow. Now, I just sneak off the train into oblivion.

Needless to say, all the members know each other, but they aren't aware that they belong to the same club. That was before; I've recently cancelled everyone's membership for not abiding by, or respecting the rule of the club which was as follows: *Under no circumstances must the Chairwoman's life be complicated with welcome home fanfare and flowers.*

My God! Flowers! For a while there, my apartment was beginning to look like a florist shop. If they didn't meet me at the station they would come to my apartment and leave flowers, letters and gifts at my doorstep followed by telephone calls.

During all this I was also seeing André, who was concerned that I was trying my hand in the florist trade. So now the club no longer exists, due to both lack of interest and too much hard work on my part. I could relate more incidents that at the time were quite painful and embarrassing, but in retrospect you would die laughing.

Happily, the club was reformed last June, this time with a new charter and limited to two members only: André and me, each one with equal status, "*Et voilà, voilà, voilà – qu'est ce qu'on peut dire? C'est comme ça la vie, heureuse.*" (And that's it, that's it, that's it - what can one say? That's how life is, happy.)

Ask Jeff to practice his translations for when you both come over. *Bon. Je m'en vais.* (I'm going now.) I'll post this in Paris on Monday.

I found the following postcard of a beautiful rainbow Rainey had received after one of her monthly excursions to Amsterdam. She always enjoyed conversing with fellow passengers on these trips. She loved to help travellers with itinerary suggestions – especially for the places she knew well. The card reads as follows:

Lorraine: A girl; a rainbow of bright new colours, a six (possibly 7) on a scale of 10 for daring (is that right?), a possible friend; gregarious, whimsical, serious, sensitive, a great companion on a train trip!

One man's tour of Amsterdam starts...

Donald

It's now 29th March, and I've been back from Amsterdam for a week.

I called you this afternoon just to hear you talk. I needed a touch of sanity and felt a bit better after it. Tonight is the first night I've slept at my place since last Monday, and now it's Monday again. Coming home tonight I almost forgot where I lived. Between Amsterdam and everything else, I'm rarely here these days.

Marcel just came by to get a jumper of his and a few cassettes. It was just a quick visit, he didn't stay. I had just arrived home a bit before 10 pm from a lesson.

It's strange, all twenty-four hours on twenty-four hours I'm running all over Paris. In the night the same and suddenly tonight I feel completely lost which is very bad, and sometimes I find myself literally walking in circles, at loose ends when I have a thousand things to do. I don't like to be like that. For someone who wanted to come back and spend quiet evenings at home, writing, reading etc., I'm never here and when I am, I'm lost because I'm not occupied and I have to concentrate to make myself relax and sit and do something … not think.

Today I was so angry inside. I felt incredibly destructive. I wanted to scream and break everything in sight. Then in the metro I must have looked fit to kill, especially with people bumping and pushing. A couple of young guys passed me and smiled as if to say, 'Smile lady, it's not the end of the world.' Then very nicely said, *"Bonsoir,"* and yours truly burst into tears. I suppose it's to do with my feelings of uncertainty and frustration in a way. André's ex-wife is in Paris, and I'm finding it difficult coming to terms with the amount of time he's spending with her.

So that was today and yesterday, but things will improve. At times like this, I need a taste of home. Can't wait to see you in July and I really want to come home for Christmas. Sometimes it gets very heavy here.

Back again. Lisa just rang wondering where I've been. We had a cup of tea and a talk, and now I'm on the 'loo' listening to Simon and Garfunkel (the price of stardom!), and thinking about doing my relaxing exercises before bed, so I'll finish this at Fiat tomorrow.

Now I'm at another society, the Solar Energy Commission, and my teaching room is being occupied by a conference. It will be free at 1 pm, so I'm waiting in the reception area. Here they sell solar energy apparatus for roofs you know, very interesting. Buggered if I know how this company survives – there's never any bloody sun here! I have a class of ten supposedly, but so far in the three weeks I've been here, I've had only six turn up. I'll expect the others when their work is less hectic.

The Manager of CBS (with whom I work three hours per week), told me that Simon and Garfunkel will be in Paris for a concert, so if he doesn't give me tickets I can get them from Frederique who works there. The concert they held in Hyde Park at the debut of their re-formation in New York is on TV tonight. I finish at Language Power at 8:15 so if I scream home on the RER I might just be in time to catch it.

The Christian Dior-clad coves are sauntering out of their conference room now, so I'll get my equipment together and set up before my students come back from lunch. I sound like a travelling circus.

On Saturday from 8:30 am to 1 pm I'm helping conduct and supervise a university entrance examination at the International School. It's an English exam and not an easy one at that. I've been coaching a twenty-one-year-old student who wants to study in the US, so I'm hoping he'll pass. I coach another sixteen-year-old boy who will also be sitting for it.

Oh, yes, I'll be starting classical guitar lessons soon from a professor at the Conservatorium here. I have decided I want to apply myself seriously.

Had another idea to work at fairs and expositions, acting as hostess for English-speaking international visitors, directing, translating, or orientating them, so I need to find a list of all these expositions to see if there's an opening. It's an idea. I would like that. It would probably be weekend work, though. Have to go now and get my act organised in the conference room.

Well here I am back again and it's a week later. André and I spent another lovely week and weekend together – very relaxing. We've been invited to a wedding in Brussels on May 3rd. We spent a weekend there about two months ago with this couple. After that weekend in the Belgium countryside, André managed to score himself one hell of a cold … lost his voice and was generally out of action. So he went to the chemist and bought one of those wonder drugs that claim to kill everything – headaches, fever, cold, cockroaches – and if there's any left over, I'm going to use it to scrub my balcony and do the windows.

We are 'babysitting' at the moment. It's the Easter holidays, and we are looking after André's niece's pet rabbit. It pooped and piddled all over his carpet last night, so it was relegated to the bathroom.

I finish at 1 pm today then I'm going to pick up my parcel at American Express and go to the post office to post some cards to you, then to see Mr Harrison to give him my invoice for last month before going home. Hope I remember where I live – haven't been there since last Tuesday night and now it's Monday again. People must think I lead a wild life. But you know I sort of feel I've finally arrived in my life. I know I could spend the rest of my life with André. I've known him now for eight months; it's not that long really, but somehow you know when you know … but slowly, very slowly.

Even if it all ended next week, I could say, "For once I arrived, but it wasn't meant to be."

André was married at twenty-one and divorced seven years later. He's very tall with a wonderful physique. He is very serious but with a great sense of humour. He has good principals and is a real gentleman. He is at the same time, distinguished, relaxed and casual – a diplomat if you like – very sensitive but direct. He was a karate teacher and now works as head of a publicity firm. Before that, he was a photographer. Many magazines are filled with his photographic work.

You'll meet him when you come. On reading this, you'll expect to be met at the airport by a knight in shining armour – actually he's very normal. It's just me, and I think he is wonderful. Anyway, he's scared of horses and gets very claustrophobic in helmets!

So there you go. We will see what we will see.

I like being free too. I'll find it hard to settle down with someone when I eventually do. André gives me space – he lets me be me. It's like we are two people all the time, but I feel he makes me more than I am and I hope I do the same for him. With him, I don't feel closed in. It's important for me to have space, light and love and for me to give more of all that. You know, I think I'm in love. I've never said it to myself because it's not something so definite, rather it's like experiencing and watching the change in yourself and the world around you.

One thing, with him my French has improved out of sight. I understand just about everything and can follow all kinds of discussions – political, psychological, etc., *and* I can wear my high heels when we go out. Actually, he is everything and more than what I imagined in a partner, but I've got my feet on the ground (between trips to cloud nine), and I know I can be prepared for anything. Even when it upsets me when unwanted experiences happen, I can usually carry myself and weather it. But who knows – who the hell knows? Not me that's for sure.

After I had fallen madly in love with Carlos, I ended up like a busted balloon when our relationship ended. He now wants to start our relationship again. I feel that I was married to him once in a past life. Whenever he calls or comes by I melt, but what we had is definitely in the past. Carlos is probably one of the most physically beautiful men I have ever met. I should write that book; I've had so many experiences – serious, hilarious, painful, incredible and unimaginable.

I'm going now. My second group of students are in conference, so I'm out of here.

See you in July. I can't wait!

It's now Friday, April 2nd, and I'm in a cafe; I have one and a half hours free before my next and last student for the day. I just ordered an *omelette nature* and *une verre du lait* (a glass of milk) and the waiter arrived with a huge glass of wine! 'Beaujolais' sounds similar when you say it, even though it has nothing to do with a glass of milk! The difference there being a sober professor or a drunken one!

André is calling for me at 7:30 tonight at work. We spent the last two nights at his mother's house as her husband is in hospital and she asked André to come by. I don't know what we'll do this weekend. Whatever it is, it will be wonderful.

Monday 5th now and yesterday we had a lovely lazy day. I slept till 11:30 am. We went to the *Champs Élysées* and sat at a sidewalk cafe watching the passing parade while soaking up the sun. Later we visited a friend, then on to the Louvre just to listen to some music. We walked in the gardens and went to a movie. It's such a beautiful time of year in Paris. Spring in all its glory! The days and evenings are sublime.

The weather is just gorgeous, and I can't wait to see you and Aunty Shirley. It would be wonderful if Uncle Len and Uncle Noel were coming too. Would be great to see them all.

Back again – now I'm on the fourteenth floor of *Tour Montparnasse*, the huge tower building near *St-Michelle*, and my student is a no-show, hence the letter.

It's Lisa's birthday next week, so I have to get the gang together for a night out. I'm the coordinator, and we usually end up seven or eight of us for the evening. If everyone has a schedule like I do, it's hard to track them all down.

Frederique gave me a whole heap of records from CBS the other day, and I took them to André's house to play on his stereo. They are great. Last night was funny, we let the rabbit out and it went crazy – kept jumping up in the air imagining that it was scaring itself, and I was in hysterics. It's adorable but insane. When it makes a mess on the floor, André calls it names and relegates it to the bathroom, but if it's not out in two minutes he goes and brings it back in telling it how cute and crazy it is. Both he and the rabbit are as cute and crazy as each other!

André is going out to dinner tomorrow night with a film producer to discuss a publicity film, then on the 17th, he is flying to Hong Kong again.

There is a new hotel that has just opened on the *Champs Élysées*, the most expensive in Paris; a suite is 37,000 francs per night, ($5,000) so needless to say, many of the clientele are Arabs. I know a jazz singer who used to be a model for Yves St. Laurent and she has just received a contract to sing there, so we are going to her opening night. We've been before to other jazz clubs to hear her sing. She is so lovely and has a great voice. She's the fiancée of the public relations guy at Language Power.

I'm working only two days a week with Language Power now and mostly with Harrison Linguistics at Fiat, also Solar Energy Commission, and CBS Record Company. I've also worked in Minolta, Kodak and Tupperware.

Well, it's almost time to tackle the metro again ... another half an hour and Christmas will have come prematurely for all the jerks in Paris. I've decided the best place for your bum on the train is to sit on it. I almost castrated one dude with my umbrella the other day. The worst time is when the carriage is so packed that you can't even breathe to speak, let alone defend yourself!

Love you.

Letter, 15th April 1982

Hi Mum

Just a brief typed note before I leave to-night I worked late so I am using the secretary's typewriter

The reason why there are no full stops or commas in this little epic is that I'm buggered if I can find them on this typewriter I have enough trouble working out the French let alone their typewriters

Sent off a few postcards between students so you should get them sometime next week My apartment is slowly coming together and actually looks like someone lives there Lisa is going home in July and that will surely be the end of an era I really would like to write a book you know which is going to be quite a problem seeing I cant even sit still long enough to write a letter So that is my latest folly Every now and again I have these wild inspirations for the middle or the beginning or to record some hairy situation I seem to have fallen into along the way So needless to say I have pieces of verbal garbage on paper all over Paris not to mention my apartment which would make a veritable bonfire on cracker night I say all over Paris as the bulk of my inspirations always seem to arrive in the Metro at rush hour when it is difficult to breathe and where one can not even move away from some jerk who thinks its feely time in peak hour on every metro in Paris

So imagine trying to get a pen out of my bag which usually hangs at bum level anyway The jerk standing next to me would probably think all his Christmases had come at once The alternative is to write it all down when I get off the train which means instantaneous trampling in the bowels of the Parisian Metro Not the most salubriously comforting thought So as a result my thoughts disappear never to be retrieved again or perhaps if my memory is still

242

in form end up on copious sheets of paper unfinished or too lengthy to be posted

One of the other teachers just came in and started to read over my shoulder and said that is a hell of a sentence

So then we decided to try and find the punctuation marks

Found the full stops and commas, and now seeing I have to go we don't need them anymore. André is waiting for me in the café next door.

This is not much of a letter pet, as I've been very busy and haven't written for a while, so I'm gathering together some things to put into an envelope just so that you will know that I'm well and very, very happy … in love even, I'm sure. It's funny. Usually I care what my friends think but this time I know I don't need anyone's approval even though it's nice when they give it.

So this letter is quick, it's a bit disjointed, but it's only a quick note to say I love you.

I can't wait to see you in July!

Letter, 20th April 1982

Dear Mum,

André left on Saturday at midday for Hong Kong. I spent the weekend with his sister-in-law and her friend at André's house. I go to Amsterdam on Friday 23rd. I miss André terribly – I really do. Can't wait till he gets back and I'm counting the days, three down, twelve to go. I hope he has a wonderful time with Tristan.

Lots of work this week which is good – keeps me busy and focused.

It's so heartbreaking. Sometimes he talks a lot about his son, and other times he clams up and doesn't want to think or talk about it. Once he told me that he cries about it sometimes.

At the airport when he left, I just stood there for about half an hour (as I always do when you leave). I always have the feeling that I'll never see that person ever again. It's terrible, but I always do.

We won't be able to go to our friend's wedding in Brussels next month as that's the day he gets back and I can't take the day off work, so I'm replying for us. I'll send a letter and a card.

On Monday I'll be going to a premiere film showing on the *Champs Élysées*. I have a friend who produced the film, and she has invited me. We saw the film *Reds* on the weekend, and I thought it was brilliant.

My student arrives at 5:15 and I finish at 8:15 tonight. I *was* going to André's place … I still might – it's close – but on second thought I have to walk from the station in the dark and it's a bit late. I'll just go home instead. I miss him so much and can't wait till he gets back. I'm using my time to relax, grow my nails which I bit off watching the movie *Reds*, lose some weight for summer and get my life without David organised. It's just so heartbreaking; for both of us but in different ways.

I'm at Mr Schroder's now. It's 23rd April, and I had an excellent acupuncture treatment today.

I'm reading a book titled *Life Before Life*, and spent an hour discussing this concept of reincarnated souls with my acupuncturist. It's an exciting and fascinating subject, and I felt as though my spirit and I had stepped into a limitless world which may take forever to absorb even a fraction of its truth. I feel that if life is a spiral, our soul *never* dies, but just moves from one life to the next … fantastic!

Well, tomorrow is Saturday and Lisa, Ward and I will take a bike ride in the country and have a picnic. It's spring and so beautiful in Amsterdam now.

Maxwell is coming to Paris to stay a few days with me before he travels to Florence, then a couple of Australian girls will stay, and André finally comes home from Hong Kong on May 3rd. We are going out now to take advantage of this beautiful weather.

The following is an extract from Rainey's journal regarding this visit. The entry is unfinished.

This trip to Amsterdam has been for me the most richly rewarding few days I have spent since I first set awesome eyes on Europe.

Leaving Paris, stressed, with barely enough time to catch the train and buy the newspaper, and yes, without the means to do so, is a stark contrast to how I'm feeling at this moment. It has been as if my spirit and I have had a wonderful time, as though we have just stepped into a new limitless world in which it may take forever to absorb even a fraction of its truth. It has made me feel young, not so much in terms of age but rather in terms of the Laws of Heaven.

It's for this reason that I feel I'm beginning, perhaps even earlier than this, in Heaven's initial stage of wonderment but if desire is part of the soul, then it seems I'm on my way. My acupuncturist is indeed a beautiful person, and our conversation was so insightful.

He's right. It is important to be 'on Earth' as it were, in Paris - especially in Paris, and especially for me – the Spirit, the Soul and the Body... our conversation was fascinating!

Interesting comment on cancer, on colours and on the Laws of Heaven. There *is* no way to defy or even shy away from the Laws of Nature and of Heaven. There is yet one path to walk with her in Harmony. Short of this is disaster …

I am not yet there, but I know it is indeed life's mission to which there is no end, at least in this earthly life. It is in the desire, the striving at times, even painfully so, the learning, the sharing, the attempting to live close to or along with the infinitely mysterious, beautiful Laws of Nature. And so if the soul be desirous and the spirit strong...

Back in Paris a week now and back into work. It has been great having Maxwell stay these past few days. He really is someone I can talk to. I think he enjoyed his stay here.

Letter, 4th May 1982

Dear Mum,

I hope you have a wonderful Mother's Day. I'll be thinking of you. I really loved the photos, especially the one of Barbie and you on the steps. I have them stuck on my kitchen wall.

André came home yesterday. My feeling for him is growing and growing but very quietly, stably and steadily. He told me he was very sad to leave his son but very happy to come home to Paris and to me. He said, "If I could put the two together it would be perfect." He is the most beautiful person I have ever met.

I'm still a bit tense as a result of the last two weeks with David. He came over again from Australia on a business trip. Last week was very stressful. It's finally over. I thought I had come down and was beginning to relax, but the first thing André said when he saw me was, "What happened? Why are you so tense?"

I think it'll take a while for me to level out, but now that André is back I feel already so different and more alive. I never thought a person like André existed in real life – I was beginning to think I was an idealist. I suppose everyone thinks their man is ideal, but then I'm so bloody choosy.

When I get depressed, I always go to the same place – the hairdresser. It's almost hereditary. I have a mother that screams into clothes boutiques and buys them out of house and home. I go to the hairdresser and let them go to town on my hair. Sometimes (depending on my mood) I don't care what they do – I figure it can only be an improvement. Then I crash the nearest plant shop, buy everything and walk out looking like a forest trying to find somewhere to lie down. Then we have a competition to see what can grow the fastest, their leaves or my hair.

I made the fatal mistake of having my hair cut just one week before André came home from Hong Kong. He likes long hair. He made a diplomatic understatement, "Oh ... you've cut your hair!"

So I said, "No, I washed it in cold water and it shrank. Tried to stretch it but it didn't work."

He's going out to dinner tonight to a business conference - I don't know what time he will be home. This morning I got up a 6 am, and he sleepwalked out of bed to turn off the alarm and forgot to reset it for himself. At 8:30 am I was in the middle of a lesson when I excused myself and called André because I knew he was half asleep when he turned it off. But he didn't hear the phone because I had carefully closed all the doors so he wouldn't hear my hair dryer. He surfaced at about 10:30 and considering he starts work at 9 am ... oops.

Well, Mum, I love you lots. It's almost Mothers' Day, and I'll be thinking of you.

Letter, 16th May 1982

I did some translating for Carlos last night. He's doing extra work in a private aesthetic clinic near the *Champs Élysées*. He is a very skilful surgeon.

I translated all his hospital references into English so he can send them or present them at other interviews. He is rolling in money now; he has two apartments, a car and looks like a walking advertisement for Yves Saint Laurent and Dior all wrapped up in one.

I worked in his office last night while he did his rounds. He kept popping in, and we talked a lot. Although his divorce came through late last year, he is trying to get back with his wife. I looked at him last night and found it so strange to be sitting across the desk from him, completely calm, when a year ago when we broke up I didn't know whether I was Arthur or Martha and was tearing myself apart. And now ... amazing.

Carlos said to me last night, "Come here and give me a big hug." As he held me, he began to cry and said he wished he hadn't let me go last year. He said he wants to find someone like me. When we left the clinic, he said, "Say hello to André and tell him he is one lucky man."

Carlos. What a history that was. I wrote my best poem about us. It's strange, whenever I see him it's like we never split up. It's so good when you can keep a relationship but on a different level.

Letter, 19th May 1982

Well here we are again – but not too happy. The other day some jerk, dick-head, turd ripped off with my bag, my big one with all my school books, cassette recorder, a new cheque book, all my Dior makeup that I had just replaced, my glasses, the lovely books I received for my birthday, and a piece of writing (about twenty pages) that I had written and was particularly happy with.

I had been hesitating to send it to you as I didn't want it to get lost in the mail, but in the end I wanted to share it with you. It was a great letter – funny, hilarious, serious and sad, and I had finally decided to send it to you because I was sick of seeing it floating around. So that little effort of two months disappeared too.

André was furious when he came home because the bag was in his car. He had picked me up at Fiat Company and driven me to a luncheon date at the Opera. He had ten minutes between business appointments, so ran into McDonald's on the *Champs Élysées* to buy a hamburger and that's when they broke into the car and took the lot – all in ten minutes.

"Did you have anything important in your bag?" he asked when he came home.

We always put my bag under the seat or in the boot. He went to the police and spent two hours searching the toilets in the area. Reckons he knows every loo on the *Champs* now!

Well, I was very calm. André was nervous and said he would have killed the guy if he had found him. Good thing he didn't, because he is a second dan karate professor and would have scattered the poor dude all over the *Champs*, I'm sure. I was okay until the next day when I remembered that my twenty-page letter with two months of writing had been in the bag. Then I cried.

So tonight at 11 pm we are driving down to a little town on the *Cote d'Azur* near *Saint-Tropez*. We both have five days holiday and will be staying with friends there, the same ones we stayed with in Brussels. André loves sport; he plays tennis. I told him I'm good at chasing tennis balls, so we'll swim! He is so brown – normally very dark – very Latin and I've slowly become a shade lighter than transparent lily white. Bought a tin of brown house paint yesterday … used two coats and I'm now just lily white. We've advanced one shade.

In the last two weeks I went out too much, drank too much and played too hard. Sometimes I'd get home after André and leave before him, so for a while there we weren't even crossing in the bathroom. And in the evenings when we got home it was like 'Oh hi, remember me?'

I'm paper hunting now. Found this on the table; I hope they don't want it. I loved the birthday presents you sent. Everyone loves the jumper Barbie, and I love the black suit – can't wait to wear it – it looks gorgeous.

I had a lovely birthday but had to work because it was a Monday. I got home late, and André had prepared a birthday dinner. We had black caviar, cocktail of shrimp avocado and grapefruit with a sauce, escargot, cheeses, a marvellous strawberry birthday tart with a big red candle, and a bottle of *Dom Perignon*! It was a lovely surprise.

We were relaxing last night when out of the blue I hear, "Can you cook?"

I try to stay out of the kitchen if I can manage it; I've done well so far. The few times I've prepared a meal, it's been with the help of the *charcuterie* (the delicatessen). All I have to do is arrange it on the plate.

"You've never actually cooked for me after all this time."

I didn't think he had noticed after five months of practically living together! In a vain attempt to deflect the subject, I responded with, "Don't push your luck, kiddo. Up till now you've been very fortunate."

"One night you'll have to."

I was a nervous wreck for the rest of the evening, but that's OK. I'll pick a day when all the veggies in the country keel over and die, when the butchers go on strike, and the electricity commission cuts the power, then say, 'Hell, what a bloody shame.'

No, I'll have to cook a typical Aussie dish. I've been racking my brain and have decided for openers that we'll have beer and peanuts, then for a change of pace and colour, baked beans on toast, then to get rid of the taste, peanuts and beer, then maybe a cuppa tea, luv, with bread and jam. Just kidding. I'll probably do roast lamb and veggies.

I hope these students don't arrive; I want to leave early. I have to pay my rent, go to the bank, buy a pair of slacks, pack, wash – how about wash *then* pack. I have a two-hour private lesson with a high school student at the library, then André will pick me up, and we'll go home to his place. We'll leave about 11 pm tonight and get there about 9 am tomorrow. Oh, I mustn't forget to buy batteries for the Walkman and take my driver's license, look for my swimming costume somewhere in the bowels of my suitcase and give myself a second coat of paint. Then on Thursday, I go up to Amsterdam. No rest for the wicked.

I'm still cursing the shit that stole my bag. André wants me to make an appointment with the optician as soon as possible for a new pair of glasses because of my work, but I thought you could get them, Mum, from the optometrist and bring them over in six or eight weeks when you come.

For my birthday, the girls (Lisa, Frederique, Denise and my two Australian friends) took me out to dinner with André on the *Isle St Louis*. We had a great night. Maxwell gave me a beautiful book of Victor Hugo in French and Lisa and Ward gave me Kahlil Gibran's *The Prophet* which walked with the rest of my gear. I had to go to the perfumery and buy myself all new makeup. It cost a pretty penny, too.

I know you would have died laughing reading the letter I lost. You may have even cried in other parts. I took a funny situation and projected it to the extreme. There was philosophy, prose and bull-shit all wrapped up in twenty pages, enough material to make *War and Peace* look like *Women's Weekly*, and the deadbeat who ripped off with my stuff probably can't even read English.

I know if we see some turd walking down the *Champs Élysées* with my bag over his shoulder, listening to my *English for Beginners* tape, reading Kahlil Gibran, sporting Dior makeup, wearing reading glasses and a pair of grey spotted stockings (I assume he would have polished off my liquorice from Australia), he probably won't even get to the part in my letter about transvestites and the price of Brussels sprouts before André splatters him from one end of the *Champs Élysées* to the other in one easy obliteration. The bastard.

André and I went shopping on Saturday. We bought a timer for the coffee percolator. You set it for the time you want and it turns itself on. You fall out of bed into the kitchen and *voilà*, you wake to automatically prepared coffee which saves us thirty minutes in the morning … thirty minutes which we consequently waste. We end up getting up twenty minutes later (because of the thirty minutes we have 'saved'), only to arrive at work at the same time with the old mad scramble of getting ready then screaming to work in the car with all the other crazy drivers. They've probably all got coffee timers like us. We'll take it back and get our money back. The bloody thing doesn't work and I'm still as late as ever! That's technology for you. They'll sell you anything these days.

I hope Fiat doesn't want these pages; they were all neatly stacked at the end of the conference table. There were originally seven sheets, now there's only one left. I might leave them one, and they can all share it at their conference. A little bit of togetherness never hurt anyone.

Now I have another hour and a half here. I do three hours on Monday and four and a half on Wednesday. I was thinking, as I work at Fiat, CBS and the Solar Energy Society, I could have a discount on a solar energy unit for my house (that doesn't exist), a car (which would end up in the rear end of someone else's if you share the road with these crazies … that's the least you'd expect), and free records to look at 'cos I don't have a record player. I love Paris, but something tells me I don't quite have my act together quite yet.

Letter, 21ˢᵗ May 1982

Dearest Barbie and Jeff,

I'm at Fiat Company again and just waiting for my class to arrive; they are seven men – three Italians and four Frenchmen – all very nice and we have a lot of fun together. In two weeks Mum and Aunty Shirley will be here – can't wait.

Yesterday (Sunday) André and I had a day in the country with his cousin Josephine, his sister, her husband and their two children. We went to Normandy, a province in the north of France by the ocean. My God, it was so cold. The Atlantic Ocean has nothing on the Pacific. André loves to wind surf and is thinking of buying a windsurfer. It's a very popular sport here.

I'm having traumas at the moment because I'm thinking of giving up my apartment and moving in with André, which I've been doing for the last six months anyway. We'll see. In two weeks Lisa goes home to California for good with her American boyfriend, Ward. My students have arrived – I'll have to stop now.

Back again. As I was saying, André suggested I give up my apartment as I don't live there. He doesn't push, he's not like that. From a living point of view and from the way we feel about each other, it's logical but I don't know. If I kept it, I would only ever go there in transit now. It's still beautiful, and I still take care of it.

André wants to buy another place depending on what we want to do with each other if you know what I mean. (I'm glad you do because I don't.) I only know I like to be free, but when I *am* free *without* André, I am lost. I don't mean when I'm not with him I'm lost, I mean if he wasn't around anymore I would be devastated, but I would pull through. It's just that … I don't know. I'm confused. Threatening to love someone so much means you're so much more vulnerable. It's so safe to be by yourself and not be totally committed – even though that's what I want, and I want that with André.

The other day he asked me why I looked so sad and I replied, "Because I'm so happy and that makes me very afraid."

We talked for a while, and he said, "Don't worry, you're not alone there." So at least that's something.

I'm getting hungry. If this accountant comes in one more time and tries to ask me out again, I'll scream. He's cute, but I'm not interested in anyone else.

I would give up my apartment if I knew our relationship would be okay and as it is now I have no reason to believe that it wouldn't be. That's my problem – I want a guarantee without the risks. David said to me recently on his last visit, "If nothing else Lorraine, do yourself a favour and talk. Give of your thoughts, your fears and your desires to someone else, instead of shutting them inside you. Take a risk for love. One day you'll meet someone that you really like a hell of a lot, and because you guard yourself and you fear so much you'll never know unless you ride with the wind a little – risks, doubts and uncertainties included. So what if you lose out? At least you'll know. The other way, you may lose something wonderful that you were too afraid to try."

I know one thing. You can't tell me Barbie, that if it's love, it's natural. I don't believe in that – even love itself for me is a decision, not just a feeling.

So now I have to make a decision about my apartment. You might not think it's a very big decision, but it is for me. It's not because of the blood, sweat and tears I went through to get it. It sort of represents my liberty, my emotional security, even though I want a life with another person. I never thought I would be so bloody difficult and so fearful. My dread of all dreads is to be married. I just want to share my love, my fears, and my life – everything – with another. I'm not even married but if I did get married now, I would still think it would be too soon. My thoughts are scaring me silly at the moment.

When I was younger I always had the dream of only ever giving myself to my husband on our wedding night, of walking down the aisle of a church to the man I love and starting out fresh with my life partner. (Well, that little hallucination melted into oblivion a long time ago.) But I never thought I'd marry someone who had been married for seven years with a five-year-old son, and with as many fears as I have. Then again, never in my wildest dreams did I think I would ever have the privilege of sharing what I have shared to date with André. If it all ended next week, it will have been the most wonderful time of my life.

So you see I *do* have my feet on the ground. I don't know what I would do if we broke up. Yes, I do … I'd pick myself up again and move to another country. No, I wouldn't … I don't know what I'd do. See how weird I am? I had another hallucination too (that melted, I don't know when), that you were supposed to fall in love and carry each other into perpetual, everlasting ecstasy. I think someone's been telling us stories; I feel ripped off. But no, if it were that easy it wouldn't be fun.

Moving ever-onward, you can still keep your ideals and dreams as long as they are not too far-fetched like mine. There at least you have a reference and hell, I'm nobody's princess in shining armour except my own and that won't get me very far. I don't even like horses, and I'm too scared to wear a helmet for fear my hair will get messed up, so don't like my chances. I'll have to find another plan of action.

I hear work is easy to find in Outer Mongolia. No? Me neither.

My students are very late so I'm going to hit the road before they get here.

Letter, 29th May 1982

Dear Mum,

I'm sitting in the train at Amsterdam station waiting to go back to Paris. It's a long weekend there, and I'd rather go home and spend the time with André. I can't wait to see him.

You know it's a year since I've known him. Remember, he was the student I got paranoid about because I saw on the allocation board that he was having lessons with another teacher at Language Power when *I* wanted to be teaching him. When you were here in October, you diplomatically asked me if he had been with me for an English lesson since I returned to Paris. Turns out, as he told me the other day, he always wanted to have me as his teacher, but because it would look too obvious, he chose another male teacher. When Lucy, the receptionist, asked him which teacher he would like to be with he would say, 'the tall blond Australian,' and would conveniently forget my name. I had no idea of this until five months later. I had admired him from afar for five months because I thought he was too nice to be single. I figured he had to have a girlfriend. Don't forget that of those five months I spent two of them in Australia and he spent one month in Hong Kong. Our relationship began very sanely and slowly. I hope it lasts. I could marry him.

I've always thought that it would be nice to marry someone where you start off only with each other – it's simpler – not someone with an ex-wife of six years and a son aged five, but it's all part of him. It's something that, however permanent or temporary our relationship is, I will learn to accept. I don't mean to accept his ex-wife or his son – no, because that I already have – it's like accepting anything. I mean to accept the fact that when he is 'within himself' about his past, his son, and quietly but obviously reflecting. I can't do anything to help him but just be there when he needs me. I mean accepting the effect it has on him.

It's a shock to realise that I can't do anything directly. I can't take the hurt away, and sometimes I wonder if I ever make it easier for him. The important thing is that whatever I can offer him, to share, to console, to laugh in the face of it all … God listen to me! It sounds like I'm going to ask him to marry me … well, given half a chance … no.

I talk like this, but when I think of having to give up my apartment, my freedom's security, I think, *Shit Lorraine, what do you want?* As the French would say, *"Cela s'arranger,"* (It will work itself out.) The train is just pulling out of the station.

I wish that shit-head jerk, unprincipled sod had kept his stinking rotten maulers off my bag; I had a brilliant piece of writing for you in there. I could really attack that rotter, kill and maim the bastard. I could cry when I think I will never see that letter again. It was incredible; you would have died laughing, peed in your pants and cried in other parts. It was the best one I had ever written; that's why I hung on to it for two whole months and guarded it with my life, too scared to post it for fear it might get lost in the mail. I try not to think about it because it makes me angry and upset and DAMNED DANGEROUS! Luckily I have this carriage all to myself at the moment. Calm, Lorraine, calm.

The Dutch countryside is beautiful, full of flowers, and Barbie, the lambs are out.

I'll tell you what Mr Schroder did the other night. Because we arrived home late Tuesday from Saint-Tropez, I didn't ring him until Wednesday morning to reserve my room for the following evening. I felt sure he would have been booked out. He said, "Don't worry I'll have something for you."

He told the guy who was in my single room that he would have to sleep on the floor on a mattress in another room because he had a lady coming from Paris who is a regular and who comes up every month!

The train has just arrived at The Hague. There's a crummy little beach here that they say has waves. Actually, it has a few little ripples, with sun and rocks and benches that you have to lie on because you can't lie on the stones on the beach. I love Europe.

Oh my! This dude just walked down the aisle wearing a t-shirt with AUSTRALIA and KOALAS spattered all over the front. I love the subtlety of the Aussies. Their discretion is unmatched, except for the Texans who insist on wearing their ten-gallon hats and their holsters in Paris. This guy probably has a kangaroo on a lead in the luggage compartment. He's still looking for cans of draught, and corks to tie around his hat to keep the non-existent European flies away.

Anyway, back to the story of Mr Schroder kicking out his customer to make room for me. The guy was an American doctor, gorgeous-looking, very sensitive, with a great sense of humour. Together we went down to the gay restaurant for dinner, and during the conversation, he told me that he's sleeping on a mattress on the floor in someone else's room because there was a girl from Paris who always comes to stay every month. Let me tell you I had been feeling guilty and was trying to avoid this person whoever he was.

Well, I got caught on my fork as I tried to slide under the table! Then I laughed and said I was really sorry. Luckily he laughed too and said, "You owe me one."

I showed him Amsterdam in an evening. We had a wonderful time, so now we're even. He was lovely. The other night André and I were reading our stars, and mine said that I would meet someone who I would be attracted to.

"No chance," said André, "I'm locking you in tomorrow; you're not going to work."

Funny … this guy was cute.

The two dames across the aisle in my carriage haven't stopped eating since they boarded. They're both as big as houses and only just fit in their seats. They are having a wonderful time with all their food. It's amazing what their stomachs can hold. I think they must be expandable. They have already polished off ham sandwiches, cheese, cake, and fruit. Now they are just continually nibbling.

When this ship jerks to a halt I'm going to launch inconspicuously into their laps and devour the remnants of their munchies. Wonder where the man with the food trolley is?

The sun shining through the window is lovely. I can't wait till you come over Mum.

Last night I had a horrible dream. I dreamt I was tired of living in Europe and I wanted to go home. I was desperate. Packed all my things and didn't tell my work or my friends. But the worst part was I couldn't leave because I didn't have a car to get there. I was so relieved when I woke up.

Some of my dreams are so weird – bizarre. Recently I dreamed I was lying on my back moving head first through a dark tunnel and I knew I was dying. There were three doors to pass through. I passed through the first, then the second door. You and Barbie were there at the entrance to the tunnel, and I knew the only one I would come back for was André, but he was not there to put his hand in and bring me back. You can't imagine how relieved I was to wake up with a start and find that it was just a dream.

I had my acupuncture appointment at 10:30 am yesterday; he also gave me some needles just to relax me and free my mind, because I dream too much, just heaps of confusing dreams. He said, "You will feel tired after this."

Then I went to the village of Baarn which is exquisite. I love Baarn; did my good food shopping and arrived back at Hotel Schroder at 1 pm. I lay down for five minutes before going out again but woke up eight hours later!

The train just pulled into Rotterdam. Next month I'll go to the beach here, it's near The Hague Sherringham. Remember Barbie, we stayed there.

The food-trolley man is back again, and I'm proud of myself, I watched him walk by. Now, in front of me is the money changer – nicest guy – he just asked me did I want any money, and it took all my composure not to say, 'Sure, if you are giving it away. How much can you spare?'

Everyone is giving him their cash. He just comes along, and people hand him squillions of money (I'm in the wrong job), then he scribbles on a piece of paper and gives it all back. Waste of time if you ask me – weird mob, the Dutch. If I were him, I would scribble on a piece of paper, give them all a number and tell them to line up at the next stop. Then I'd get off and run like a bat out of hell.

It's a six-hour trip to Paris; André will meet me there at 5 pm.

I'm reading a book in French titled, *Freedom in Love*. (I think that's how it translates.) It's about marriage communication from the kitchen to the bedroom. I never do any of the things that this book says you are supposed to do, and I do all the things that you're not supposed to do. It's really depressing me and what is worse, I think they might be right. I think, *Oh shit, this bloody book is making me crazy*. Makes me feel so inadequate, but it's good reading.

I think everyone would believe that they were the world's greatest lover for their boyfriend, then husband. They mistitled this little number. It should read, 'How to Make You Feel Inadequate in Two and a Half Pages' and that's only the introduction! I've read a bit further on, but I keep telling myself to put the bloody books back on the shelf and just live and relax. But then there are things to learn – it doesn't all come naturally.

Take me for example. Just because I like food doesn't mean I can cook it. I spend more time in the delicatessens and restaurants than I do in my own kitchen, *et voilà*, the problem of most couples. No, it's a *potential* problem, and it's all about communication.

Most couples can discuss at length and in intimate depth the reason for the excessive gas bill or where to go for their holidays, but with personal needs and intimate aspects, it's like, 'Who me? I'm fine.' Shit. It's true, isn't it? I'm tired of that. I want … no, I *need* a total communication. It takes courage, patience, active input and a lot of time to achieve that.

We've all heard of the marriage guidance councellors who have never been married. They are too scared and have such grandiose hopes and ideals for perfection and idealism that on a human level they know it's going to be bloody difficult if they do get to that point in their relationship at all. They would rather pass on their fantasies and keep them wrapped up in their perfect, untouched, incommunicable wrapping. I think a lot of couples live like that.

With as much as I feel for André, I'm just as scared really. So when I say, 'I have arrived,' I mean I have arrived at a point from where I can start.

Love isn't a resting place; it's a moving growing space where we communicate from the essence of ourselves, and only there can we find *true* love.

Bring on the violins. I'm getting rather intense here, so I'll change the subject.

Can't wait to watch them unpack the luggage from this train, and watch this dude's kangaroo jump out. It's probably wearing the same t-shirt.

This will definitely be the last page as I'm getting writers' cramp. I've been writing since the train left Amsterdam at 11 am and now it's 12:40 pm and I haven't stopped yet.

Roosendaal now ... still in Holland. We'll probably go to a movie tonight to see *La Maison du Lac* with Katherine Hepburn, Henry Fonda and Jane Fonda. How do you call it in English? 'On Golden Pond', I think. I know you saw it and loved it. I saw 'Reds' twice and loved it. If you get a chance, go and see Monty Python's 'Life of Brian'. You'll pee in your pants. It's brilliant. Jeff, you would love it, I guarantee it! If you don't, I'll pay your fare to Europe ... how about your taxi fare to the airport ... or can you go by bus? If you promise you'll walk I'll buy you a coffee when you get here. No just joking. But seriously, if you haven't seen it, go. 'The Holy Grail' is good too but not as good as 'Life of Brian'.

Newsflash! The two fat ladies are drinking liqueurs out of the lid. Now they are smoking, which could mean it's the end of the first gourmandisation or the beginning of the next – it could well be the latter. They could be thinking about mugging the trolley man, as they may be out of supplies. Never trust hungry, fat old ladies.

The man sitting in front and across the aisle is all class. He has a Dunhill red and gold cigarette case and gold lighter. He's wearing grey trousers and a blue jacket (it's the 'uniform' here). Oh, *and* a red striped shirt with white cuffs.

The ladies are asleep now. They remind me of a remnant from a Roman orgy – the food part.

I'm tired now, I think I'll sleep.

Take care. All my love.

Chapter 9

Letter, 18th June 1982

Dear Mum, Barbie and Jeff,

It's Friday afternoon, so just a quick note. I'm at Language Power again and my next student will be soon here. Today at lunchtime I bought a lovely pair of olive green and gold shoes. They have a low wooden heel – very smart.

On Sunday, André and I are driving to Deauville on the Atlantic coast for the day with a family group. It will be nice.

We just had a quiet night at home last night. I did the shopping across the road from my place and then took the train to André's. The bag was heavy and when I got to the suburban train station, it burst. The toilet tissue rolled away, followed by the round of camembert cheese, whose lid went in an entirely different direction, promptly followed by a French wolf who, no doubt was thinking, *Voila! I'll take charge of this situation.* He picked them up while I watched and asked if he could carry them for me. I said,

"What ... the toilet paper and the cheese?"

No, but he did offer. Been there, seen this, done that. I remember the last time a Frenchman offered to carry my shopping. Three weeks later I cried myself silly because we had split up. So thought I, *I can carry them all by myself this time thanks, but if you like, you can bring up the rear, just in case we lose the lot again.*

I'm so happy being with André. He didn't want to talk to you on the phone the other day, Barbie because he's very timid when speaking

English. The only time I speak English now is at work – it's good, I need the practice. It was great to hear you on the phone. Ring whenever you like; André said anytime, any hour, day or night. He told me you sounded so cute and that you had such a young little voice.

Maxwell sent me a postcard to say he is in Australia visiting his parents for two months while waiting for his Dutch working papers to come through; then he will begin his dentistry practice in Amsterdam. I go there again on Thursday, June 24th through Sunday 27th.

Can't wait till you meet André – he's really lovely. Can't wait till you come over; there are only fifteen days to go. The weather is beautiful now. You need relatively light clothes, maybe a jumper or cardigan. No coats this time! Don't bring too much, pet, as I'll be moving to André's and I'll need a convoy just for the first load. Every few weeks I have a big throw-out.

Denise is so excited about your invitation to Australia. She's at the Australian Embassy today, getting all the necessary paperwork organised. She can't believe what a fantastic offer it is and is very moved by your generosity.

Sacré-Coeur from my balcony is so beautiful at night … pity I'm never there to see it these days. I don't want to give up my apartment, but I do want to spend all my time with André. When I used to be at my place I always wished to be with him at his. My absence of logic scares me.

Letter, 18th June 1982

Dear Mum Barbie and Jeff,

Well, another holiday, another spectacle, but this time we did it with heaps of style and carried it off like a little beauty, at least I thought so. It was one of those experiences where you can't decide whether you surfaced a winner or were traumatised into indelible, irredeemable failure. I don't know, but I sure as hell know I wouldn't do it again for anybody – not even for André.

Time: Four weeks ago.

Place: Sun drenched *Saint-Tropez*, where the whole transit population is out to impress themselves first and everybody else next. So one dons one's new purchases, poses and struts, you name it. I made a nice big red hole in my bank account doing just that; at least it tries to look like a bank account most of the time. It does for a couple of days while my monthly cheque sits there waiting to be distributed among all the French *horribles* like the tax collector, the rent, the electricity bill, the TV man – ad infinitum – the list is endless. Then it just melts into oblivion.

So anyway, back to my story. Firstly André's taste in clothes ranges from the sublimely ridiculous to the beautifully classical *vis-à-vis* his mood or humour at the time. His cousin enjoys the latest, modern, way, way out Parisian fashions that have to be seen to be believed. She had just purchased an emerald green cotton seersucker ensemble – very short – with loads of large, wide, horrible green frills, with a matching green 'straight jacket' as an excuse for a bodice. I must add she wears them beautifully. André thought the outfit was wonderful. In fact, everyone except me thought it was wonderful.

So, as we were packing to go to *Saint-Tropez*, it found its way into the suitcase to the tune of, "You can wear this in *Saint-Tropez*!"

I dutifully packed it to the silent tune of, *Like hell I'll wear it,* having already taken a look at it and thinking, *In Australia, they would probably put me away.*

Scene 2: The morning of our pose in *Saint-Tropez*, and while pondering over what I would wear and how well I could impress myself while wallowing in the glorious privilege of sipping cold martinis on the beachfront in salubrious *Saint-Tropez*, in terror I discovered the poo-poo green frilled creation stirring in the bowels of my bag.

Enter, Beloved.

"Why don't you wear Josephine's green ensemble?"

Panic stations! Why didn't I say, 'It couldn't stand the sight of itself and drowned itself in the toilet.'? Thought that lacked heaps of style, so holding up my latest elegant and expensive purchase I said, "I had thought of wearing *this* actually."

Beloved: "Just try it on."

So we just tried it on, and he went into raptures, said I looked fantastic and that he could even eat me. I thought it a sacrificial duty to wear the monstrosity. The couple in whose house we were staying, didn't utter a word when they saw me. I haven't quite decided whether they were trying to suppress their irrepressible laughter or were just politely disgusted … I fear it was both. In retrospect, it was either that or paranoiac shock. They were my sentiments exactly, except *I* didn't think it at all hilarious.

By this stage, Beloved is having passionate fantasies at the sight of me, and believe me, it was a sight! He said he could eat me. I thought of offering him the dress to eat, and taking a rain check on me or vice versa, but I think the deal was me in the garb.

Sitting in the car, engulfed in the masses of poo-poo green frills and matching straitjacket, I felt like a dressed turkey waiting to be eaten. I was praying that *Saint-Tropez* would turn into a fancy-dress parade for loonies and crazies before we arrived – even then I would have been overdressed for the occasion – or that his passion would get the better of him and he would eat me in the green mass and put us both out of our misery. But no, it was not meant to be.

Arriving at the scene of the 'would be if they could be' bar (I don't remember how I got there) I was in a state of utter shock at this stage but consoled myself with the fact that at least I was half hidden under the table, and only the top half of me could be seen. I thought I might pass it off by occasional spasmodic twitches of the head, and if I wrapped my arms around myself people would still notice, but probably stare with more compassion at the 'crazy' in the green straitjacket who got lost on her way to a 'come-as-you-are' party. I remember once at home, when I knew I was going to be invited to a come-as-you-are party, I wore the same thing from dawn till dusk for a week for fear I would be caught unawares, and when I arrived I wished they *had* caught me unawares, because when I got there I felt like a pimple on a pumpkin.

Well back to the *Saint-Tropez* spectacle ... circus ... whatever. That's right, isn't it? Where everybody laughs except the clown? Imagine the scene in *Saint-Tropez* – from one 'would be' to a 'could be.'

"*Cherie*, what is that?"

"Don't be ignorant darrrrrrrrrrling, it's a green dress and ... *mon Dieu!* ... there's somebody in it!"

The climax of the afternoon was a suggested promenade around the port, in other words, join the passing parade. I figured this would be my cue to faint, collapse, die or melt. At one stage along the dreaded walk, I thought of closing my eyes so that I could fall over and get lost in the frills so no one could find me.

Saint-Tropez boutiques have the unforgivable habit of putting mirrors in their shop-front windows. I looked into one by mistake and scared myself half silly.

At least it's something to write home about. Unfortunately, I'll never be able to brag about my sojourn in *Saint-Tropez* with the fervour of most people.

André will be here soon to pick me up. He suggested we live together and that I give up my apartment as I was never there and his flat becomes *our* flat. Well, I can assure you, the panic that set in at the thought of giving up my little palace was disturbing, to say the least. I thought of putting on the green dress to take my mind off it. I do want to live with André – I have been, since January practically, and that's what's so wonderful.

Actually, he was very diplomatic and subtle about it, but it landed like a ton of wet rags, PLUFF, when he asked, "How much notice would you have to give on your apartment?"

He was in the bath at the time, washing his hair with his eyes closed. Good thing because I turned red and white at the same time. I was sitting on the bidet and almost fell in! I know I want to live with him, but I can't imagine giving up my little castle on the eighth floor.

I've decided I will make an irrevocable decision with the strength of character that even surprises me, and my commitment is ... a definite

MAYBE, an un-debatable PERHAPS, with a powerful WE'LL SEE tacked on for good measure. See how I've changed? I've become a purposeful, adventurous, unafraid little devil, who rides with the wind and needs no guarantees for the future. It's okay … don't rush me.

Denise sees more of my place than I do now; she's staying there. I had to ring André at work recently to ask him for my phone number so that I could ring and ask Denise for the combination number to unlock the main door of the building. I've got signs on every cupboard in my apartment now: underwear, jumpers, etc., because I can never remember where things are. Denise has become my secretary and cleaning lady. I don't live there anymore, I just visit. I still love my little castle, but I love André more.

There's nothing like being in competition with an apartment to put a hell of a hole in your ego. Fortunately, he doesn't have a big ego – it's just me.

I returned to Paris in July 1982 to spend four weeks with Rainey, this time with my sister Shirley who had arrived several days earlier. On my arrival, I was surprised to see how tired and drawn Rainey looked.

Shirley and I stayed in her apartment on Rue La Fayette, and she was with André in the north-western suburbs of Paris. Denise was staying downstairs with another friend, Adriana, while we were there.

The first morning after my arrival Rainey came to the apartment on her way to work. She came again on the second morning, and Shirley had gone out early. That was when Rainey told me about her pregnancy. I was instantly elated – until she added, "But I have to have an abortion."

"No Rainey, no – I will come over. I'll stay and help you."

She was devastated about having to have the pregnancy terminated and explained what the doctors had told her; that it would be too risky to both her and the baby to proceed with the pregnancy because of the chemo-therapy drugs she had been given. There was a strong possibility, they said, that the baby would be deformed and that growth hormones released during pregnancy could stimulate the growth of cancer cells within her *body.*

"I know this little soul so well," she told me, *"It's free to come and go whenever it pleases. I know when it's with me and when it's not. We are so happy together. Now I believe it knows that I've decided to have the termination because it comes less and less. I believe it knows, and I can feel its sadness."*

The following day I accompanied her to the hospital where she had her pregnancy terminated.

I still feel her pain and her grief as I write today – over thirty years later. The following poem was among her papers.

It is perhaps a bud crying out to bloom
Knowing at heart something that will never be.
A voice pleading to share a part of us
A part of life
A small heart beating – yet unformed
A voice so strong – yet there is no sound
A voice without a sound
A bud without the sunshine
A feeling
Eyes that cry without a tear?
Yes it is all of this.
A soul without a choice as yet
Who, like the flowers and with the sunshine,
Will bloom again in time.
Conceived in love – born in tears.
Les yeux pleure sans pleurs.

-Lorraine, July 1982

That month in Paris was for me, a time to experience all manner of mixed emotions, feelings of joy and of deep sadness. I was so glad to be there, and to be able to give Rainey the level of support with the love and understanding that only a mother can give. It was a devastating decision they had to make.

It was wonderful to meet and to get to know André, understanding the love she felt for him and to see the love and regard he had for her. They were very much in love and eagerly looking forward to the future together.

That month passed all too quickly. I was not able to spend as much time with her as I would have liked as her daily routine was very busy, but we did manage, with Denise's help, to show Shirley much of Paris and take her to many of the places she wanted to see. We would often meet Rainey for lunch or coffee during her breaks between classes and spend time at weekends with her and André. That month seemed to fly, and in no time I was back at the airport saying a very reluctant goodbye to her once again.

Letter, 12th August 1982

Dearest Mum and Barbie,

With all my love, always. Well, I thought of you all the time while you were on the plane Mum, and I was very upset and sad because the four eventful weeks we had here seemed to pass so very quickly. One thing's for sure; if ever you get bored you can just come over and I'll sparkle up your life, one way or another.

André came home that day at about 4:30 pm, and with Tristan, we left Paris for Arcachon around 5 pm. Tristan is a gorgeous child, a physical replica of his father, and he and I are getting on famously.

The speciality at Arcachon on the southwest coast of France is oysters, so André and I were in our element. We also went up to a place on the Atlantic coast of northern Brittany – *La Cote du Granite Rose* – a most amazing place. The coastline there is lined with huge pink granite boulders, which over time have been eroded into fantastic shapes.

The countryside was gorgeous but there was not a lot of sun there. We spent time sailing and swimming, André went windsurfing, and the three of us had a wonderful, relaxing time.

I'm back to normal now, health wise. I feel much better - no more pain - no more cramps and I feel everything else is becoming more gentle if you know what I mean, softer with time, and of course André is so wonderful. I'm so glad you know him, Mum. Now when I talk about him in my letters you will know and feel exactly what I say.

I love you both very much and really miss you.

Letter, August/September 1982

Dear Mum,

Well, where to start. I'm very concerned about André. Sometimes I feel I'm helping him, and other times I feel so helpless, so awkward. I could cry because there's nothing to say – it's all understood. His little son, Tristan, left us yesterday to visit other family members before going back to Hong Kong on Tuesday. I cried when he left. He's such a beautiful child. André is so depressed. It's as if he doesn't know what to do. He's explosive and interiorising everything at the same time, and Tristan hasn't even left the country yet. I know it will pass, but for now I feel so helpless.

Now Wednesday and Tristan left last night to return to Hong Kong. André is empty, but I know I've helped him just by being here. I'm usually home when he arrives in the evenings except when I have a late class. Then he picks me up from work. He was better than I thought he would be. The first night after Tristan left was the worst, but I feel I did help him.

It was so good talking to you on the phone the other day, Mum.

On Thursday I'll be going up to Amsterdam again for my next acupuncture treatment.

I have a new private student beginning in October. He's the accountant at Fiat and has been offered the position of European Marketing Manager with trips to other European countries, and to the States where it's necessary to speak English.

September 4th

Now I'm on the train returning from Amsterdam. Well, I had my long overdue appointment with the acupuncturist. The constipation has gone, but all this has put my spleen out of whack; I could hardly walk yesterday. The acupuncturist said not to worry, it will get worse before it gets better. Great! That's comforting, just what I wanted to hear! I have a bad ache in my left arm from the shoulder down to the fingers. It's the colon meridian that's reacting. Imagine if you went to the GP with that; there's no way they could find out what it was. My next appointment is in three weeks' time.

I didn't sleep at all last night; hope I can sleep on this train back to Paris. I have two books, two apples and a sandwich. I wrote a note to Barbie and it's strange; I used to write such interesting and creative letters, but lately I'm not inspired.

The acupuncturist asked me how I felt during those months of my pregnancy and I told him it was one of the most beautiful times I had known, but that after the abortion I felt empty, mentally, physically and spiritually. I felt alone and so different.

I remember the first night at home after the operation; I was dog tired but didn't want to go to bed by myself. It wasn't even enough to be next to André – I had to hold on to him. I didn't realise then that I was trying desperately to fill the void. It was just a feeling, but that's what it was. I felt so depressed, so lost and alone.

The acupuncturist explained that during this time of pregnancy there is an incredible amount of spiritual, physical and mental energy (it's true), and that after an abortion it's a great shock to the mother, physically and emotionally.

It's strange, you may think I'm overreacting, but now at times I know that the little soul helps me. It's here with me and I'm very conscious of it sometimes; not just being aware of it, but as if it looks after me at special moments when I least expect it and most need it. It's quite beautiful.

I asked the acupuncturist, "Do you think most women react like me?"

He said, "No. It doesn't mean that the spirit doesn't communicate with the mother – it's a question of *sensitivity* and of *listening* on the mother's part."

The thing that made me most upset during that time was that towards the end of the four months the little soul went away, even while I was still pregnant and would only come back sometimes. And I was so glad when it did. The acupuncturist was surprised when I said that, but I *know* it happened.

I love you Mum, lots and lots.

Rainey's need to express her innermost thoughts and feelings came via pen and paper, and at these times writing was her outlet. She was sometimes guarded when writing to us, always keeping her letters bright and cheerful. The following was not in a letter but on a loose page, undated, which I found among her papers. I feel it must have been written around this time.

I don't wish to be morbid, but at times I get the feeling that I will die at a young age; or if I live, then André will die. Maybe it's not that, but something...

I hope André doesn't die of a heart attack ... I know he has a weak heart. If he did die I don't know what I'd do, I really don't. I'm crying now ... how stupid I am. Maybe I'm scared of losing him. I know I am. I wonder what my baby would have been like.

I'm scared of losing my freedom. I'm scared of being caged in like a bird. I'm scared of having too much freedom. I'm scared of being in love ... out of love ... I guess I'm just scared of being hurt.

I'm so very tired. Sometimes I feel like I've been living a thousand years. Maybe I'm one of the ones they keep sending back for a second go at life, just never getting it right.

I wonder what I'm supposed to learn here and if I ever wanted to be born. Sometimes I feel like a little soul myself on a borrowed adventure, on borrowed time and in a borrowed body, wanting to give it all back till I end up where I belong, where ever that is, but I know it's not here. I don't really think anybody belongs here; it's just a practice ground for elsewhere. I wonder...

September 8th

I'm at work now in *La* Défense, writing this at Language Power while waiting for my favourite gay student. He's lovely. I always seem to be somewhere waiting for someone. On Friday I have an appointment at the American School, hopefully to enlist more private students, and then I'll be more financially secure. I feel much better this afternoon.

September 13th

No, I don't think I'll bother about lessons with that accountant at Fiat because he likes me and I don't want any drama. I prefer to have my students from the American School with no problems.

André, Denise and I are going to see Neil Young in Concert tomorrow night; I got the tickets for half price at CBS. Yesterday I went with André and a friend of his while they went windsurfing on a lake one hour from Paris. That was a nice break. We went out to dinner too many times last week, and I've put on weight I'm sure.

André is going to Hong Kong for Christmas. He wanted me to go and said we'll spend Christmas with Tristan, his ex-wife and her husband because she wants to be with Tristan at Christmas. That really annoys me. She has him all bloody year, and all his childhood for that matter, and there's no way I'll go. I remember how I was when she came to Paris and André took photos of her in the park and took her out to dinner, so I'm not wrapped in spending Christmas with them. I would prefer to spend Christmas with Maxwell somewhere. That reminds me, I must ring him – he chased all over Amsterdam looking for me that last weekend, but I was too sick to move. I'll have dinner with him next month in Amsterdam. He's a good friend.

Through Denise, I've had an offer from a tour director to work at the airport as ground hostess for English tourists on Monday and Friday afternoons ($100 for ten hours). It's with Paris Travel, the agency where she works. I'll be working as a transfer hostess, meeting passengers at the international airports (there are two, Orly and Charles de Gaulle) and bringing them into Paris by coach. I'll work between both airports (but obviously not at the same time), hold up signs with the passenger's names, put them on a coach and give them a guided tour on the way into Paris to their respective accommodations.

So now I'll be working as a ground hostess, teaching at Fiat, CBS, Language Power and Harrison *Linguistique*, plus my private students. I have six private students at 100 francs per hour payable in advance. I'm tired of kids ringing me up at the last minute and cancelling their lesson. I keep my time free for them, and they pay. If they miss a lesson, it's up to them to put themselves out to replace it. Plus, living with André, I have to be more organised. I can't scream in anymore and leave the place looking like the wreck of the Hesperus if I'm running late.

It makes me frustrated because for the amount of time I've been here and for the hours I work, I should be more financially secure.

Actually, Monday was panic stations. I had to find another job as all my companies still hadn't renewed their contracts. I visited six tourist agencies, went straight to the top and asked them for a job, but I think Denise's offer is the best one.

I'd love to go home for Christmas, but even if I had the money, that would still drain me financially; I hope Maxwell doesn't have any plans for Christmas. We can spend it rolling in the snow in Amsterdam.

It's sad with Lisa gone and Denise leaving soon. That's one part of our lives over … or perhaps just beginning. But lately, I've been waking up feeling very lonely, alone and vulnerable. Before, I was different. I had that 'with the world at my feet' sort of feeling. Now it's changing; I love André and I want to marry him, but don't ever tell me that when you fall in love everything melts into instant organisation. The time we've spent together has always been wonderful but never all sugar and spice.

I'm going to miss Denise terribly; I already miss her, and she hasn't even gone yet. We've been spending more and more time together and talk for hours over coffee. I'll miss that.

Several months ago we found a Revlon hair care company that had professionals giving demonstrations of all kinds of treatment for the hair, and they needed models. So Denise and I applied. They said they would love to use us as models and welcomed us with open arms. It was to sit and have your hair styled, then model it. That must mean we're famous – or would have been if I hadn't had to go to Amsterdam. It was rather strange to think I was having traumas last year when Doctor Schwarzenberg advised me to shave my head. Instead, I just watched my hair slowly fall out for those four months. Funny old world isn't it.

I remember when my hair *was* falling out last year I used to go to the hairdressers a lot to boost my morale, which only lasted until Vivienne would touch it like she was handling the crown jewels. Then to the lady who washed my hair, she would say, "Do it gently, we don't want to lose any more."

I used to go there and pretend I had squillions of hair, except that when it was wet I looked like nothing on earth. Well … now that I'm beautiful and famous …!

I don't have many English-speaking friends; Carlos is one. Recently we had coffee together and he said to me, "Lorraine, I think what you have is wonderful. Hold on to your happiness and never let it go."

I like talking with him, and we laugh a lot together. My friend Frederique speaks only French, and there's Philippa from New Zealand. She's nice, but Denise and Lisa were like sisters. Marcel too is nice, but Maxwell is my favourite.

Sherbet, when I start making a list of my jobs and my friends … oh, I do have lots of other friends plus all of André's, my other acquaintances, and students that I go out to dinner with, but I mean *real* friends which are hard to find anyway. This is such a transient population – the ones who speak English I mean. I'm speaking less and less English now; I speak English at work and French at home and socially, except for talks with Denise and with Maxwell in Amsterdam.

Barbie, you have no idea how difficult it is sometimes to be with someone who doesn't speak your language. I love André dearly and maybe one day we'll be married, but as stimulating and as exciting as it is, it's also frustrating.

Take this morning for example. Well, take Friday for starters. I spent about three hours at *223 Rue La Fayette* talking with Denise; she's living in my apartment now. I left my keys behind, so she said she would put them in her pigeonhole at work for me to collect. As she'd be arriving at her office at 9 am, I could spend an hour with her before starting classes at Fiat Company at 10 am. This meant if I wanted my keys, I'd need to get up at the crack of dawn to take the Metro and the RER so as not to be late for Fiat. I wanted to get my application for the new job, which was also in her pigeonhole, along with my bank statement.

Denise had read it to me over the phone, but not before she said, "Lorraine, I hope you are sitting down, because you only have sixteen dollars in your account and the other letter is from the tax man and the bastard wants to take it all," and we burst out laughing.

So the story of my life was in Denise's pigeonhole, and I told André the night before that I would be leaving early.

At 6:30 this morning I said to myself, 'Self, it's morning, the bloody sun's not up yet, but *we* are.'

Then I had a revelation! If Denise doesn't carry her pigeonhole around Paris with her, I can get it at my leisure, whereupon I felt relieved but got up anyway because I had too much on my mind. Had to have a shower, wash my hair, iron my clothes and prepare my lessons, plus write a list of the friends I had left in Paris, to give me moral support. So I did all that when André woke and said, *"Je comprends rien."* (I don't understand, you are supposed not to be here.)

"I know, but I changed my mind."

"But why did you get up so early – what have you been doing for an hour and a half when you should have been sleeping?"

I *felt* like saying, 'Contemplating the joys of life … like having all my best mates leave the country, looking for more work, trying to build my bank account, deciding what I'll do about my apartment, pining over the loss of my Pollyanna state of mind, and rejoicing in my new found state of domesticity, that all the love stories say I'm supposed to love as much as I love you.'

I think someone's been telling us stories; that's probably my problem. I prefer the fairy tales where the good are justly rewarded, the baddies get their just deserts, and everyone lives happily ever after.

So instead, I told him the story about my keys and Denise, which is horribly complicated even in English and even more complicated at 8 am in French, to someone who was having great difficulty waking up, let alone deciphering my French which I speak painfully when I'm preoccupied.

He said, "Oh Lorraine it's too complicated. Besides if you didn't want to go to her office, you would have slept," then came the crunch, "You must have had another reason to get up."

I thought, *be calm, be calm … SHIT… give me a break, I don't need this.* And I just simply said,

"No."

My speciality, of course, is complicating simple issues, but then I suppose I *should* have stayed in bed. So then he woke up in a bad humour which is not abnormal at the moment, and he seemed to be sure I was planning an elopement with someone else or moving out or something like that. Then because I was ready, I buried my head in the four hour straight lessons I had to give today at the Fiat Company because when I feel confused I must be organised, otherwise it can be a catastrophe (more of a catastrophe than usual). Then he announced that he was going to the toilet.

"I'm going at Fiat," I said.

He thought I meant that I was going to leave for work without him. He always takes me. The look on his face said it all (because in French the words *to* and *at* are the same) and he looked at me as if I'd just told him goodbye forever. Then I realised.

"No silly, I'm going to the *toilet* at Fiat."

Then at 1 pm today, who should be waiting for me at work at lunch time but my beloved.

"Oh, what a surprise. What are you doing here?"

"I came because I needed to give you a kiss," And he spent his lunch hour giving me kisses, then drove me to the Opera where I spent two hours with Denise over coffee in the restaurant near her office.

She is coming around tomorrow. We'll spend the afternoon at home over tea and bickies, and when André comes back, we'll have a quick bite to eat then go to the Neil Young concert.

School is back, and a Japanese girl has been added to my fold, plus another Egyptian boy and four other Americans, so my schedule will be tight.

I talked to Mr Harrison, and we decided we would take our students to England for the long weekend in November. Fly to London and ... shit! I can't do that. I'll never get back into the country! Well, we'll have to sort that little number out. One thing's for sure, there's never a dull moment here.

I now have a renewed contract with Fiat Car Company through Harrison Linguistics, with three times as many students – an average of eight in each class. Mr Harrison is beside himself with joy and said he'll give me a handsome commission. That could be half my fare home for Christmas.

On Mondays I work at Fiat then like Superman, I'll soon have to change into the Paris Travel uniform in the nearest telephone box, which will be a catastrophe if we keep eating in restaurants the way we do. I won't be able to fit in the box, let alone the uniform. Then it's out to *Charles de Gaulle* International Airport telling the tourists how wonderful Paris is.

On Tuesdays, teaching at CBS, Energy Commission and private students.

On Wednesdays, teaching at Fiat, and private students.

On Thursdays, teaching at CBS Recording Company, Energy Commission and private students.

On Fridays, I teach at CBS again, then to the airport to do my ground hostess act. Oh, and Language Power gets fitted in there somewhere. Plus, I work at Harrison Linguistics a couple of hours per week. I'll need to practice turning around super fast like Wonder Woman so I can be everywhere at the same time. I'll tell you more in my next letter.

Now it's the next day, Tuesday 14th, and I'm at CBS waiting for my student. After the lesson, I'll get the tickets for the concert tonight then have coffee with Frederique in her office. I'll sign up for the part-time job with Good Times Travel Agency as well.

Oops, it's September 21st.

I had a letter from Maxwell today. I'll catch up with him in Amsterdam on October 1st, and this weekend André and I are going up to Brussels. Saw Denise and Sammy today as well – she's madly packing and so excited to be going to Australia.

André is at Aikido, the Japanese martial art of self-defence. At fifteen, he was the youngest person ever in France to have gained his black belt. He *teaches* Aikido now, but when he had Tristan by himself, he gave it up. He told me that during that traumatic period after his divorce, a guy provoked him in a car accident; he hit André and André hit him back putting the guy in a coma for a week. So I guess I'd better behave myself.

The highlight of my day today was a call from you Barbie. I figured Mum must have told you that I had lapsed into a severe state of depression and you decided to call me. It made me want to come home for Christmas, so I'm going to try and find a job on weekends and see what happens.

André is fairly *au fait* with your malady of writing half written letters, then discovering them months later in the bottom of your handbag. He said to me this morning, "Thank God she's not a journalist."

"Why?" I asked.

"Just imagine, September 21st, 1982, the war in Germany has just ended and President Kennedy has been assassinated. Australia has gained her independence and something about someone landing on the moon."

That reminds me – I was due to meet five planes at different times last Friday, all of which were delayed due to fog, so British Airways shoved everybody onto three other aircraft and sent them over, all at the same time to two different airports, Charles de Gaulle and Orly. They were on different flight numbers to those I'd been given, which put me up shit creek. I was panic-stricken as it was my first day and I wanted to impress the agency. I lost Poms left, right and centre. So last Friday there were squillions of little panic-stricken Pommies on the loose in Paris. God knows how they got there; half of them can't even organise themselves to find a toilet. But I've still got my job!

On Friday I'm going to try and lose a few more panic-stricken Poms. I hope British Airways get their act together this week.

Letter, 24th September 1982

Dear Barbie and Jeff,

Now it's Friday, and I'm at the airport once again playing ground hostess for Good Times Travel Agency. I must try not to lose them all like I did last week! I've had two job offers for hostessing, this one with Good Times

Travel, and the one with Paris Travel where I'll be replacing Denise. I was lucky. Denise recommended me to the London director, and he phoned yesterday to say I could start Monday. It'll be two afternoons a week, and then I'll be able to give this crazy one up.

The new hostess job will be very similar to this current one; I'll start at the meeting point in Paris where I put everyone on a coach, go to the airport with them and put them on a plane back to London where they belong. Then as they're going through the gates to board their flight, the arriving Poms come screaming out; I put this lot on the same coach, which is waiting. On the way into Paris, I talk on the microphone telling them how not to get ripped off by wealthy Arabs and rude Parisians, how not to spend the whole week in the maze of the metro tunnels trying to find a way out, administration details, etc. I direct the bus driver to each person's hotel and go with them to reception to make sure everything is hassle-free.

My trial run with Paris Travel is with Denise on Monday. The Paris Travel uniform is a navy-blue skirt, white blouse and a red blazer. I was thinking of buying a UK flag and wrapping myself in it. There's not much difference.

My first plane for this afternoon arrives in ten minutes at 1:30 pm, then I have another one to meet at the other airport at 1:35. Don't like *their* chances of being met I can tell you ... then the next one at 3:30, then 5:30 and 9:25. I get home in a taxi at 10:30 pm and we're supposed to be going to the movies tonight. Don't like my chances there either.

Tomorrow André and I are driving up to Brussels for a party and staying the weekend. The following weekend we're going to Amsterdam. I go up on Thursday afternoon, and he'll arrive on Friday night. We'll have dinner there with Maxwell, and I have two girl friends from Brussels coming up also on Friday.

I keep looking at the arrival board, but my next plane hasn't landed yet.

Airports are interesting, and thank God because that's where I spend my Fridays, although I didn't start till 1:30 pm today.

Denise told me that the night before hostessing we must have all the hotels organised in terms of the route the bus driver takes. We have to 'work it' she said. I know Paris better than I know Sydney now. Strange, isn't it? I also thought it would be glamorous being a ground hostess because you have to speak both French and English, French at the airport and in Paris, and English to the Poms. But no, it's not at all glamorous. Oops! My plane has arrived – back in a minute.

Well - TOUGH! That lot is lost and gone to their uncertain fate in Paris. If you ask me, they should all stay at home. They embarrass me more often than not. Some of them are cute but classless.

I really look forward to the last planeload when I pile them into a taxi, get a free ride home and have the driver drop me off at my front door. Every Thursday I go to the office to collect my schedule, the list of names and 100 francs per couple per taxi. That's about 1000 francs which equates to $500, and every Thursday I have this nagging impulse to take the money and run! Just kidding.

Next week we'll have a farewell dinner for Denise. I'm slowly getting it organised. Not having it at my place because not everyone likes scrambled eggs on toast, even if I went all out and chucked parsley all over it, so we'll go to a restaurant. We will be eight: Marc, a friend of ours from Language Power who has just returned from three months in the States (he's been working at LP for as long as I have), Frederique, my French girlfriend from CBS who knows Denise well, Joelle, another French girlfriend, Denise of course, and a gay friend of hers with his boyfriend. André and I make eight.

Another one bites the dust. First, it was Lisa leaving and now Denise. We are (or were) in the same 'gang' in Paris, the originals being Lisa, Adrianna, Anilu, Denise, and yours truly. We all met while working at Eden perfumery. Lisa is home in California and married now to Ward, Anilu is home in Mexico and married, Adrianna is getting married in May, and there's just Denise and me left. Now everyone has gone home and left me here by myself – the buggers! We were thinking of having a reunion (the League of Nations) next year or the year after and Australia looks like it will have the privilege as it is closest to everyone except me. Actually, the closest geographically would be somewhere in the African jungle, but I don't like the jungle's chances – or mine for that matter.

Back again. I just managed to rescue four Poms out of six that time, which is not bad going for me and a never to be forgotten catastrophic experience for them. This tourist agency will probably be glad to see the end of me. I keep losing their clients, left, right and centre.

Last Friday I left the airport at 10 pm, tired, empty, and crying, and the Poms who shared my taxi felt sorry for me saying it wasn't my fault. Now I have a new philosophy to retain some semblance of comportment and self-preservation. It's called 'them's wot gets met, gets met, and bugger the rest.' I don't get paid enough to scream between airports in a panic-stricken state, only to miss the plane and be embarrassed by the other passengers.

André came up with a good idea, but before I tell you, here's a little information about the uniform. The name of this travel agency is *Good Times* (it's English) and the t-shirt, which I flatly refuse to wear, has *Have a Good Time with Me* written in bold lettering all over your boobs! But then if I did wear it I'd probably make a fortune, and I wouldn't even have to work for *them*. It had to be a Pom who thought of that little number. Anyway, André said, "I've got it! I've solved your problem of losing all the passengers. You go to the sex shop, buy one of those inflatable ladies and put her in the T-shirt with a sign, 'Wait here fellas; be back in a minute.'"

Yesterday was so funny; it reminded me of Candid Camera. A man was standing on the corner watching me walk up to a phone box, open the door and make a call. As I was talking, I noticed that the whole panel of glass was missing from one side of the box, which he couldn't see from where he was standing. I walked out through that side of the box, and the look on that guy's face was classic. He gaped at me as if I was magic. His eyes were as big as saucers and his mouth fell wide open. I thought it was so funny because moments before, he'd been trying to act so disgustingly cool and suave to attract my attention.

My next plane arrives at 4 pm – it's late – that's okay. Then there are another couple of hours before the next source of embarrassment arrives. My first four clients were the name of Curtis, so I'm standing there holding up the sign that read 'CURTIS.'

A guy walked past and said to me in French, "His first name wouldn't be Tony, would it?"

I felt like saying, 'Try Martha, George, Bertha and Clive.'

A short time later I saw him again on the taxi rank (he's a cabbie) and after I had squeezed the passengers all into another cab, he came up to me and said, "If you ever need a taxi in an emergency, or if there is ever anything I can do for you, just call me," (yeah, I'm sure…) and he gave me his special cab number.

Now, what else can I tell you? There's twenty minutes until the next group arrive.

I have a friend who is an international tour guide. In fact, she's going to Columbia next week to pick up her group, bring them to Europe and spend two months with them travelling around France. There was a time when I would love to have done that, and now that I have the language and the contacts, I only want to be with André.

I was saying before that I look forward to going back in the taxi with the last lot of tourists because it's a bit like old home week. We talk about the price of eggs in London, the footy, all sorts of interesting stuff, and the wife doesn't say anything because she's still in shock. It's the first plane ride she's ever taken in her life and she thinks she's still in it. Sometimes it gets even more interesting when they discuss who it was who forgot the toothpaste. And then, "Oh, how much is toothpaste in Paris – very expensive?" and, "Are hotels costly?"

That's when I tell them about the metro, that if they sleep there, they don't have to pay anything and that the winos who live there can't help you with toothpaste, but they'd be only too happy to give you a bite of their sandwich.

My God! Wonders will never cease I didn't lose anybody that time. The whole six of them arrived on that flight except that it was to no credit on my part, because they all found *me*! Thought I had plenty of time so went to have a cup of coffee, and as I was fighting my way through the crowd coming off the plane, I literally bumped into two of my passengers by mistake.

"Oh you must be from Good Times," they gushed. Thank goodness, I was wearing my badge.

I don't understand this job at all. Last Friday I ran around like a panic-stricken idiot and lost all of the eighteen except two. Then this week I'm wandering around, head in the clouds, and couldn't care if they all ended up in the middle of nowhere, go up for coffee when they're arriving and bump into six of them by mistake. And they wanted to give me money because they said I was *so nice*. I still haven't quite worked that little number out, but things do seem to be improving. I must have done something right. Buggered if I know what it was.

The reason I've started to write with a red pen is that when I decided to go for a coffee, I left my blue pen on the seat. After I bumped into the tourists, gave them my spiel about Paris, organised their tickets for the taxi, put them in three different cabs and talked to the taxi drivers, I came back to arrivals half an hour later. After re-arranging my papers in the ladies' room, I sat in a different area as I needed a change of scene.

Then lo and behold, a man appeared in front of me and said, "*Excusez-moi Madame, mais vous avez laissé votre stylo sur la chaise là-bas*," He told me I had left my pen on the seat. My God, he must have followed me everywhere for the past thirty minutes just to give me my pen! International airports are so interesting.

Now I have until 5:30 before the next lot of panic-stricken Poms arrive, then the next arrival is 9:30. I always check the weather in London the night before, so that I know if I'll finish at a civilised hour. If there's no fog in London, which is a miracle in itself, I can expect all my flights to arrive on time.

This will have to be the last page. Twenty pages are acceptable. Mum told me in her last letter Barbie, that you had noticed a half disintegrated letter stirring in the bowels of your handbag the other day, begging to be let out. If I can still read it – please send it!

I wonder what movie we'll see tonight. Have you seen *Mad Max*? I thought it was brilliant. Go and see it; you will either love it or hate it. We loved it, and for me, to hear the Australian accent and to understand the humour was just great. I embarrassed myself by laughing when no one else did. But it was fantastic.

I hope tonight's not too late because we're leaving for Brussels tomorrow morning.

I've decided to give up my apartment now. I've found André, and I've thought about it a lot. I'm never there these days, and as Denise is leaving soon it wouldn't be practical for me to keep it. If I sub-let it would be for at least six months, during which time if anything happened the responsibility would be mine. I suppose I'm only keeping it because I'm scared something might happen between André and me. If it ever did, I don't think I'd want to go back there anyway. I would have to start over again, psychologically too. And the other reason is that besides being a gorgeous little French apartment, it represents all I've fought for over here after a very difficult year: my freedom, a place of my own, a haven and fabulous memories. And what I went through to get it was something no one would believe.

So now I'm fighting for something else, a chance to love – really love – a chance to share my all with … to live. And this is not without its problems either, problems beyond both of us. But we have each other. I think you understand. And now it's another time and place and motivation, time to move on.

It makes me feel like I'm giving up something that means a hell of a lot, for someone I love more. For me, never having been in that situation and knowing how much I have a horror of being tied down, ironically my feeling towards my apartment is tying me down. I feel that as soon as I get married means I'm getting older. Shit! We can't have that! But it's different with André; I really do love him so very much. Actually, I must if I'm giving up my apartment. It's not just four walls and a roof.

For me, it psychologically represents my freedom, my other life before I started living with André. It's the commitment I didn't make to anyone or anything, no commitment, no risk, all play and ... well... I think you understand. I'm almost on the ground between bouts in the clouds with my beloved. My God, I must be running out of things to say.

I'm sitting in a café near one of the arrival gates, watching the world go by. One man is holding a box of red roses – he's apparently waiting for someone. Remnants of the only time I ever received a box of a dozen red roses, all in deep red bud. That was one of the most exciting, romantic, moments of my life. I guess because I was in love at the time – as much as I knew how to be. I was young at nineteen, even a little naïve in love.

Those roses were beautiful, but they stayed in bud and never bloomed. Just like us I guess. I still think of Luke now, quietly, six years later. I still can't believe he's gone. I have so many wonderful memories of that time. In fact, I went to him in a dream that same year he died. That was another time and another place.

I know that was one of the experiences that made me hard with men – aloof and always ready to stand up to anything – just anything after I went down so hard then. I wonder why he had to die.

Please write and tell me about your plans for everything Barbie, from your land to your house, to your family, to the trip you are planning. Sometimes I feel out of touch with you – never mentally – but with your life. Hurry up, for God's sake and get your act into gear and get over here.

When Denise comes to Australia, take her skiing and show her places. She is a beautiful person. I know you will love her. I miss her already, and she hasn't even gone yet.

Thought I'd finished this letter, but I'll just tell you this little bit. There were four tourists I was supposed to meet. I got two, and the other two got away. By this time it was the fifth planeload of Poms I'd met today. (Don't show this letter to any of your English friends, they'll think I'm racist. I'm not racist – I just can't handle the tourists.)

By the fifth group I'm a little raw around the edges. The first two passengers were okay and while I was looking in my bag to give them their pamphlets, I asked the wife to hold up the sign for the others. She thought all her Christmases had come at once and held the sign high above her head. I was telling her husband how to work the metro and where to find the toilets, etc. when another Good Times client arrived and began asking the one holding the sign impossible questions.

Pointing to me, she said, "She's the leader, I'm not."

"Yes, I'm the hostess," I said.

"Well, she's holding the sign," was the abrupt response.

I lost my cool, and said with some authority, "Well, *I'm* wearing the badge!" No class.

Meanwhile the husband, who saw the funny side, was laughing so much I'm sure he was wetting his pants. And his wife who thought she was running the show with the board was still holding it high above her head. But everyone had arrived anyway.

Well now it's 6:40 and my next plane is due at 9:30. I think I'll call home and tell them to go to the movies without me. When this flight arrives, I'll have to wait till all my passengers get out of customs, go into Paris with them to their hotels, and pick up a jumper from *Rue La Fayette*. By then it could be morning. I should have brought a sleeping bag.

Remember to take Denise to that fabulous French Patisserie in Five Dock. They sell excellent croissants that go down well with coffee or with champagne and orange juice.

I'm going to buy a French cookbook now. I'm improving. I can cook a nice pepper steak in sour cream sauce, and veal in sour cream with mushrooms.

Postcard, 2nd October 1982

Dearest Mum, Barbie and Jeff,

I'm in Amsterdam again. Love you lots and lots. I had a great acupuncture treatment today. Thank you ever so much for the money – it was a lifesaver. I'm okay now as I get a full salary and have all my private students, plus the Paris Travel job.

After the acupuncture yesterday I came back to Hotel Schroder, went to sleep at 5 pm and woke at 8 am this morning. I love coming up here to Amsterdam. It's worth every penny.

Mr Schroder is packing up to leave for Spain next month He's invited André and me to visit him there. We said our goodbyes and I felt very sad. He and Herta have been such a special and important part of my life over here. It seems like the end of an era. It won't be quite the same without Mr Schroder.

André will meet me in Paris and we'll go out to dinner with Denise. She goes to England on Tuesday then flies to Australia soon after.

In September I had written to Denise inviting her to come and stay with me for a holiday at some stage in the future. She accepted, and immediately began making plans for the journey. I was surprised that she came so soon after my invitation and wished I had said to come with Rainey in December, as I know Rainey would have missed her friendship and support. Even so, they were both very excited about the prospect.

Denise fell in love with Australia, the sunshine and the beaches. She stayed for ten years, gaining her Australian citizenship during that time.

The following letter from Denise is dated 1st October

Dear Yvonne,

Thank you for your letter and all the information. I'm feeling so much better now. In fact I'm in top form, so please don't think I'll be arriving on a stretcher. Anyway, it is good to know about health coverage. I'm surprised the embassy here didn't give me any information about that.

These past few weeks have been quite hectic. I've seen quite a lot of Lorraine lately, and she is looking very well, although always running as I suppose Paris life demands. I've been over to André's place a couple of times for dinner and one evening we all went to a Neil Young concert as Lorraine had free tickets. André wasn't too impressed, but Lorraine and I assured him Neil Young really was a good musician – we just arrived ten years too late.

I expect Lorraine has told you that I got her a 'little' job with Paris Travel. English travel companies are not known for their generous pay, but it's better than nothing and will go towards her fare and perhaps she'll be home for Christmas. Every little bit helps anyway. This weekend she is in Amsterdam, and I'll see her next week before I leave France.

It was my last day at work today. It's really sad to say goodbye to everyone. I didn't realise just how many people I knew. At the *Gare du Nord* train station I had kisses from the porters, a Mars bar from the sandwich man, drink from the ticket controllers and more kisses from the coach drivers. Basel, the postman stopped his moped and whisked me into a café for a farewell Coca-Cola.

On Monday I have a farewell "do" at the office with all the girls. I've got great references from Paris Travel and France Tourism. I went to Eden Perfumery to ask the infamous Monsieur Riccard for one. I was halfway through my conversation when he kissed me on both cheeks and said, "Good luck in Australia, darling," and literally pushed me out of the way (I'm sure you can imagine the scene).

I wasn't going to get down on my knees and ask, so I left. Anyway, I have a letter to say that I worked as a bilingual shop assistant. The worst of all is having to say goodbye to my special friends like Lorraine, Sammy and George, but as they are special to me it will never *really* be goodbye.

I was very lucky with my luggage as a coach driver took them from Paris to my mum's house in London and I only have two suitcases to carry. My mum is arriving tonight and we are leaving for London on October 5th.

A friend of a friend works in a travel agency in London that specialises in cheap flights to Australia, so I'll go and see him and let you know the dates. This might be a help for Lorraine too. Is there any time you would prefer me to arrive or not to arrive? Write to me at my Mum's address. Also, if there is anything you would like me to bring, please don't hesitate to mention.

I had a lovely letter from Lisa. She has started her teacher training course in LA and Ward has been sent to Japan for six months. She seems so happy to be married and will surely miss him. She also said that Anilu, our Mexican friend from the perfumery, is getting married soon to an American. When I told Lorraine we both looked at each other as if to say, 'Only two to go!'

Take good care of yourself, and I'll see you soon.

Love,

Denise

Letter, 2nd November 1982

Dear Mum, Barbie and Denise,

It's now 8:30, and André and I are sitting in the lounge room contemplating the prospect of having to go to work after three lovely days off this long weekend. I'll be starting with another company this week. Language Power gave me a new contract, the Gaumont film Company at *Neuilly*, about four miles from the centre of Paris.

Today I'm having lunch with Marcel and with Marc, an American teacher from Language Power. Next week is a long weekend and André and I will go to Amsterdam for four days. I must get my act together and have everything organised so they'll let me back into the country.

Denise, we went to *Clignancourt* markets to see Sammy on Sunday. He is well, and wanted to know all about you. He asked me to pass by again before I leave to come home for Christmas, so I'll do that.

Now 4th November and I've just finished a lesson at the American school. Denise, I miss you so much. The place is not the same without you. How are you enjoying the blue skies and summer sun of my home country?

Well, the buggers finally confiscated my chequebook. I went into a *Credit Lyonnais* bank to withdraw some money, gave them the book and they wouldn't give it back. Then to make matters worse, I went to the *Monoprix* and as the girl was totalling my groceries (my head in the clouds as usual), instead of putting the already checked items in the trolley, I was going hell for leather from the front throwing all the unchecked items into my Mary Poppins bag when I heard, *"Oh! Madame, s'il vous plait!"*

My God … the embarrassment! Then a week later I received a rude letter from my bank, and another from *Monoprix* to say my cheque had bounced. Moving to André's house was a good idea after all – at least there they can't find me!

Winter is already in the air, it's icy today. I dug out my thermals from the bowels of my underwear drawer to find they had almost disintegrated into oblivion out of sheer embarrassment. Can't wait to see you – I'll be home the first week of December.

I'm really ready for a recharge so I can come back and face the masses.

Postcard, 8th November 1982

Dear Barbie and Jeff,

I'm so looking forward to coming home in the first week of December – really – you have no idea. I love it here, but it's very intense … very heavy. I plan to come home and vegetate my month away being a total bum – spending lazy days on the beach in the sun (if I recognise it), even saying G' day. What bliss! We have so much to catch up on.

I'm at the airport again now, having a coffee while waiting for my last load of tourists. I hope they all come to the right place. They were all drunk when I picked them up last Friday, so half of them might not even turn up, either because of memory loss or sheer embarrassment – probably the former. On the way into Paris they consumed another bottle of wine and kept applauding and shouting after each sentence of my orientation speech, so it took me ages to finish it. They wouldn't have remembered anything I'm sure. It was hilarious. I was doubled up in uncontrollable spasms of laughter. It was an absolute riot. They all *fell* out of the bus when arriving at their respective hotels, and couldn't recognise their suitcases.

I really can't wait to come home. I feel I need to.

Chapter 10

Rainey was coming home for Christmas and Barbie and I were overjoyed. We could hardly wait to see her. Our anticipation and excitement on the day of her arrival knew no bounds. It was so wonderful to finally see her coming through the arrival gates at Sydney airport.

With Denise, we spent the next couple of days together catching up and reminiscing. The house was filled with laughter. It was so good to have her home.

On the third day after her arrival, I went with her to an appointment with Professor McCarthy at Sydney Hospital for her check-up. She had written asking me to make the appointment before she left Paris.

After the examination, his expression was quite serious.

"Lorraine, I am so sorry that I don't have good news for you. I can only give you six months at best".

I gasped.

Rainey, calm and quietly composed, showed no sign of emotion. She just put her hand gently on my arm and said comfortingly, "Mum," then resumed the conversation with Professor McCarthy. He advised that the need for surgery was imminent – a radical axillary clearance – tomorrow.

My thoughts were numbed. This was too much to comprehend ... surely there must be some mistake. Rainey's joyous Christmas home-coming had suddenly become a nightmare.

Both in shock, we left and crossed the road to sit in Martin Place. When Rainey asked me, "What will we do?" I felt so hopelessly useless because I didn't have an answer for her. I had to pull myself together – I had to know *what to say. When the girls were growing up, I had an answer for everything. I could always fix things and make them better. Even in their later years, I could offer alternative suggestions in difficult situations; but not this ... not this nightmare.*

Even though the surgery was to take place the next day, we both felt that there had to be something else, an alternative out there somewhere, but we didn't know where to turn. Then Rainey quietly said, "Please take me to a beach."

We went to Cronulla where we sat just watching the waves and the ocean, and as I watched I began to understand why Rainey wanted to come here. Somehow, watching the waves' continuous motion and listening to their sound crashing on the beach seemed to take us away from the present to a place of calm where we could collect our thoughts and prepare for tomorrow.

Arriving at Sydney Hospital the next day, we were taken to the oncology ward where two doctors explained the procedure to us and answered our questions. When they left, I stayed a while talking with Rainey behind the curtain before she was transferred to theatre. As we both left the ward, I was aware of the other patients looking at me in disbelief and I heard several soft gasps. It was obvious that they were expecting me to be the one wheeled away to the theatre.

After the surgery, we called André from the Post Office in Martin Place, and Denise spoke to him. He was in shock, and we called him later to reassure him and answer his questions. I can only imagine what he was going through at this time. Denise translated for us but it was not ideal. I'm sure he was left with unanswered questions and a feeling of utter helplessness.

I feel that my thoughts need to be added here for the reader but how can I express them? How can I describe on paper such agonising thoughts – the unbelievable reality of this situation? There are no words to describe my feelings – the fear, the despair, and the feeling of total helplessness.

And what of Rainey's feelings? Her outward composure and inner strength at this time was remarkable, but perhaps her thoughts, splattered over loose pages during the two weeks of her recovery in hospital, will give an insight into her innermost feelings.

I found nine faded brown pages when sifting through her letters and papers after deciding to share her story. Her thoughts were scribbled at random over the first few pages, and as the days passed she seemed to have found the presence of mind to draw these thoughts together and write the following.

December 1982 - Sydney Hospital

If prayers are heard in Heaven, this prayer is heard the most...

'Dear God, please, not cancer.'

I had been living in Paris for three years and decided to treat myself to another taste of home and family. Not a day went by that I didn't dream of seeing my family and friends and some sun again. The thirty-six-hour trip from Paris to Sydney via Riyadh and Singapore seemed like an eternity – endless – then finally a wide swing to the left brought the Sydney Opera House and the spectacular harbour into view. What a wonderful sight! Then finally, touch-down - Sydney.

The plane wheels hit the tarmac at 180 mph. I was home! The prodigal daughter had returned. I was concerned I wouldn't see my family among the sea of people, but soon dismissed that thought.

Those few days of the immense joy of my family reunion appear to have been lost in the intensity of events. Four days later I would be lying in a bed in Ward 16 in the melanoma unit of Sydney Hospital after major surgery. Diagnosis: Metastatic melanoma.

For the moment my only thought was, didn't I solve that problem a long time ago? Wasn't I clear? I had been told I was clear.

I was numb and would remain so for quite a while to come.

Lying in that hospital bed, my thoughts were trance-like, hazy, and emotionless. I had barely enough strength to hang on to the moment at hand, let alone delve into the past or dabble in the future, for I had just been told that I had none. In clearer moments I re-enacted the scene in my mind.

How do you tell someone they are dying? I'd often wondered... gently? And worse, how would they accept it? How would I accept it?

The process was unreal. The fact was, I was dying and I had six months to do it in – and worse – I felt like I was already dead. Hell, why wait six months just to go through the motions? I couldn't believe it. But then I had a hazy memory of my surgeon saying the same thing to me in his rooms the day before.

A man sat at the end of my bed and began by saying (very matter-of-factly) that he was so very sorry, but I was dying and at best had only six months to live. Then everything went silent. It was as though I was in a vacuum.

I don't remember anything of what he said after that – I was too busy watching a rerun of my life; it flashed by so quickly... it almost seemed like a non-event that was suddenly over in a flash. After all, thought I, there is only so much you can squeeze into twenty-nine years.

When I returned to the moment, he was still sitting there at the end of the bed and I noticed his expression had not changed. His lips were moving, but someone had turned off the sound. Maybe I had missed something? My hopes rose. I was almost thankful for my temporary paralysis. Did he say he could help me?

"No."

"But are you certain?"

Still, his expression did not change. Yes, he was certain. There was nothing more that could be done.

And then something about my mother having to be told – delicately – something about the hospital counselling service to help family members cope with death was ... and could I cope with that... it would be better coming from me...

My mother! How do I tell my mother? Please God, this is not happening – or maybe it's one of those horrible nightmares. Maybe I'll wake up soon and it will all have been a bad dream. It's almost 2 o'clock, visiting hours, and she will be here soon.

I watched him get up and move away. I felt paralysed. It was almost like charades, but somehow all the guesswork had been taken out of this one. Another part of me was computing the fact that, yes, I've had a good life; the Isle of Capri had been my holiday haunt and I've been tripping the light fantastic in Paris for the last three years.

Five days ago, I was sitting in a little café on the left bank with my fiancé watching the world go by...

It was then in that split second ... oh my God ... no ... please, not cancer ... André. I can't die. Oh God, this isn't happening! How would I tell him? A telephone call at this point would be disastrous; I would wait till I was more composed.

Halfway into the night, I remember thinking if I stay awake day AND night I would have twice as long. Then it was back to the same question. How do you tell someone you love that you're going to die?

Lying there, a thousand thoughts raced through my mind all vying for pride of place, Why me? Why me?

Then suddenly, from somewhere in that twilight zone, somewhere between trying to make some semblance of sanity out of all this, came, Why not?

The nurse just came by saying, "You've been slaving away on that for a couple of days now. It must be a last will and testament."

I made a mental note to be a little more mindful not let idle words falling from her mouth affect me, and continued writing.

If ever there was a time to hope it is now. There is no need for doubt, no need for fear. At this point I don't have a plan of attack, but I know I have a faith larger than life, a belief in myself and a whole life to share – you'll see.

There and then I felt as if I had just turned around. I had made my dream, I gave my commitment, and it would come to pass. There was no question that somewhere in a quiet corner of my mind, I had made a pact with myself. I decided I would not die, but would instead live. I would entertain no negativity, and those who wanted to play along would have to play by the rules.

Rainey was discharged from hospital in time to spend Christmas Day at home. Even though she was at times quiet, pensive and withdrawn, she did enjoy being with family and friends.

So began our search for alternative ways of fighting this disease. After much reading, intensive research, many phone calls and enquiries, we finally found The Hunters Hill Cancer Support Society. There we found the emotional support we needed and together began learning all we could about organic diets, dietary supplements, special teas, wheatgrass, meditation, just to name a few of the alternative approaches to the treatment of cancer.

This was the beginning of Rainey's long and arduous road back to regain her health. It was all new territory for Rainey and us. Barbie and I were totally dedicated to its worth. At this stage, it seemed the only option we had.

There at Hunters Hill we met Martin, a man in his 60s who was also fighting cancer. He was a great help to us from the outset with his encouragement, advice and invaluable support. Over the next eight months, while following the strict dietary program, Rainey slowly began to regain her strength and vitality. Later in the year she was asked to speak at the meetings of the cancer group at St. George Hospital. This she did several times.

Rainey spent many hours with pen and paper, writing letters to André and her friends in Paris, pages of her thoughts, feelings and plans for the future. She also wrote and submitted several articles for travel magazines.

In July she was interviewed by Karen Allison, a journalist from the Sun Herald newspaper who was herself fighting cancer, and although the article was not published until 28th August, I will include it here as it gives an overall picture of the eight months following Rainey's surgery in December. This article titled, 'Fighting Cancer: My Energy is Poured into Positive Thoughts' expresses her total commitment to complete healing, to survival, and to her future with André.

The Sun Herald August 28[th,] 1983
Fighting Cancer: My Energy is Poured into Positive Thoughts
By Karen Allison

There is much controversy over the use of alternative therapy for cancer treatment. Recently, Prince Charles was criticised when he officially opened a cancer help centre which uses methods such as meditation and special diets. Meanwhile, cancer patients throughout the world are looking at these methods. Lorraine Walton is one.

Tall and willowy with long blond hair, 30-year-old Lorraine Walton has the classic good looks of a model.

She also has cancer – malignant melanoma considered in its latter stages to be one of the most severe forms of this dread disease. Lorraine was given a 40% chance of survival over six months to two years.

That was a little more than eight months ago.

She had been through the horrors of chemotherapy treatment as a preventative measure more than two years ago, and decided after an operation late last year to take matters into her own hands and fight cancer with alternative therapy.

"I wanted to play my own part in the healing program," she explained, "By being involved both mentally and physically, I don't have time to be afraid. My energy is poured into positive thoughts and actions, making it easier to cope with the disease."

Lorraine said hers was an educated decision made after the initial shock, horror and despair had passed. She read as much as she could on alternative treatments, obtaining most of her information and contacts from the Hunters Hill Cancer Support Centre.

By following a rigid diet, taking mega-doses of vitamins and minerals, cleansing her system with enemas and colonic irrigation, exercising and practising meditation, Lorraine hopes to rid her body of toxins, in order to stimulate her immune system and improve her metabolism.

Emphasis is on fresh, organically-grown raw vegetables and fruit made into juices and salads, grains, sprouts and brown rice. The only

299

cooked food Lorraine eats is a vegetable broth, rice and an occasional baked potato. Vitamin and mineral supplements taken daily include vitamins C, B, A and E, a mineral compound, kelp, thyroid tablets, and a protein form of spirulina and kyolic.

Besides the vegetable and fruit juices, she drinks herbal teas and wheat grass juice. The wheat grass grows profusely in boxes outside the kitchen door.

While her diet is worlds away from the gourmet food she loved to eat in France, any cravings for the good life vanish when she compares the way she feels now with the miserable state she was reduced to while receiving chemotherapy treatment.

"The chemo started after a check-up with an oncologist in France while I was living there in 1980," Lorraine said.

"I already had a mole removed in Sydney with good results, and felt I had nothing to worry about, but the oncologist in Paris suggested chemotherapy as a preventative against the potentiality of recurrence.

"I didn't even know what chemotherapy was. After four months treatment I had lost a lot of my hair and I was a walking skeleton, vomiting for hours after each treatment."

When a Sydney Hospital specialist advised that this treatment should be stopped, Lorraine faced a difficult decision.

"Medical experts in Switzerland and France told me the chemotherapy was saving my life, but others supported the Sydney Professor's opinion. I was the only one who could make the decision."

She stopped chemotherapy and resumed normal life in Paris teaching English and travelling around Europe. Then a quick sun and surf holiday home last Christmas turned to drama after a hospital check-up. Several days after her arrival, she was in hospital undergoing major surgery for the removal of malignant growths.

Clinically she was told to wait six months after the operation to see if growths recurred. That time was up in June and her condition since then has been regarded as satisfactory at the Sydney Hospital where she has been checked monthly. She has also undergone a non-toxic form of immunotherapy at the hospital, so she has not completely turned her back on conventional medicine.

"I accepted it because it is non-toxic and because my doctor is aware of my diet and other forms of treatment," she said.

Lorraine has just left Sydney on a trip to America and Europe encompassing two important aspects of her life – a study of natural medicinal treatments for cancer and to be reunited with her French fiancé, André, in Paris.

In California she will study the methods of Ann Wigmore, a doctor of naturopathy, well-known for her treatment of degenerative diseases with natural medicines, in particular wheat grass.

In France, with André, she will undertake the difficult task of continuing her stringent dietary program before returning to Australia next year for medical and alternative therapy check-ups.

Since the beginning of this year Lorraine and her mother have visited doctors, naturopaths, herbalists, acupuncturists and others offering treatment and help for cancer sufferers. Without a car, they have had to spend long hours travelling by train and bus to locations all over Sydney, an endurance feat some days for Lorraine, still recovering from the surgery.

Even on the most exhausting days Lorraine finds hidden strengths.

"I've changed a lot in my attitudes and come down to grass roots level," she said, "My faith has strengthened and helps me greatly and I am much calmer. My hopes for my life in the future keep me going."

Lorraine's program for the day includes drinking many glasses of carrot, apple and green leaf vegetable juices, and wheat grass juice. (She prepares them herself using a specially designed hydraulic juicer imported from America.)

She may have two coffee enemas a day and a wheat grass implant – both of which she prepares herself, or she may travel to St. Ives from her southern suburbs flat for a colonic irrigation treatment administered professionally.

Exercise consists of a gentle work-out on a mini trampoline recommended for use by cancer patients. The aerobic exercises are designed to improve the lymphatic system and stimulate circulation. A light workout on a slant board includes deep breathing exercises. Relaxation, combined with visualisation and meditation should be undertaken each day in Lorraine's holistic approach to treatment.

Outings may include a visit to the acupuncturist, a hospital check-up or an appointment with a doctor who has studied alternative forms of treatment at American clinics.

For more information on her diet and therapy program contact the Hunters Hill Cancer Help Centre.

Extracts from an unsent letter written in late May, to a friend in Paris

In terms of my health I have a lot of examinations in June. I'm sure I'll have good results. I'm feeling good – a bit tired, but good.

I'm so looking forward to coming home. I'm counting the weeks now. But I have become so used to such fantastic support systems here, like the hospital, Professor McCarthy, other doctors involved with me, groups of people with the same condition as myself, and the ever-changing information and help that comes from them. I will miss all that terribly. I'm very active in all directions, and there is yet so much to learn.

Sometimes I feel a little afraid to leave all this support, and other days I feel I can do it, even in the face of everything. On the other hand, I want to go … like tomorrow. Then I tell myself that in the final analysis, it's MY responsibility, and given that responsibility I can and will do it. It's comforting to know, that that confidence is there somewhere. Sometimes we have to dig a little deeper to find it.

There really is nothing to be afraid of - except fear itself. It's so true. It's also a question of confidence. Deep down I know I *can* do it.

If I had chosen to be an unconditional host to this disease through fear, through need, through ignorance, through anything and to just depend on hope, time and others to get me what I want, I would die. I know that. For my part, I must play an important role in my healing process before I can advance. I could decide to sit back, but it has to know I'm here. I'M NOBODY'S HOST. I would be stupid to sit back and do nothing.

You know, for a short time back in December my life suddenly looked very, very short. Since then my medical reports and all the information that led to my prognosis haven't changed. But, I HAVE. I'm *not* going to let that happen because I really want to live. So with all this, I guess I've learned how precious life really is.

What a speck in time we are! There's no time for regret – no time to dwell on the past – none at all. If we do, it must only be to sieve out the worth, the lessons and the laughter and use them in the NOW, positively for good. And as for the future ... it doesn't belong to us and never did, but it's full of dreams and aspirations, and I guess we use the NOW to fulfil them.

It's a strange thing about time – today I feel as young as I did ten years ago, but with a few more experiences added on instead of years.

André came to Sydney to see me. He had only two weeks and spent one week here and the other in Hong Kong with Tristan. When he arrived, I walked around in a semi-conscious daze wondering was he really here or was it my imagination. By the time the realisation finally sank in, the week had gone by, and I was putting him on the plane to go to Hong Kong. It was so wonderful to have him here, even for that short time.

To understand what's happening in regarding this disease was one of the main things I wanted for André. He came with me to see Professor McCarthy and to acupuncture. I also wanted him to understand the scientific nutritional principals behind my diet and therapy regime, to make an educated decision as I had done after weeks and weeks of reading, enquiries and talking to people who have had the same experience. He is now quite well versed in the alternative approach, understands, and believes in what I'm doing.

I love living in Paris. I love Australia too, very much, but my heart is in Paris with André. There will have to be some changes made when I return. I won't be running myself into the ground, keeping down four jobs trying to keep my head above water and my bank account happy. In fact, I won't even be working for a while when I go back, and after that I'll take a part-time job.

Ideally, I'd like to return to a part-time job already organised, hopefully from Australia … being sent over by Qantas perhaps … I could handle that quite well. After all, André and I need something extra to support our habit of flying from one side of the world to the other.

So I'll be here in Australia until August. I must put my health first above all else. Without it, I'm not much use to anyone or to myself for that matter.

All this to say it really is a challenge – a challenge that I intend to win.

Letter, 10ᵗʰ July 1983

Dear Uncle Len,

Finally I will be on my way back to Paris and to André. In less than four weeks I'll be winging my way, leaving on August 5ᵗʰ and will arrive in Paris August 30ᵗʰ. Between times will see me in California, where I plan to stay at Hippocrates, the clinic that deserves credit for the most part of my new health program. Three weeks of study and participation there will be great, and I'll catch up with a few friends in San Diego as well. Lisa, with whom I shared my flat in Paris, lives in San Clemente so there'll be lots of reminiscing of times passed. You'll probably hear us laughing. We had such riotous times there.

On looking back over the last eight months here in Sydney, I don't know where the time has gone. It's been a most incredible time for me. I'll probably write about it one day, but until then I have a lot of work to do for my health. I really think I've changed in that time ... not drastically, but I guess we all change through our experiences.

I could rave on forever of what I've learned about cancer in these last eight months. I believe if caught and treated *before* the body's metabolism is not able to be reversed, nobody need die of cancer, nor be subjected to the atrocities of chemotherapy and other orthodox treatments. It's quite a study, and there's so much to learn.

I understand much more now and only wish I'd had this knowledge before I had the chemotherapy. Well, it's never too late, even though I've been given a pretty disturbing report and the statistics, according to my specialist, are stacked against me.

It was ignorance that brought me this far, ignorance of the disease, believing the doctor, a GP, that my first operation needed no follow-up in terms of everything – diet, lifestyle – everything. One of my mistakes was allowing my body to be pumped full of poisons with chemotherapy.

All that's water under the bridge now, and I'm glad I've learned so much along the way. I've taken on an alternative approach to cancer because my potential of falling into a terminal stage is very high, but I believe – I really *do* believe – in the natural alternative program I have chosen.

This diet is very severe, very strict and very limited but I'm happy with it as I don't have a choice. It's very complicated, and I guess to a person unfamiliar with its basic principles, it's all too simple. And it is, but there again the most revolutionary truths are.

I have every faith in myself and this program. I can't begin to explain it here. It's taken me many books and learning, and now I know where I'm going. It will take some time, lots of energy, positive action and thought, and I know I will make it.

I've since learned that the 'art' of having cancer is not just accepting it and going along with everything that has become socially and medically accepted, like chemo, cobalt and radiation; it's knowing how to *live* with it and keep it under control *naturally*. Chemotherapy, etc., has become our best bet in the whole hypothesis. Really, nature's laws are the only tools to live by. Chemotherapy and the rest just buy you time.

The treatment I'm currently having at Sydney Hospital is a new one, a 'non-toxic' immunotherapy. My professor told me they can't guarantee anything, but I won't lose anything either. I'm taking it because it's non-toxic – it's not chemical poison. They didn't offer me chemo or the like after my surgery in December as the disease was too far advanced, so in the meantime I was told to just wait.

Can you imagine? In my most critical time, I can only *wait*? That's not quite my style. I'm sure that if I follow in the wake of the treatments that bore the statistics which my doctors gave me, I know in my heart of hearts that I would be dead within a matter of years or even months. I know that. I can't tell you *how* I know — I just do — and it's not fear because I'm not afraid. It's a gut feeling, probability and logic.

The good news is I've been invited to apply for a job in the Australian Embassy in Paris. I know a guy who works there, and he said whenever I want, to just apply. Gough and Marg Whitlam will be living on the top floor as of September 1st, and if I take the job I'll be rubbing shoulders with the celebrities. How about that?

Take good care and lots of love.

Chapter 11

O n 5th August 1983, Rainey boarded a Qantas flight to Paris via Los Angeles and San Diego, California. It was so very hard saying goodbye to her – she would be on her own now. Of course, I did worry; how would she cope? She was so happy to be returning to André and so positive with regards to the outcome of this health program.

For the past eight months, we had been working together sourcing and accessing outlets for organic fruits and vegetables, preparing her food and juices, and finding as much information as possible on alternative therapies, some of which she had already begun here in Australia. She had also been continuing her acupuncture treatment. She had been through so much during those eight months. On this new dietary program, her health and strength gradually improved. Her courage and dedication were inspiring and she had strong and positive convictions that she would be a cancer survivor. I too was convinced. This was going to work.

At the airport, because I was Ansett staff, I was able to accompany her along the passenger boarding bridge to the plane where we were met by the purser. He assured me she would be well looked after on the flight.

Rainey and I said our goodbyes and the purser asked me to wait. After a few minutes, he returned and spoke with me. He wanted to know about Rainey and what he and the crew could do for her. He said he would radio Air France to make sure they had received all the information for her forward flight to Paris in three weeks' time. I felt very reassured knowing *that she would be in such good hands. She was treated like royalty on that flight, and I was so grateful for the thoughtfulness of the Qantas cabin crew.*

With our friends on the observation deck, Barbie, Jeff and I watched until the lights of the plane were out of sight.

Letter, 5th August 1983

Dearest Mum and Barbie,

Well, here I am on the plane with three seats all to myself. I'm so excited, but I just don't believe it's true. One minute I'm at home and then…

In retrospect, the last eight months and all that has happened seems just like a tiny speck in time.

I must have only breathed twice and I've had two stewards and a 'hostie' come up to offer me extended service throughout the flight and on the ground. As if that wasn't enough to make me think I'm famous, lo and behold Simon from the TV show, *Simon's Wonder World* accompanied by Mrs Simon's Wonder World just walked by. I hope they don't sing, *Welcome to my Wonder World* all the way to LA.

The movies *Tootsie* with Dustin Hoffman, and *The Year of Living Dangerously* are showing in first and business class. We in economy get to play charades and I spy. We might even invite Simon down to show us some of his wonders.

I can just hear Simon now on his next TV show telling us about his trip to Los Angeles and about the young lady who boarded the plane in Sydney with so much baggage; how she went straight past check-in, past 'go,' but didn't collect two hundred dollars …

'Instead, she came complete with picnic hamper and beverages, and then to top it all off, on reading the dinner menu threw a tantrum and a boiled potato at the steward. She then held what appeared to be a plastic microphone to the steward and asked him to comment on the situation. Economy of course, played charades, while the young lady in question preferred to interview the passengers on what they had for lunch. I did, in fact, have the chance to be interviewed by her. She asked me if I would like to make a clean swap – no questions asked – three boiled potatoes and a banana for a prawn cocktail, filet mignon and Bavarian chocolate cake with coffee ...'

They just announced that the luggage is unusually heavy tonight – 361 tons – and to think I represent one-third of it, and that's just my cabin baggage! Oh Mum, thank you for everything!

Well, that's as far as I got with my letter when the plane took off. I saw you all waving. Actually, the highlight of the trip was Tahiti. Just before we landed there, I remembered that the cabin crew had told me I could have anything I wanted, so I thought I should ask the purser for a big round bathtub, a bar of Cussons soap, and for the pilot to circle so I could sit in the tub, look out the window and say with that gracious air of superior sophistication, 'Tahiti looks nice,' just like that ad on TV.

Looking down on Tahiti, it really was beautiful with all its white sandy beaches and softly waving palms. We had a stopover there. What a glorious place; I could live in a climate like that forever. It's a French colony, and now I can understand why every Frenchman's dream is to go there. The weather is just perfect, the setting is like the backdrop of an exaggerated stage production and the people so friendly and welcoming. It had the feeling of total relaxation. The airport lounge was dreamy with everything decorated in shades of purple.

The Qantas service is fabulous. I feel great and not at all tired. The acupuncture needles to adjust my body clock must be working well. I'm so looking forward to seeing Lisa and Ward when I arrive in San Diego.

So I send you all my love now and always. I can't wait to see you when you come to Paris in exactly eighteen weeks. I just checked my calendar.

Letter, 8th August 1983

Dearest Mum,

I'm settled in now at Hippocrates Health Clinic in San Diego. It's really great here and the days are full and very busy.

My job for one hour every day this week is cutting the wheatgrass for the masses. It's not tiring, and you learn while you do it.

We have three lectures a day and drink rejuvelac till it comes out of our ears. Rejuvelac is a fermented liquid used to improve the digestion of food. It's made from sprouted grains such as wheat or rye and has high vitamin E content. There's so much to learn here. We drink two glasses of wheatgrass juice every day as well as taking two wheatgrass implants. Daily exercises are part of the program too, and we begin the fast tomorrow. One holiday Mum, you and I must meet in California, and we will go through this program together. That's a must.

10th August

At the moment I am lying on my bed. I rest frequently through the day, especially while on this fast. I've just done an enema and wheat-grass implant, which makes me feel quite nauseous. It's detoxifying. My God its potent stuff! One smell of wheatgrass in the juicing room and I gag. When I drink it twice a day I feel ill for ten minutes after. On the fast, it must go straight through your system as there's nothing to absorb it. I think my body must be in shock.

Every day is a very full schedule which also includes lectures. We drink rejuvelac every hour. I've had one colonic so far (it's on the premises) and will have a lymphatic drainage next week. All this surely has to keep me off the streets and out of trouble.

Letter, 13th August 1983

Dear Mum,

The highlight of the week arrived in all its glory last night. Everyone (all being too weak to stand and mingle) gathered in a circle on chairs, and guests were asked to think about offering their talents. It reminded me of summer camp in fourth grade at school, and charades in economy on the flight here.

The first to come forward was Ester who disco danced to the tune of John Travolta's *Saturday Night Fever*. Seeing that it was only Friday night and Ester is seventy-five years old, there was something that didn't quite gel. It didn't seem to faze our Ester though; she was really getting in there, giving it her all. God only knows where she found the energy to do that – we were all hanging limply over our chairs.

Then came a violinist who produced a 'hey down hoe down' and a 'do-si-do' while we bodies clapped, tapped and nodded heads. A Mexican lady stood behind her chair and sang a song about someone loving somebody, even though they had pimples (in Spanish). Then Jethro produced his 'geetar,' and all joined in to the tunes of *She'll be Comin' Round the Mountain, By the Light of the Silvery Moon,* and *On Top of Ole Smokey,* etc.

When it was almost time to watch the video, Ester insisted on teaching everyone the polka. She ordered the chairs to the wall for more room and proceeded to dance the polka to music. I don't think she noticed that she had it all on her own and the rest of us were still hanging over our uprooted chairs. So tonight was a social night, and someone saved the day by showing the movie, *Heaven Can Wait.*

Next day now, and it's like a blessing because it's a free day – no lectures, no being in a certain place at a particular time. Today I slept in 'til 8 am, did my kitchen duty, had a colonic, signed up for a lymph drain, did my washing, deposited my bed linen and collected fresh sheets, cashed my traveller's cheques and now I'm about to do my enema. I had an hour's rest too.

Back again. Not too many people are here today, a lot went home yesterday, and the new 'first weekers' will arrive tomorrow. Being here really feels like home and everyone is your family. There was one guy here last week who I spent a lot of time with. He left yesterday, and I really miss our conversations.

I'm learning so much here … about the skeletal system, elimination, detoxification (both mental and emotional), food combining (which is superbly incredible) and pain control, just to mention a few. The third and final weeks will be a consolidation of all we have learned and revising lectures from weeks one and two, plus new lectures. I've worked in the wheatgrass rooms and the kitchen so far. We are all very weak on this strict dietary program. I've lost more weight, and a lady told me that I remind her of Grace Kelly and someone else thought that maybe I was a model. So it has been an interesting and a great week.

Another highlight of this trip is meeting up again with Lisa and Ward. There are lots of memories for us to catch up on. They were there to meet me at the airport when I arrived in San Diego and will come to visit tomorrow. They'll have a tour of the place, sit in on a lecture and stay for dinner but I think Ward will have to bring a backup supply for that.

It's incredible isn't it, that Lisa who I first met at the Eden Perfumery in Paris three years ago, lives just over an hour away in San Clemente. It seems that Time and Circumstance are weaving loose threads together somehow. Nothing happens by accident – everything happens for a reason, and I'm so glad she is here.

Most meals at Hippocrates consist of lentil sprouts, mung, fenugreek and buckwheat, greens, sunflower seeds and alfalfa sprouts with a special sauce, and raw squash – it's all varied. The sprouts are not grown in soil but sprouted in water until the sprout is as long as the seed. Apparently they have optimum value at that stage. We also have cooking demonstrations of recipes. Breakfast to date has been a huge slice of watermelon and juice of the same. I've had two colonics so far. I'm learning so much and I make notes in my journal every day.

Afton, the secretary here, had cancer in five places and couldn't walk. She was told by the doctors to go home as they could do nothing more for her. After eight months on this program she saw only a slight improvement as she was very, very sick. Now after seven years, at the age of seventy-one, she is as spritely as a chicken and demonstrates on the trampoline.

There was a psychologist here who gave one of the lectures. I thought he was about fifty, and we all stood aghast when he said he was seventy. He's been a vegetarian and later a raw foodist for fifty years, since he was twenty. So imagine what I'll be like when I'm seventy - trim, taught, terrific ... AND cute.

You must come here as I said, one holiday, we'll both meet here at this Health Institute instead of Paris, and go through the program together. Three weeks here and you become well. It's a recipe for life, and you get to live an extra twenty odd years! Pretty good deal if you ask me.

My room is great. I don't know how people manage with their enemas, implants and their rest-time while sharing a room, let alone four in a room. I'm so glad we booked a private one. It has a nice big double bed with en suite and walk-in wardrobe. There's lots of lovely greenery and flowers outside my window too. This place used to be a retirement home.

My duty next week (I chose it) starts at 6:30 am. It's better at that time, and when the duty is finished in the morning it means a relatively free day, so I'm happy with that.

Today is Sunday. I was up at eight, did my trampoline exercises (not for too long as I don't have much energy), then breakfast (watermelon and juice of the same), then I had half an hour of clean-up duty in the kitchen, which goes really fast as everything is super organised. After that, went down to iron my clothes that I'd washed yesterday, but the iron must be as old as Ester and sometimes tears the clothing. Then to the office to buy some more post cards after having received the fan mail you had posted to me.

I didn't watch the movie last night. I sat outside and talked with two of the other women here. Joan, the girl next door, just popped her head in and said that if I go to the beach this afternoon with Lisa and Ward she would love to come. Then we would come back and listen to Eydie Mae Hunsberger, who is a cancer survivor. Her lectures are really inspiring. Tomorrow there'll be an influx of new-comers when we start again with more lectures.

I'm losing more weight. I pile my plate up at mealtimes and eat in over an hour, very slowly. I didn't sign up for lunch or dinner clean up because I need the whole hour to chew this raw food. Last night friends at my table said, "You must be hungry!"

"No, I just don't want to fade away to a shadow of my former self," I replied.

I love it here. I'm going to be sad to leave, which seems to be the story of my life. I was sad to leave Paris, sad to leave Australia and now leaving here will be the same.

I'm looking forward so very much to returning, and especially to be with André again. I'm like a cat on hot bricks ... a skinny one.

Here at the clinic, I'm working very hard in these three weeks. It's just fabulous being here. I'm concentrating purely on this clinic, and even though I'll be with André in two weeks, I'm calm as calm and laid back, making the most of the NOW, and when that NOW comes over to Paris, I'll be right in there with it and that's a good way to be.

I should make this the last page of the letter as I don't want it to be too heavy. Lisa is bringing me some aerogrammes this afternoon, so I'll use them next to write my little reflections in the plane on the way to Paris, funny reflections, and leave the rest to tell you what I did with my free Sunday afternoon.

So here I am back again, much, much later. Lisa and Ward came, and with Joan, we went into San Diego down by the beach to a most luxurious and expensive international hotel where we were subjected to all the wonderful temptations of the outside world; restaurants with tempting sea-food platters of oysters, prawns, calamari and sips of white wine. Regardless of how good this program is, I'm human. I love food and wish I'd looked after my body more so I could share all that wonderful food with André. I'm off junk food forever now.

I thought Hippocrates would have turned on something special for the guests tonight, being Sunday, but they didn't. We had buckwheat and sunflower sprouts, lentils, mung and fenugreek sprouts with a tiny baby tomato and a horrible carrot sauce over it. Oh yes, plus we had a carrot loaf, and that was it. Never an entree, never fruit after a meal – the only thing you get after a meal is a glass of rejuvalac, or water two hours later. So you see I have to be strong and I don't mean strong so I won't cheat, because I never have and never will, but strong so I don't get too upset and angry and sorry when I can't enjoy what I would like to have, like steamed fish with chives and parsley sauce for example. Sometimes it gets to you, but you go the whole way because that's the only way to go. It's easier here and in Australia, but when you get out and smell those wonderful aromas, and everyone is indulging except you, well, I admit I really wish I could have something like that. But I'm very fortunate to have come this far, and I have to do what I have to do, and that's that.

So I need to find something to channel my energies into, an outlet, a hobby ... an occupation. I'll work on that leisure and accomplishment area when I get back to Paris. I know I do need that *something* that I can concentrate happily on. We have each other, André and I. I have my program, and he has his work, tennis, aikido and restaurants, and we have friends and movies, but that's not enough. I need a personal hobby, leisure, something ... ambition outside of what I will be devoting all my waking hours to. If you think of something, tell me. Reading maybe, writing definitely.

Anyway pet, we had a good afternoon. I think I'll crawl into bed with a book now, and then it's up at 6:30 in the morning to begin another full day. Could you file all my letters as you did before when I was in the States?

Back again. It's now 15th August, and I'll finish and post this letter today.

This clinic is fantastic. I'm doing well, although the detoxification the first week was so intense that I, along with most of the other guests, was very sick but that's a good sign they tell me. It's no holiday here. Some people are so very ill when they arrive and you have to see the improvement to believe it. It's really incredible. This program works. I am learning so much here.

Letter, 16th August 1983

Dear Mum,

What a lovely day it's been. André rang, and I ate my dinner in the office waiting for his call. He had rung earlier but no one could find me, so he left a message to say he would call back, which he did at 2 pm. He's so excited, and so am I. He's so funny. I said, "I want to make love to you."

"I think I've forgotten how." Was the reply.

No one in the office could understand French of course.

Your letter arrived today with the information about the coffee. There is an outlet in San Diego for all seeds, and they ship all over the world – they will even ship them before you pay if you tell them the need is urgent because these people are familiar with the program.

I called Air France in Los Angeles, booked my flight and all is set. It's a full flight, but I'll speak to the purser anyway. I've ordered uncooked food and a fruit platter for the trip, and requested an aisle seat, also baggage assistance at both ends. They said I would need to speak to the check-in guy about my excess baggage, but I'm sure it will be fine – I know it will – I shouldn't have to pay excess baggage. See ... positive thinking! That works too.

I'm getting so excited. I feel great on this program, and I believe I've learned enough of the important considerations to make my health improve even more effectively. The timing of food and food combination is great and varied.

There's so much to do when I return to Paris. It boggles the mind just to think about physically and mentally setting up my new lifestyle there. I bought Eydie Mae's cookbook and know what foods I have to go easy on and what foods to avoid.

I was in the office talking to the secretary after André called and when it was time to leave for the next class which was on beauty care, I said to her, "Well, I'm going now to learn how to look beautiful," and the guy standing behind me, who works here said,

"You can skip it then."

So I told him how wonderful he was and gave him a hug.

The atmosphere here is superb – so loving – we are all like a family. I wish the world was like this, but that's our job to make our own world loving and relaxed, however large or small it is. So there's the bell for dinner, and now I'll go and 'pig out.'

Love you Mum, I'll write again soon.

At this time I received a call from Rainey, telling me about a clinic in Chula Vista. She explained the program they used (the Gerson Therapy) was a non-toxic, natural, alternative treatment for cancer and other diseases. She wanted to spend some time there to learn more about it before returning to Paris and was very excited about the prospect. I told her it was a great idea and agreed with her decision. Her health was the priority and she would fill me in on the details later.

Letter, 25th August 1983

Dear Mum,

I'm so excited - I'm floating. I can't believe that in the last five days I've organised my life around this Gerson clinic, Totality House. Had tests done at Hospital La Gloria in Mexico, medications ordered and set to go. Spent a day at the clinic (the Gerson halfway house), studied the Gerson primer from cover to cover, studied the timetable and made it out in greater detail. I know what and when to take everything. Scheduled my five daily enemas and organised half my gear into my apartment there.

Joan is coming too, and will do the first five days with me. She doesn't have cancer but just wants to detoxify. Lisa and Ward will visit, although I don't see many free hours in this clinic's fourteen hours per day program. There's a lovely park nearby, which, it seems, will be the limit of my social activity for the next little while.

I'm so glad I've had eight months transition diet at home, and especially so blessed to have been able to study here at Hippocrates for the last three weeks. I've learned so much, it's unbelievable.

This has all happened so quickly. I talked to André to explain to him why I'm not coming straight to Paris and felt as though I took his last breath away. He literally faded away on the phone. Tristan leaves tomorrow to go back to Hong Kong, and I know André rang because he was feeling down, but he agreed that I have to put myself first at this time. So now I have the okay from all who count. I'm on such a high – it's great. I'm psychologically prepared and feel wonderful after these last three weeks at Hippocrates.

I've organised Joan into this clinic too, also two other people from here as well, and today when I called Narelle the director, she said, "I will have to put you on commission if this continues."

I really have my act together now, and a direction that is so clear and I will be forever grateful for the way it all came about.

When I spent the day at Totality House with Joan, Narelle said, "I don't know what your plans are, but have you thought of working in the field? We need help here, and eventually I would like to open another clinic."

Well, I know I'm okay, and I have a direction.

I have another appointment with the Gerson doctor in Mexico in two weeks' time, and I'll be opening a bank account tomorrow in Chula Vista. All this has happened in five days – I can't believe it. Oh, and I love my chiropractor. God, he's wonderful. He has magic hands. After my treatment, we gave each other a big long hug. I swear he has given me energy that I didn't know I had.

Well, I'm so happy. I'll go directly from here and move in on Saturday afternoon 27th. I'm ready for anything. I'm going to give it my all, and Mum, you made it all possible. I just know I'm not going to want to leave that place; it's even going to be hard to leave Hippocrates. The story of my life it seems.

I love you Mum, and it's so great to have your support. I know you are thinking of me and I don't feel alone. This is all so fantastic the way things have fallen into place.

Letter, 27th August 1983

Dear Mum,

I'm just so happy and feel terrific after the past three weeks at Hippocrates. Would you believe I feel like a different person! I feel so well. I feel healthier than anyone. I feel like I'm just bouncing and ready to take on anything. I can't believe it – I really can't. I don't know what those three weeks at Hippocrates did for me, but I can't believe the change. In fact, I lost count of the number of people who told me just in my last week there that I looked absolutely radiant – and I *felt* radiant. It's just a miracle. Never knew I could feel so fantastic. I have so much ambitious energy. I'm always doing, but I can't strain or even make much of an effort physically because I don't have that physical busy energy – it's just in my mind.

I can see ahead so clearly now - I know my direction. I know deep down what I must do, and that is why I feel so well and look so great. I've been shown my path… all the channels are laid out, and I've relaxed into it.

So here I am at Totality House, having just finished my enema, sitting on my bed ready and waiting for a healing reaction. I have learned that God gives us only as much as we can handle with his strength. Oh Mum, I'm so happy here – I look and feel great, my skin is perfect, and everyone at Hippocrates said that I was a beautiful person and deserved to get well. I made so many friends there.

Ward came up from San Clemente to help me move. Joan is here and everyone is so helpful and supportive. You must come and spend a month here. I can see myself wanting to stay. I'm truly in the right place. I feel so blessed to have been shown the way here and to be following the Gerson therapy wholeheartedly. After several years I'll go on the Hippocrates diet. I can't believe how blessed I am. This is truly divine intervention. See what the power of prayer does!

Letter, 28th August 1983

Dear Mum,

You would never believe this healing haven, it's great. It's my second day. Up at six and did my enema, I've had three so far today and will have five per day. It *does* seem a lot, but that's part of the Gerson therapy and I will follow it religiously.

I have a lovely room, and the apartment is superb and sprawling. I share it with a German lady, Rosita, who is very nice and very discrete which is what I need. We each have separate bedrooms and bathrooms.

The rooms are beautifully carpeted, spacious, light and airy. We are upstairs on the first floor and surrounded outside by lovely trees. There's a park across the road, although we're so busy with this schedule, we may never get time to use it.

I'm surprised to find that not all of the twenty-four patients here have the same positive attitude as I have. Some are negative, some sceptical.

The meals are FANTASTIC, just scrumptious! You'll see when you come. As a patient's carer you would only pay $10 per day; that's your three meals. You pay nothing more to stay in this beautiful apartment and watch the super smooth, efficient running of the place. Oh, I'm bouncing off the walls! I feel that one day my vocation might be in healing… somewhere, sometime.

It's said that melanoma patients respond best to this treatment, and please tell Karen that eight out of ten people on this program have had chemotherapy. I would truly love Karen to be here. I think of her so often and would love to go through this program with her. Is she is still writing for the newspaper?

Well here they say to eat, eat, eat, drink, drink, drink, and detoxify, detoxify, detoxify, and that's what I'm doing. We have all the fruit we want. We just go to the big cooler and help ourselves around the clock, and the variety is amazing. The director told me to eat as much as I can between meals within reason – fruit, fruit juices, soup or oatmeal – all available around the clock, to build myself up. Rebuilding she said, is just as important as detoxification so that when I DO get the healing reactions and CAN'T eat, I will have some reserves. So there you have it in a nut shell.

At Hippocrates you can't rebuild on sprouts, salads, greens, and only three juices per day and no eating between meals. Plus you detoxify slowly, lack energy and where is the rebuilding? I think Hippocrates is the ultimate diet for healthy or not really sick people. I think the wheat grass is God's manna too. We have that here at the Gerson Clinic in the green juices.

What I intend to do after *X* number of years on the Gerson therapy, when I'm free of disease and have boundless energy, then and only then will I go onto the full Hippocrates raw food program.

I feel as if it's all coming together for me and can't remember when I've been this happy, this relaxed, this focused and this directed. What a blessing! I really feel like me! I can truly see a beautiful future in every way. And let's face it, through all this experience and the whole range of feelings from thoughts of dying, isolation and fearfulness, through degrees of positivity to NOW when I'm so full of *wonder* at the complexity, beauty and simplicity of it all, it surely must be for some reason.

It's amazing. I was taken through the whole thing, from the first feelings of being told I was going to die back in December, to now when I'm bouncing with joy. I just marvel at that.

When I recall that day, nine months ago, in Professor McCarthy's office when he told me I had only six months to live and I thought I wouldn't see André for much longer and wanted to do *so* much before I died, I start to cry. I guess it's because I didn't cry then. But emotion has to come out, so I let it… I must. And then when I stop crying, or even while I'm crying, I think how blessed I am. I don't dwell on it or get glum, but let it out and push those feelings of reflection and pain toward the wonderful future I have ahead because you must not keep emotions in.

It's strange, but when we detoxify, we also detoxify emotionally, and lately, especially at Hippocrates and even at home, I would cry at the drop of a hat, here at Totality House too. I don't know why, but I know its emotional detoxification the body is throwing off.

We don't look at the little poops and say, 'Now where did that come from?' We just let it out. It's the same with emotional detox. In fact, if we haven't detoxed emotionally, then we must work on that too.

Now it's 4 pm and time for the liver juice drink … equal parts of calves' liver juice and carrot juice. It's my favourite. We have thirteen juices per day delivered on the hour. They are all different. One of the kitchen staff comes to the door of each apartment, rings the door bell, enters and places your juice in the kitchen. You must drink it there and then as it's not allowed to stand.

I have all my medications; they're all so easy, and this afternoon I'll be learning how to give myself the vitamin B and crude liver extract injections. Now I have to read more of the Gerson book, *The Primer*. I'm underlining things, and I'm going to make it my bible.

Mum, I love you for making all this possible. It's just so wonderful and I feel so blessed to be here. Give my love to Barbie and Jeff.

Excerpt from my Letter to Rainey - 29ᵗʰ August 1983

Dearest Rainey,

How are you love? Today would be your first or second day on the Gerson therapy. I think of you all the time. Do let me know how you are coping and if you need me to come over.

Your story appeared in yesterday's paper, and the response to it has been overwhelming. It's amazing how many people want to speak to you. I just had a phone call here at work from Jeannie at Hunters Hill Cancer Support Group. She told me that an Adelaide TV station called, asking for your phone number. They wanted to fly you to Adelaide to be interviewed on their program next week. She said they were hoping to get you before you left and were so disappointed. They asked if anyone else could go and I think she or Martin will be going. She said the response to Karen's article has been incredible and that she had to take the phone off the hook to go to the bathroom. Martin also rang and said he had been answering the phone all morning.

"Aren't you proud of your beautiful daughter?"

"Martin, I always have been."

Chapter 12

Letter from Lisa, 1st September 1983

Dear Yvonne,

It was great to hear from you and thank you for your warm invitation. Who knows, maybe someday we may be able to take you up on it. Thought I would write and tell you how Lorraine is doing.

I was so happy and relieved when she said she was going to this new clinic, I couldn't see how she would be able to follow such a strict program and diet in Paris. Ward moved her in last Saturday. I had to give a bridal shower for my sister that day.

I went down on Tuesday and spent the afternoon with her. This clinic is great and I am so happy she is there. They encourage everyone to eat as much as possible, and I was happy to see that.

Lorraine shares her apartment with a lady of about fifty-five years. It's a real apartment. The clinic, in fact, is a twelve-apartment complex.

I don't think Lorraine has lost much more weight and her colour is much better. You should see her at the clinic! She is so happy and enthusiastic! It radiates from her. I plan to go down once a week to see her. It's an hour and a half from our place in San Clemente. I have a few things to take down to make the place look homey.

Yvonne, try not to worry too much. Lorraine is in good hands, she is in good spirits, and I'm glad she chose to stay there. I told her that if she starts to feel sick, I would go down and stay with her for a few days. I think she will be just fine.

Yvonne if there is anything you want me to do, please don't hesitate to ask. Take care of yourself and try not to worry too much.

Our love to everyone there,

Lots of Love.

Lisa and Ward

Letter, 1st September 1983

Dearest Mum,

It's almost time for breakfast at 8 am. We eat like kings here. I've done my gentle trampoline exercises. I go lightly because my energy is being used for detox. I don't even lift my feet off the trampoline, but I do it for ten to fifteen minutes three times a day.

Yesterday after my 5 am castor oil drink and black coffee enema, I didn't think I was going to make it to breakfast. Rosita's husband, who is here to settle her in, knocked on my door when I hadn't surfaced for the breakfast hour, to ask if I was okay. I was sick, nauseous and weak after the castor oil, but it lasted only four hours. That happens every second day so one must be organised and prepared, bringing in coffee, peppermint tea, gruel and fruit, etc., the things I may need because I know when I'll be too sick to leave my room. I feel we are so in tune with our bodies here. Being your own doctor can be fun. I see a healing reaction further down the line for me. I have, after all, been slowly detoxifying for nine months now, fasting and cleansing, so...

I would love to stay here and eventually help Narelle, the Director, to run the place or to set up a facility like this in Paris. She's already put those ideas to me. She has suggested that I work with her when I'm well, to work out of this building after two years of intensive therapy, and maintain my diet and the therapy from here. But I think to set up a clinic in Paris would be wonderful.

I've opened a bank account, and when the advice comes I'll send you the account number and find out the cheapest way to forward money.

I'm well organised now – my room is like a little haven. Lisa came down to bring me the money you sent, and she thinks the place is great.

My time at Hippocrates was one of the most intensely beautiful experiences in health and healing that I have ever experienced, and here at this clinic, I'm using all that I learned there – especially the mental and emotional detox.

I'm keeping a diary of all that happens to me during the day in terms of healing and reactions, things to remember, and the daily organisation which is very important and time-consuming. It's great to be completely in charge of your return to health.

Letter, 2nd September 1983

Dearest Mum,

My energy levels are really high. I'm up at either 5 or 6 am every day. To-day is castor oil day again. This happens every second day at 5 am. Two tablespoons of the stuff followed by a coffee enema; then five hours later, castor oil again plus another coffee enema. My coffee is currently brewing for today.

I'm putting on weight and feel almost like my old self in terms of not feeling that I have a disease. One of my many affirmations that I work on daily is, 'I am experiencing optimum health and have no further use for cancer, or any functional impairment. I am healthy NOW.' Affirmations are great, and I have lots of others.

I'm working hard on meditation too, and the other night I really 'tripped out' experiencing out of body feelings and floating and just euphoria that I'd never experienced or felt before. I actually got to a point where I no longer felt in control and got scared and came back.

So now I'm working on letting go completely. Letting go of illness, worry, everything, and then finding a balance, but the letting go is very important.

It'll be great when you come in December, and I thought of a wonderful idea. When you come, you might like it so much that you may decide to stay permanently, live in one of the lovely apartments and work in this Halfway House helping Narelle run the place. You don't need to stay in Sydney for anything. This could be a lucky break work-wise and life-wise, a real change of scene. See yourself in an entirely different living situation with a different set of references. Visualise it, and it will happen. Then you could stay here, and you'd be closer to me in Paris. The flights are not that expensive. Think about it. It could be the change you need and deserve. Southern California is even more relaxed than Sydney. The climate here is perfect, and it's geographically beautiful. I think it would work. Then when I open my health clinic in Paris, you can come and work with me! Anyway, when you come you will know.

Letter, 3rd September 1983

Dearest Mum,

While writing, I'm drinking my green juice with potassium. I can't believe I'm here doing a program that is the 'Stradivarius' of all cancer treatments *and* giving myself my own B12 and liver injections. Joan and I practised on an orange before we 'shot up' on ourselves! The first time I did it, Joan would help because it was quite traumatic for me. She would say, "Okay, NOW!" and on the NOW I would stab myself. Then I'd get paralysed and couldn't move for fear. I would shake and tense up and sweat and I'd forget to breathe. Then she'd say things to calm me like, "Think of it going in and doing wonderful things to you."

Last night I did it myself, and I've really improved. Sometimes I talk to myself to be relaxed, and as I'm pressing the needle in I say mind boggling things like, 'Hey Lorraine, you're doing so well.

Everyone, come and watch her technique – so smooth - and it doesn't even hurt!'

I still have to say things like that because it's pretty weird. Last night I was standing in the bathroom with the needle in my bum injecting, and sometimes I still feel nauseous but I know it's only psychological. I thought, okay, it's time to talk to myself. So aloud I said, "Very good - for this examination in injection technique I'll give you nine out of ten."

And I'm deadly serious. Pretty soon it won't faze me. I'm doing so well. It's a great accomplishment to give yourself your own injections, and somehow doing it puts you 100% in control – complete conscious control of your own healing. It's *your own* responsibility and totally comes from your inner self, and that is so powerful. When I finish giving myself the injection, I walk out of the bathroom thinking, *I am in absolute control of my healing process. All I want for myself is coming to fruition. My highest aspirations for myself are all coming to me. I'm doing it myself, and that's incredibly powerful. I'm doing it all.*

When you begin to open up, to work with and to expect your highest hopes from the God within or your higher self ... *wow!* You sure do open the way to let it flow. I'm growing spiritually, emotionally and mentally here. It's just amazing. I can't believe just how much personal growth I'm experiencing and have achieved here. All this is really mind boggling.

Letter, 6ᵗʰ September 1983

Dear Mum,

Well, it's that time again – juice time on the hour with all the goodies. It's 5 pm and today the two people arriving from London, expressly to come to La Gloria Hospital, and who I spoke with last week on the phone, would have just touched down at San Diego airport. This lady has advanced liver cancer and last week her son William, flew to the US in desperation to search out a clinic and while here stumbled across the

Gerson Therapy. Don't we all? So when Narelle saw him last week he was literally beside himself – didn't know where to turn.

Narelle asked if I would meet and talk to him, which I did for an hour. Then the next day Joan and I got him on side, and after a short while, I have never in all my life seen hope completely transform an individual. He was still even more disoriented and would literally be turning around in circles. Joan couldn't believe this guy. I could because I know what both intense confusion, and hope in the face of potential death can do to a person. He would turn around to reach for something, (say a pen) and just keep on turning!

He went back to London, and last night I was in the main kitchen when the phone rang. One of the staff answered it saying, "Sorry, Narelle isn't here. Oh, Lorraine, yes she's here." And the man passed the phone to me.

It was William asking if he and his mother could stay here at Totality House before they checked into La Gloria Hospital, just to orientate his mum. I said that while I couldn't speak for Narelle, I didn't see why there would be a problem, and suggested they come here straight from the airport and have dinner with us. He almost jumped through the phone with joy. When I returned to my room, I was so full of emotion. Having been in the same situation, healing myself and now being able to help others in the most intense way there is, offering them a spark of hope in life. It was all so beyond me, so overwhelming and I just burst into tears.

You see, William is beside himself because he believes his mother is dying and she only likes England and her own doctor, so he believes that she won't settle in here. That I cannot understand, but when you see how all this affects some people, you must understand.

God, I would go and live in Outer Mongolia and eat sawdust if it would save my life. One thing I've learned is that not everyone here reacts as I do and I still can't understand that. I thought that when your life is threatened, you would do anything – I mean ANYTHING.

It's now five hours later, and William and his mother have arrived – they are in the wing opposite me and are just settling in. I was the welcoming committee along with Narelle, and we will see more of them tomorrow.

So I ate too much as usual at dinner tonight and am sporting what is known as 'the Gerson belly' - some days it's worse than others. The food here is so fantastic.

I'm so lucky to have the support of some good friends here. Lisa bought me a beautiful hanging plant when she came down to visit last Saturday. She and Ward have been great. Joan and I have become so close. We've shared so much together. Then there's my other friend Bill who also has melanoma. He's very nice, and so much like me in character. He's from the advertising world in New York and now lives in San Francisco. We spent two weeks at Hippocrates together, and I know he'll come down every now and then to see me when he goes back to San Francisco. Whenever I give him a big hug I feel somehow that I'm home, that I have arrived. It's weird but lovely. He left Hippocrates a week after Joan and I left, and then arrived here at the Gerson Clinic on Saturday. He and Joan went to the hospital, and when they came back we all went to the beach in his car between juices. He rings me, and we talk for hours.

It's strange, but since I've been here (and I will say it has nothing to do with Bill) I feel that my destiny is not in France and that somehow, I might never get back to Paris or to André. That thought scares me so much that I think it must be the poisons floating around in my body, or the fact that I always seem to be going another step to prolong my stay here. I can't explain it, but I will say it's weird. I really feel that, and I'm very quiet about the whole situation, almost in a weird state of acceptance if that will be the case, and whoever is going to change my destiny (whoever that Divine Being is) is also going to give me the wherewithal to slip into it and accept it. I said to Joan it's almost like I'm in a waiting zone ... and it's stronger than me.

I often wonder if and when I will ever get back to André. I don't know ... somehow at the moment I can't see it. Maybe this feeling is temporary. I don't know. I feel like I'm treading water and being prepared for something else. I love André and I want to be with him, but this is something I can't explain. I've never felt this way before. In short, it's such an incredibly strong feeling that it's all beyond me. I'll leave it open, ever hoping to understand.

Letter, 13th September 1983

Dear Mum,

I feel like I've been here forever and that everything else is very far removed. It's great; it's because I'm so intensely involved in everything here.

I have my cheque account now. Some people accumulate wealth, books etc., my forte seems to be empty bank accounts, so I'll send you the details of my only claim to fame in this country. You know, they sent me nine chequebooks! I thought, what the hell am I going to do with all these?

I talked to Narelle, and if you wanted to come and work here she would welcome you with open arms. There are several couples here where one does the program (the patient), and the other who is healthy (the carer) stays with them and works either part or full time to earn or subsidise part of their cost.

Now what I had thought:

A. When you come over in December, you could just stay here, relax and enjoy; see what's going on and pay just $10 per day for meals, room and board

B. OR you could also stay here on a holiday basis; do some part time work, i.e. juicing or general errands which would pay for much of our accommodation and food for the month, with a view to deciding what you'd like to do in the future here – if anything. You could then go back to Sydney after having checked it out and come back later.

C. OR you could come here for the duration of my treatment, although that wouldn't be practical as you wouldn't have your job at Ansett Airlines to go back to. So you would, in that case, move house and start anew – a fresh start in California. I think it's a fabulous opportunity. You would, Narelle said, work with her in this halfway house and she would guarantee you work all the time for as long as you wanted it, and I have a visualisation of you being very happy here.

She also wants to expand this clinic to the coast, in which case you would go with her. If you couldn't live on the premises due to lack of space, you would have an apartment close by. I can see you being a vital part of the program. The closest beach here is fifteen minutes away, swathed in palms, and Paris is just ten hours and $580 away.

There's a lot to consider, and I don't think you'd lose anything. I think it would be fantastic. Think about it. I can see it as a very real possibility and probably the big break you need. Or instead of moving here permanently you could come just for the duration of my stay, however long. It would be great for you and would financially enable me to stay longer.

I'm going through a period of immense creative development at the moment. I'm writing letters to TV stations and want you to send me the address of the Adelaide television station that wanted me on their programme. I can use my writing to further awareness of the alternative approach to cancer. I know I can. It can be my medium, and maybe speaking as well. I feel I'm really being shown the way to my own health firstly, and my divine purpose in this life secondly. They are both as important, but my health must come first at this time.

For some reason, France and André seem to get further and further out of my reach.

Undated entry from Rainey's journal:

Why do André and France seem never to be mine anymore? I can't explain it. I feel serene, and just like my dream I don't know what will happen, but I have this overwhelming feeling that it won't ever come to pass for us, as much as we both want it. I know I'm on my right path. Now I must stay in touch and be prepared to follow my destiny whatever that may be.

'Faith is the substance of things hoped for and the evidence of things unseen.'

Affirmations are so important. Here it is so wonderful. I'm learning to let go completely. I've conceptualised it, and now in meditation I can feel it. Through all this I can see perhaps a place for me. I'm growing, changing, and this really is a turning point in my life. It's so delicate that I can't write about it to anyone but myself, in case my thoughts stop free flowing ... being they must flow.

I truly believe we can mobilise ourselves mentally – we must, otherwise our situation is transient, lasting only as long as our new physical limitations. But as long as we are in touch with our inner self – our source – our life force, our horizons are as infinite as the life source within us.

Following the publication of the newspaper article in August, an incredible amount of interest in the program had been generated.

This ultimately resulted in a minor influx of Australian cancer patients to Totality House.

In late September, I went to Hunters Hill Cancer Support Society for the first time since Rainey had left. The room was full of people, and I was told it had been like that ever since her story was published.

Her name seemed to have become a household word among the people there. I was talking to a lady who had been recently diagnosed with leukaemia. She told me she didn't know what to do or where to go and said,

"It was the story in the paper about this beautiful girl – such an inspiration – we think she is just wonderful. My husband took the newspaper to work and did lots of photocopies and sent them everywhere – to New Zealand (where we come from) – to Brisbane – to the UK - just everywhere. Her name is Lorraine – did you read the story?"

I also met another couple, Paul and Susan. Paul had recently been diagnosed with advanced liver cancer, and after reading the article they wanted to know all about Rainey and the Gerson Therapy.

Letter, 19th September 1983

Dearest Mum, Barbie and Jeff,

I've become quite attached to my enema bucket (no pun intended). I inadvertently caught myself lying on the bathroom floor in the process thereof, resplendent with foam lie-low and pillow – attached to both walkman and bucket, grooving to the music of Ray Charles in Concert, while reading *The Cancer Syndrome* by Ralph Moss, and eating a banana. On seeing myself I was speechless, and it was further complicated by the fact that I was enjoying it all immensely.

It's there, lying on the bathroom floor that my inspirations tend to manifest themselves as they have no respect for time or place.

Being one to capture these rare moments on paper, it was all stations panic when paper and pen were nowhere in sight. Paper? Paper's no problem thought I – there's a whole roll of it here somewhere. Pen? My kingdom for a pen! The callisthenics involved in reaching for a pen at this point defies the imagination, but let it suffice to say that the process is swiftly interrupted by a most inopportune fart… Suddenly Ray Charles is a source of intense annoyance, and I don't see the flowers on my lie-low anymore.

Oh yes, such is the innate character of these precious little half hours scattered intermittently throughout the day, and each has its own story. It really is comic relief as long as you don't count de-pooping the bathroom after each stint. I mean really, one can take just so much of *La Vie Parisian*, can't one?

I feel so good and so healthy. I have an insatiable appetite. I eat, eat, and eat and I'm putting on weight. I can see me leaving here fat and happy. I go to the beach occasionally; it's only fifteen minutes away. I have a nice lifestyle here and love it. Up at five or six every morning – busy in the day on the hour with juices, medication, enemas, trampoline exercises, meditation, skin brushing and alcohol rub-downs to stimulate the skin. I also write a lot.

I just couldn't get my act together to write to André after he called me at Hippocrates. I felt so saturated, and couldn't pull myself out of that feeling to write. It was weird. I was happy, and strangely, for a while, I was on such a 'high,' it seemed that France didn't exist. I saw myself being called further afield to something else, but I didn't know what or where. I had so much going on in my mind. Then André rang me at Totality House and said, "If you ever do that again (no contact) I'll smack your bottom."

I felt like a naughty girl. Apparently he had telephoned Hippocrates but couldn't understand them, so asked his sister Renée to call her boyfriend in New York who called around to trace my whereabouts. He even tried to call you, Mum. I told André he should have been an undercover agent and that if the offer to have my bottom smacked was still open, I'd take two. I thought it was funny.

I'd really like to stay here at Totality House for a long time. I'm so happy here. My friend Bill in San Francisco rings me often. Lisa will come down again this weekend. She and Ward have been wonderful and are so supportive. I spent a lot of time with William (the guy from London) while he and his mother were here, and he's invited me to London to spend forever. He's even planned an organic vegetable garden – the works. But here I have my own space. It's great. I've always wanted this, a perfect space where I can be myself. No hassles, no intensity, just a relaxed, productive space in which to move. Here I have it.

I often wonder if I didn't have a personal stake in getting sick. I'm sure we all do – however deep we have to go to find it. Now it's a question of how I can have all this and be well at the same time. I'm working on it. It's quite a study, and I never cease to be amazed.

An extract from Rainey's journal

Here is about the only place I know where the general flow of conversation revolves around the contents of your last enema return or the reason you arrived late for dinner was that the 6 pm castor oil/coffee enema ended up everywhere except in the toilet bowl.

It's the only place I know where on castor oil treatment day, over dinner in the dining room, the air can be pierced with an almighty fart followed by a panicked exit and nose dive for the loo, emerging after twenty minutes in a whole new outfit to resume the conversation where he left off without batting an eyelid.

It's the only place I know where that kind of frivolity is accepted at the dinner table and doesn't appear to interfere with appetite ... and the food still tastes great.

Yesterday said it all: involvement in the program to the point that it saturates and permeates everything you do; the main thrust being adherence and survival through this program.

The bathroom is a haven. I've covered mine with plants. I've moved my private library from the lounge room to the porcelain top of the toilet bowl. My letter writing is done there - also my meditation. And of course, my walkman and cassettes are there too. I've noticed this in every case. It looks like the inmates here have literally moved from their apartment to their bathroom.

I had the phone technician come yesterday. I'm having an extension cord long enough to reach into the bathroom.

We were discussing the possibilities, and I said to him, "Maybe it'll be a whole lot easier to have one outlet – yeah – just put the whole shebang in the loo."

This guy, I swear, thinks this place is a loony bin.

"What! In the bathroom?"

"Sure," I said, "When can I expect it?"

"In a few days," was his stunned reply.

Then after some reflection I heard myself say, "And please make it a white one – not beige. I'd like it to match the toilet."

And the sad part is, I was serious ... hell!

A few statistics might help to put the picture in perspective. We use two rolls of toilet paper every two days – spend about five hours per day there – can't move on healing reaction days - you may never get out. I tell you, if ever I survive through this program I'm going to have to write that book! And you know what the funniest thing in all of this is? It's all true; I'm not making any of it up.

Anyway, back to the bathroom. So I was lying on the floor and had decided to relax and meditate listening to the music of Jonathon Livingstone Seagull. I'm completely immersed in what I'm doing without actually being conscious of it to the absolute exclusion of all else. So, I've got my Walkman and my enema bag and unconsciously realise that both apparatus need the same kind of mechanical organisational process to work. Both need to be set up plugged in and turned on to work. I swear on a stack of bibles that for a split second total confusion reigned. What do I plug into where? There seemed to be a total array of chords, plugs, holes and for a minute it all looked too much. But then I must have figured it out because I stuck the plastic hose in me bum, put the earphones on, released the stopper on the enema tube and waited for the music.

I'm thinking, I know there's a break before the music starts, but I didn't think it was this long, so I looked at all the tubes, cords and switches. I swear I was so confused. I followed the trail. "Fine," said I, "Enema bag, tubing, me - earphones, Walkman. So far so good. Earphones switched on..." then I burst out laughing at the whole situation and couldn't stop myself.

The other day I went down to the store and bought four plants to decorate the apartment and couldn't understand why it still looked bare, then realised I'd put them all in the bathroom.

This place is a world of its own. It's history in the making and so exciting to be a part of – smelly, but exciting.

God, it must be getting to me. I thought, tonight I need to get out of here. I need a break.

For the moment my escapes are limited to the San Diego beaches. I went down there the other night just to walk on the beach, and decided that instead of looking at the water I really preferred to be IN it, so I stepped out of my shorts and played in the ocean under the stars. I was in my element. On this programme you aren't supposed to swim in salt water but I admit the passion was infinitely stronger than I. I felt like a little girl who had just stolen a candy bar... God did it taste good!

I crept back into the clinic hoping no one would catch me. I kept thinking, now what will I say happened? A large dog? No... fell in a puddle - a big one? No. It hasn't rained around here for months. Then suddenly I was back in my apartment, and I slept like a baby.

Letter, 23rd September 1983

Dearest Mum,

Paul and Susan, are here. The welcoming committee consisted of Narelle and myself. We were waiting for the flight at San Diego airport, and I said to Narelle, "Do you realise we are here to meet people we've never seen before?"

The passengers were coming off the plane in droves, and suddenly I said, "Look that's them – let's go."

She looked at me as though the program had finally taken its toll.

It *was* them. We had hugs all round. It was so exciting. Even now I'm jumping up and down. They haven't stopped talking about you Mum since they arrived. They said they feel like they've known you all their lives.

We settled them into the apartment below mine and talked non-stop over breakfast this morning. I'm beginning to feel like a celebrity because Susan keeps saying, "And fancy seeing you in person." I think it's funny.

Well, they are a bit overwhelmed and pretty saturated with all the information I've given them: books, tapes, supplements, etc.

Tomorrow, Karl (another patient here) and I will lead the excursion to La Gloria Hospital to hear Charlotte Gerson give a lecture. If you had told me that I'd be involved in all this six weeks ago, I probably would have thought you were crazy. We'll have to start up our own Gerson halfway house, Mum.

Love you.

Letter, 29th September 1983

Dearest Mum,

Paul and Susan are now settled into La Gloria but were rather overwhelmed by the whole show. They're fine now, although they're having a difficult time getting used to the bad (that's a bit heavy), I should say, the relatively primitive conditions there. It used to be an old Mexican hotel before it was turned into a hospital. Paul and Susan were a bit … well if things aren't shiny clean as one would expect in a hospital … I can't blame them I suppose. When you've come so far only to find yourself in a fourth-class hospital, but I guess it's not everyone who can disregard their surroundings for the sake of living. The problem is that first class hospitals around the world wouldn't even consider including this program, even when *they* have no further treatment to offer.

How was I to know that Paul and Susan expected Totality House to be an annexe of a big white modern hospital? I guess the name 'La Gloria' *does* conjure up fantastic imaginative images of grandeur. I should have guessed when she donned her white gloves and that outlandish hat. Yes, they were shocked, and I couldn't help feeling that maybe I'd been a little too enthusiastic in my letter when I wrote telling the Hunters Hill group about this place.

Well, how do you expect to feel when your life is being saved? I thought everyone in this situation would feel that way. Anyway, the fact of the matter was, they were dumbfounded when they arrived at the

Hospital La Gloria. I said to them, "This program could save Paul's life. Don't worry about the colour of the walls and the carpet. You are here for the therapy. Just get in there and get well."

Well, I guess it all would have been okay if, just a few nights ago, the electricity in the hospital hadn't croaked for forty-eight hours, and Paul found himself in a fourth-class hospital somewhere in Mexico, giving himself a cold coffee enema by candlelight. But as fate would have it, he did. What more can I say?

Some people just don't realise that this program works, but I guess we all have our own hang-ups to overcome. I took nine months to get over mine. Paul was just thrown in at the deep end without a life raft. For him it was case of sink or swim ... he swam. But who the hell cares who threw you the life raft? To me, the name of the game is survival.

Mum, let the support group at Hunters Hill know not to paint this place as being fantastic – just paint the *program* as being brilliant. I must admit though, for all I'd heard about La Gloria, I too was a bit taken aback when I first saw it, but not for long. I'll forgive them first impressions – after that I expect people to concentrate on what they're here for. Not what colour the carpets are.

Now I guess I know why I've been taken through the mill when people like Paul miss the mill and go directly from the diagnosis and poor prognosis straight to Mexico. I don't suppose you can blame anyone who's had no breathing space.

I'm very tired today. André's sister Renée called me from Paris. André is panicking – he imagines me in Mexico being ambushed by banditos and sold into the white slave trade. That's what he said to Renée. I talked with her yesterday. André is apparently ... I don't know ... I don't think I realised how far we really are apart and the things that play on one's mind. I know he's worried about me. I wrote him a long letter yesterday and posted it.

I love you, Mum. Narelle said you are fast earning your stay and you aren't even here yet.

Letter, 3rd October 1983

Dearest Mum,

We have just welcomed another Australian couple, Alan and Nancy. I seem to have ranged from a tour hostess, coordinator for Susan, counsellor with everyone, and ground hostess at the airport. Also, I'm finding that I have Florence Nightingale tendencies with sick patients.

This morning Narelle asked me, "Are you sure you don't want to stay and help me run the place, or I could put you in charge at weekends?" And she was serious.

Well I had forgotten who Alan was, and said to Narelle at San Diego airport, "Here we go again, meeting people we've never seen before." When I saw Alan at the airport I recognised him and thought, *What is he doing here?* Then I realised in a split second that he was the reason we were there.

We are going to have to open up an Aussie wing here soon. When they cut the ribbon, they'll probably just use enema tubing. This place must surely be worth a book. I must admit though, the best medicine is to be able to laugh at it, in the knowledge that you are getting better and better.

Letter, 5th October 1983

Dear Mum,

I don't feel very much in the mood to write letters lately, so this typewriter shall be my incentive.

It's strange, I've developed an uncanny sense of knowing who in this place needs a lift - be it encouragement, knowledge, or just someone to talk to. I usually come up with the goods, and oddly enough my needs are always met a thousand-fold. It's amazing how that happens. I'm convinced that this must be one of the laws of the universe: you get back a thousand-fold of what you give out, whether it be word or deed. At least that's what I'm finding here. The key factor is attitude. It's a fearless giving, sometimes even in the light of lack. It's all in the attitude.

Another universal law is that if I don't turn the stove down while I'm preparing the coffee I'll have to clean the kitchen floor, and that's one law that's as black and white as they come.

And if you're wondering how I procured an electric typewriter for as long as I want, I've been visualising one in my apartment for the last three weeks and low and behold, I got it. That's another universal law, and believe me, it works. I have discovered so many incredible things in my hours of meditation, it's just mind boggling, and I can't wait to share them all with you. This atmosphere is so wonderfully conducive to discovery and healing.

My world over here runs on beautiful things like laughter, and heaps of it, constructively in all things, smiles and lots of quiet moments for reflection. There is no space allocated, in even the idle moments of the day, for anything negative. I've learned to recognise those kinds of vibrations from afar, and that's the good part. But the not so good part is that I'm a thousand times affected by it when it *does* happen. So if when you get here, you feel a 'baddie' coming - whether it's a thought, word, or deed, just smile and say, 'cancel, cancel.' They are the only house rules.

A friend from across the hall left last week, and I really miss him. He was a swami from an ashram in Canada and was here caring for his father. We had many good conversations, and he was great to listen to and to talk with. We laughed a lot together. I miss that. Some people here make you feel like you shouldn't be laughing, but those people I avoid like the plague, only because I find I have to. It's like anything else I suppose.

All in all, it's great, and I know once you are here you'll probably set up a whole new set of rules to live by, the same as I'm working towards doing. It is, I might add, a lot easier to do here … it's like taking time out from the outside world - something which I badly needed. For me, this is a little haven, and my work here is far from being finished. I believe I'll know when it's finished and before that time you'll have to put a bomb under me to move me. Even then I'd probably fall right back down here again.

I'm not ready to go back to Paris, or even into the big wide world for that matter. I haven't landed the big one on André yet. He's still getting used to the fact that 'she didn't come home when she said she would'. Quite frankly the time that I have to lay all my cards on the table and say something like, 'see you sometime in 85' or 'how about 'Christmas' 84, hasn't come yet. Somehow it still has the same hollow ring. I guess it all boils down to 'see you when I see you.'

I don't think people realise that whenever I write to André, at some point I always end up in tears at the frustration of it all. I don't think André does either for that matter. That's the only thing that weighs heavy, and I'm tired, so very tired of trying to please everyone in this whole situation. I have to decide what's right for me – Lorraine - and not make any compromises in the name of Lorraine and André. There is no room for compromises in this game. For us to be together, I literally need to beat this and live.

I've just spent four weeks watching Rosita, the lady who shared my apartment, die. And then I had to tell her husband and watch him die on hearing. I never cease to be amazed at the seriousness of this disease and the incredible suffering it brings and leaves in its wake. Now I'm crying.

When I think of André on the other side of the world and me over here at such a crucial time in just about every sense of the word ... I guess subconsciously I always think of Paris as where I 'caught it' as Madam Gaba would say, and I'm just not ready to be thrown back in there, even if I did spend twenty-five hours a day attached to my enema bucket. As long as I think of Paris as the woods into which I would be involuntarily throwing myself, then I figure I'm not ready. It's also a question of security ... but then so is cancer. I just feel so safe here, and until I have that feeling about Paris, I won't leave.

I guess if André would write I would feel a lot closer to him. The fact is he hasn't, and I'm seething mad. Then I think – bugger it, what the heck. I sweat and cry writing a letter to him, and he hasn't written to me since my birthday last year. He rings occasionally. At this point I don't accept excuses, and I told him so in my last letter. I'm tired physically, and I'm tired of waiting for the postman to bring me his letters. I don't even expect them anymore.

Carlos rang me yesterday. I was hoping that his phone call to André asking for my telephone number here would have been enough to spur André to put pen to paper, if only to tell me that he wasn't impressed with my choice of friends (like he did the last time Carlos called him in August asking for my Sydney phone number).

I was just thinking, my truly wonderful 'being in Paris moments' lasted about eight weeks, and from then on it seemed if I wasn't fighting for my life, I was fighting for a franc. André is wonderful and I love him so much, but if I went back to Paris now it would be like going back to the scene of the crime, and I mean that. I guess in the end it all caught up with me.

It's strange, I thought I was ready to go back to Paris when I left Sydney in August just two months ago, but now I find Paris is the last place in the world I want to be right now. I couldn't handle the stress or the intensity. I hope by the time I *do* get back, André will have got his act together too. There's no way I could handle his extended family problems right now. I have enough trouble handling myself at the moment let alone André and his estranged family relations, which I can well do without. I desperately need a letter from him.

My friend Bill from Hippocrates will be coming down from San Francisco on Wednesday to go to La Gloria Hospital and then to stay here at Totality House. We get on famously. He's my age but lives too close to consider any kind of serious relationship. Among my considerations is the pertinent, 'Where do you live?' If it's less than ten thousand kilometres away, they don't have a hope in hell. Twenty thousand kilometres and over, then they're up for consideration and have a fighting chance. Twenty-five thousand kilometres and they've won me ... and I don't care what they look like. Chances are I would only ever see them once in a blue moon. I bet you think I'm kidding. Just look how well it's worked so far.

Bill rings me every week, sends me letters and cards and is already making plans for a drive down to the beach between the hourly juices when he arrives. Then there was William, the one from London – a lovely guy. We spent a lot of time together when he was here. He keeps sending me beautiful letters that I almost melt over, and cards and gifts to boot, and from the man I love I've had neither sight nor sound (minus a few phone calls) since last May. If he doesn't play his cards right, I might get a better offer. You might think I'm kidding there too. Actually, any offer would be worth its weight in gold right now.

I can hear the phone ringing downstairs – I wonder if it's a lover from afar – but which one? Carlos is moving house, this time to New York. It was great talking to him yesterday when he called. He and I have one thing in common. We've moved around so much that he's now given us the title of 'Citizens of the Earth,' and it seems to fit the bill. I know he'll come to see me when he moves to New York.

William wrote in his last letter, and I quote, 'Why don't we go and spend Christmas up in the mountains in Nevada in a cabin?' He would fly over from London, so you see I'm not short of offers. I wrote back and said that seeing I'd been there and done that once before with Luke in Aspen, would he consider Outer Mongolia without me. Or failing that, if he couldn't think of anything else, could he send me a return ticket to Paris. I haven't heard anything on that yet.

Then there's Bill, who recently said to me, "Why don't you move up to San Francisco after this so we can do the treatment together?"

Hmmm ... and what treatment did you have in mind, Bill?

Hell, that's the best offer I've had in months, apart from the cabin in the mountains deal. If I'm not around when you get here Mum, just call Bill in San Francisco, William in Outer Mongolia, or failing that, Carlos in New York, and if you call Paris just lie low on the Christmas festivities, okay?

Tsk, tsk, and you thought I was just practising my cynicism for the letter I'm about to write to my friend in Paris. Actually, cynicism I don't need as such. The way I see it, when you're fit to kill, maim, or injure as I am at the moment, it gets thrown in as part of the deal at no extra cost.

I don't think I told you, wait for it – I wrote to Luke's family – a beautiful letter, if I do say so myself, but I'm not really waiting for a reply. I wonder if that has anything to do with the fact that I check out the letterbox every day looking for a letter bearing a Maryland, USA postmark. I'd even settle for one from Paris for that matter. Who says I'm fussy? It appears I'm asking the impossible in both cases.

If nothing else, we have accomplished a 'first' – a typed letter that you can read without calling in the national deciphering squad. You see, progress is being made even in the face of turmoil, and I'm speaking of the turmoil André will be in when he receives my next letter telling him I'll be going to Nevada via Outer Mongolia and New York for Christmas and that he's welcome to tag along if he can find me. Failing that, I'll probably see him Christmas '85, but not to hold his breath. I didn't realise I could be so catty. Besides, I have to have someone to pick on and talk about, and unless my enema bucket develops ears and a mouth overnight, I'm stuck with talking to the typewriter.

So, what else can I tell you? Paul and Susan have returned to the throng, ever so happy to be out of La Gloria Hospital. He went through some rough patches there and still has a long way to go, I'm sure. It was like a homecoming when they unexpectedly arrived as I was dropping the garlic into my soup via the garlic crusher.

One thing I like about this place is that there's no one to impress here. After parading like a mannequin around Paris for the last few years, I actually enjoy parading around here looking like the wreck of the Hesperus. I mean where else can one fall out of bed, fall into the bathroom, then fall into the breakfast room still half asleep and looking like death warmed up?

Love you lots Mum, and can't wait to see you.

Chapter 13

Letter, 17th October 1983

Dear Mum,

You would be proud of me. Not only do I hold the distinction of enjoying multiple credentials here, i.e., lecturing on the Gerson Therapy, initiating the uninitiated, head of the welcoming committee for the Aussie expatriates, ground hostess at the San Diego Airport (with the occasional tour thrown in at no extra charge), I've now joined the illustrious ranks of public relations officer. At least I will have in about ten minutes from now when I ring the director/doctor of La Gloria hospital in Mexico.

My mission is to try to resurrect the bad vibes between this clinic and the hospital, while assuring him that the Australians are not actually taking business from them by dividing their stay between the hospital and here, and that they can't have *all* of the money *all* of the time. I'm astounded by how much that hospital in Mexico runs on the almighty dollar.

Narelle is getting the flack, so she asked me to soften the blow by explaining the circumstances. I think they believe she's taking all their business.

Alan rang me this morning to say he was checking out of the hospital this minute, and was not staying a moment longer. The cost is astronomical and the services there are not that wonderful at times, and they seem to want to keep you there pretty much until your money runs out.

So this morning I had one irate Alan on my hands as Narelle is in hospital. I rang her and said, "Any excuse to get out of work. Either that, or it was one hell of a good weekend."

But no, she fell off her bike and broke her foot. So I'm expecting Alan around 1 pm. Paul and Susan also checked themselves out so I can see why the Mexican doctors think Narelle 'has her hands in the till,' so to speak. I'm going down stairs to arbitrate the matter now. She said from her hospital bed this morning, "If you do this, you can have anything you want,"

I replied with, "How cute is your doctor? On second thought, forget it."

Back again. That was fast work ... I must have done something right. The hospital director even said he could possibly find a way to have me work on commission for all the people I send them. I'm feeling a little cynicism creeping in here. What he seems to be suggesting is not what all this is about. It's about the fight of your life - *for* your life.

I laid it on thick, I must admit. Told him I write about the Gerson Therapy for various cancer support groups in Australia and about the article Karen wrote which was published last month resulting in the recent influx of Australian patients. Well, he grabbed that. I guess it doesn't matter who the hell I am, as long as I come good with the product. Regardless of all this, I along with so many others believe in this program and what it can achieve for cancer sufferers when all other options have failed.

The director said we could talk more about it when I see him for my next consultation ... and you thought I was just a pretty face. It just goes to show what a bit of fast talking can do. So far six Aussies have arrived – that translates into a lot of money to the hospital if they stayed three weeks. Knowing how money hungry they are, they'd probably push a quarter into my hand and say something like, 'The border toll is on us, and don't forget to bring back the change.'

Seriously though, can you imagine putting someone on commission to bring patients into a hospital? Here I can. It boggles the mind and is quite disheartening.

I've finished typing my little thesis on cancer. I really think it's great, but possibly a bit too outspoken for the media in Australia; they would probably end up toning it down if they printed it. I thought they could use the Cancer Convention in Sydney as an alibi to print it in its entirety and perhaps get away with it.

Mum, I hope you are sharing my letters with Barbie and Jeff as I don't have the time or energy to write two letters saying the same thing.

All my love.

I suppose we could understand why Rainey allowed herself to become so involved in the running of Totality House; this was her nature and she had such a passionate belief in the Gerson therapy.

Perhaps she felt in some way responsible for the Australians who came as a result of the newspaper article about her. She seemed to be their focus; her story was their motivation for going there, and I suppose they reached out for her support, which she gave instinctively and without hesitation.

Knowing that her health and remission from the cancer was her ultimate goal, I became very concerned that too much was being asked of her by the director of the clinic. I was worried that her own thirteen-hour day program was suffering. Rainey was on her own at this stage, managing her own daily routine and the time-consuming preparations without the help of a caregiver.

The following is an extract from one of my letters written in September urging her to put her health and her program first.

"... Rainey love, I must stress how vitally important it is that your all-important therapy must not take second place for anyone or anything. If you are being asked to be put in a position where this is happening, the answer must be no, and an alternative solution found that does not jeopardise your own healing program. I have felt that the arrival of Australian patients would

*put certain demands on you. I know that you are ever willing to help, but that must not be at the expense of your own program, your own health and your own goal. You must be forever mindful of your physical limitations, and your energies must be poured into rebuilding yourself. You still have a long way to go, and the help you give others must not be at the expense and sacrifice of your own program. The others have their carers, you are doing it alone and you must be careful that you do not allow yourself to be imposed upon. I know you will help others – that is your nature – but be aware of **your** needs. You must rest and not get tired running around after others and doing so much for Narelle. Your therapy and health **must** come first. Please Rainey, concentrate more on your own program and your own healing. I'll be there soon ..."*

Toward the end of October, Martin, one of our friends from the Cancer Support group in Sydney phoned me. He had written to and phoned Rainey about this as well.

"I just spoke this morning to your beautiful daughter!" he said.

"So did I," I replied, and we compared notes.

He said he had received a letter from someone at the clinic who mentioned how Lorraine was doing so much to help everyone. Martin said, and I totally agreed, that she must stop doing so much for others and concentrate on herself.

"She is defeating the whole purpose by doing all these extra things. Everyone else there has their carer, Lorraine has not," he said.

He too was concerned enough to write to her and to call her.

Letter, 18th October 1983

Dear Uncle Len,

It's really fantastic to be here. I spend my time attached to my enema bucket on the floor in my bathroom, drinking miles of juices, with the occasional little jaunt to the hospital in Mexico. It is after all, illegal to cure people of cancer in this country. Too many people stand to lose too much money.

It seems my newspaper article is reaching far and wide. The director and yours truly met two more Australians at San Diego airport yesterday, and we went down to Mexico to settle them into the hospital there. Soon after, they too became initiated into the joys of the programme. You haven't lived until you've taken a coffee enema, and according to this programme, you won't if you don't.

It is, from my experience, the only place where talking about the contents of one's last enema return is not only acceptable but educative and enjoyable around the dinner table. This place must surely be worth a book.

I must admit though, the best medicine is to be able to laugh at it in the knowledge that you are getting better and better... and I am. It's great. This whole thing has in fact, been a blessing in disguise.

Well, I have in front of me my last literary effort that I hope will grace the pages of many a journal, newspaper and magazine. The topic, *The Politics of Cancer* or *The Cancer Syndrome*. Either way, it all boils down to one thing: big bikkies.

I think of you and love you lots.

In September Rainey began writing at length in her journal about her thoughts on the politics of cancer. She writes from the heart with a no holds barred approach, some passages being quite controversial. I will include here, some non-controversial excerpts.

Excerpts from Rainey's writing on cancer

It is not my intention, nor is it the time nor place to delve into the political considerations involved in the so-called cancer syndrome. Nor is it my intention to condemn the medical profession at large; however, until we are able to expand our horizons beyond these limitations, and raise our consciousness to at least question the rationale behind closed minds that will neither entertain nor explore alternative fields of endeavour, then I fear we must be content with the five-year survival as a conventional milestone for cancer patients, punctuated with the agony this disabling and socially stigmatised disease seems to attract.

Surely the time is right to explore, in all objectivity, and with the utmost discernment, an alternative approach to one of the most unresolved crises of our time.

If we are to find a cure for cancer, it is necessary to examine all alternatives. Clearly, something radical is needed – an approach that is fresh and daring. Where will these new ideas come from? Many people believe they will come from the well-funded orthodox research centres. It is only logical, they reason, that those with the highest credentials, finest equipment and amplest research funds will make the significant breakthroughs in cancer. While no one can say with any certainty that this will not happen, it is much less likely that the administrators of large programs, at the centre of a highly centralised bureaucracy, can generate the kinds of ideas that are needed.

What is most urgently needed for problems of this kind is an abundance of new ideas, and these are most likely to come from the imaginative and intuitive scientists, innovative clinicians, or small research laboratories which have the advantage of independence, so vital to a creative scientist.

The current crisis in cancer cries out for radical solutions. People are confused, frightened, restless and on the point of rebellion against the current ways of treating the disease. The growing personal and national cost of cancer – the incredible tragedy and suffering, plus the staggering financial waste of it all, make new direction not a dream, but a necessity.

As I write, the intense detoxification taking place in my body has surely taken its toll today. It is by no means an easy road, and there are no shortcuts. Meeting the physical and emotional detoxification process head-on, in an already debilitated state, requires courage and steadfast dedication.

There is no mystery, there are no secrets to this treatment, but there are some pre-requisites to its successful implementation: an open mind, fearlessly ready and willing to learn, and a belief in the therapy and in the body's innate capacity to induce complete metabolic reversal.

I am speaking of the Gerson Therapy and its initiator, German physician, Doctor Max Gerson. His book, A Cancer Therapy – The Results of Fifty Cases, was published in 1958, but Doctor Gerson did most of his work before that time. Yet during his lifetime, and since, his work has been virtually ignored by the medical profession.

He elaborated to detoxify the body, kill the tumour masses and to absorb and eliminate them. He found a way to restore the liver, if not too far destroyed, and repair the destruction caused by the tumour masses. In his treatise, A Cancer Therapy – The Results of Fifty Cases, Doctor Gerson expands upon the theory and practice of his therapy in most elaborate detail.

If you are a cancer patient, who like me, has experienced the anguish of surgery, chemotherapy and radiation without success, I would strongly encourage you to participate in this program.

I have metastasised melanoma and a 30% chance of surviving six months to two years. I am thirty years of age. My chances are slim. My hope, my determina-tion, and single-minded dedication are at an all-time high, for I have reason to hope. I believe cancer is not just treatable, but curable.

I speak from experience when I say that the road to renewed health is long and hard for those who contemplate turning the cancerous metabolism around naturally. But then the stakes are high – in fact, the highest of them all – life in the face of potential death. And if it all seems incredulously simple, it's because it is. It is also ours for the taking and if someone, somewhere, on reading these pages is moved to see some light in a seemingly dim situation, my efforts will not have been in vain.

Here at this clinic, I see terminal patients being carried in on stretchers and walking out again. I also see people die. It is not a miracle cure per se, although the body, once given the wherewithal to induce and to mobilise her intrinsic powers of healing, will in some cases execute the miracle of life in the face of potential death.

If I may venture to add, we so often stumble across the simplest of truths, pause for as long as it takes to pick ourselves up and resume life in the fast lane, where, by its very nature, there is neither space nor time to stop. Yet we have in our midst, a power so near, that it is overlooked, a power so simple in its operation that it is difficult to conceive.

I can truly empathise with those of you in conflict, or in opposition to these statements, as I have experienced both modalities of treatment. My wish is that the powers that be on both sides, orthodox and holistic, open their minds to the fundamentals and truths of each other's approach and integrate their knowledge to find a more effective and truly holistic approach.

As I write from the confines of a clinic in Southern California, my thoughts turn to home, where a dear friend has just lost her battle with cancer. For her children, Laurie and Pete, I wish the gentle understanding and acceptance that only time can bring – and for Karen herself, perfect peace.

As a journalist in her own right, and through her writing, Karen touched the hearts of many, bringing hope, inspiration, and the motivation to question the status quo. To myself, she brought friendship and the inspiration to put my thoughts on paper and to speak out in the hope that someone may glean a little of what Karen would have us share: strength and hope – hope in the face of potential death. Hope is a catalyst – it is life's spark itself – without it, we have and are nothing. Yet, once armed with this precious energy, we have the key, the wherewithal to explore limitlessly.

Letter, 28ᵗʰ October 1983

Dearest Mum,

Your job will be here when you get here – we are all waiting for you! This will be a whole new and wonderful program of health for you too, Mum.

I'm astounded at how this has worked out. It is just a perfect situation, and we can be here sharing it together. It's a study in health for us both, and a fantastic job and scene change for you.

I haven't really had any major reactions to this treatment – not at all like the ones I had before leaving Sydney. I've had minor reactions here, and I'm writing it all down so I can hopefully see a pattern later on.

Now regarding Alan and Nancy – Alan doesn't look the bundle of health he was when he arrived. I told Nancy she had best warn the troops on the home front before they arrive back. It's strange, with chemo and all the other orthodox treatments, people expect to get very ill and suffer to a ridiculous degree, but with a natural treatment, they expect to get well – like yesterday – and painlessly. I haven't quite worked that little number out yet. Take Paul, for example. Now he expects to be able to get out of bed and walk around, in spite of himself. He said to me, "I'm not going to let this treatment take hold of me – I'm going to fight to stay on my feet as long as I possibly can."

I told him, "Paul, no you are wrong. Do you believe in this treatment – do you have faith in it?"

"Yes."

"Then you must surrender to it on *its* terms, not yours. This is no time for headstrong statements, it's a time for letting go – let go and let heal – stop fighting. Relax in the healing and trust your body and the treatment. You have nothing to lose, so give it all your energy, give it your best – just relax."

I hope he does.

This morning at breakfast, I listened to Nancy talking about how important it is for her to be here with Alan and how she could not understand the partner remaining on the other side of the world. She said, "It's the two of them in this together like everyone else her. Couples here are united, they are one. The dedication to each other is unbeliev-able ... they work on everything together. It's beautiful."

That was over breakfast. I had to leave. I went up to my room and sobbed. I'm okay now though. I wish I could feel that way about André and myself, but I don't.

Maybe I should have asked him to come here. I don't even feel as if we are together enough to ask, or hope, or even expect. I'm so damned tired of making all the moves, of pouring out my heart and feelings about all this on paper, and not getting any feedback. I mean nothing. He rings occasionally – I know he loves me but we seem to have lost all sense of communication. I know it's not easy ... why does it have to be so complicated? Why can't it be made a little easier? I'm going to ask him that.

Please, don't you or anyone else write to him. It's already complicated enough. Besides, I don't want anyone else to interfere. I sometimes think inwardly or subconsciously, that perhaps this is the way I want it. I always seem to be running away from someone, even if I don't want to. Who knows?

Here there is a space in her letter before she begins writing again with the words, 'So now you know.' It was at this point that I believe Rainey had decided to stop writing to André and to call him.

My phone rang. I answered, but there was no reply. I knew it was an international call, because of the unmistakable echo sound that was always heard. Several times I said, "Hello? Is that you Rainey?"

There was still no response, but I could hear breathing, and I knew it was Rainey. Still, she did not answer. By now I was beginning to realise that something was very wrong, so I launched into a one-sided conversation.

"Rainey, I know this is you. I know that you must be very upset and I'm right here for you. I'm just going to talk, and you don't have to say anything until you're ready, but whatever it is we can work it out together."

With that, I heard this terrible scream ... a cry that seemed to come from somewhere deep within her, from her very soul. It spoke of unbearable grief and anguish – a scream that is forever embedded in my memory and in my heart. She was now losing control of her breathing, and I knew I had to get her attention.

"Listen to me Rainey ... listen to me ... we are going to breathe together ... breathe with me ... breathe with me now ... slowly ... in ... out ... in ... out." We breathed together until she became calm enough to tell me about her phone call to André. It affected her deeply, both emotionally and physically.

I called her back a few more times that day and the next day.

Her letter continued, possibly some days later.

So now you know. I'm numb. I hurt. I'm shocked. I don't know what to say ... it defies words.

I rang André, and you know the rest. I could never in my wildest dreams conjure up a more unreal situation. I keep thinking I'm dreaming. All I know is that I have to deal with this very carefully, because I want my life. At this point I'm in control, completely, for I can choose, literally, whether to live or die. What an incredible power that is. We all have it. Having this choice makes it clear.

Letter, 1ˢᵗ November 1983

Dearest Mum,

I love you. As I write I'm preparing to make a quiet exit ... destination Paris. I hope you were sitting down for that. If you weren't, you probably are now. This is something I have to do. Trust me. I have never been so calm, so self-assured and so decisive in my life.

This is my destiny at this time, believe me. The same God who brought me here is going with me there. Send me love, prayers and light, especially for André. Some have written him off as a bad investment and maybe he is, but I'm not going there to tell him how much I love him. I'm going there *because* I love him. Someone has to make a move to salvage this relationship, to find whether we *do* have a future. Then when I find out what the hell is happening, I'll decide whether or not I want it.

I'll tell you one thing though, from here on it will have to improve if I'm going to have anything to do with it. But I want to give us a fighting chance, and that means making a move. Left to him to lose himself in his puddle of wallow, nobody gets a look in. It will take some working out. I'm going with no expectations for us; I go only to help him see the light for himself. After that, only time will tell.

I never thought it possible to love someone so much, to only want what is best for them, even if it doesn't include me. It's surely one thing to say that, but another thing to really mean it and I do ... it's that simple. It hurts – it hurts so much – it hurts more than I love him. This must be one of the biggest lessons of my life, and to date I'm coping beautifully, that is after I had my screaming fit. Hell, I was calm when I rang you.

Send me all things positive, I can't use the worry, and please, no phone calls. Don't call me – I'll call you. I mean that. I'll call you when I get there. At this point I'm so dedicated to a cause, that whatever happens will be a blessing.

My suitcase looks more like a pharmacy. My health will be fine because I'm taking the therapy with me. My schedule is worked out down to the last detail. I even have a placard to wear on my back that reads, APPROACH WITH CAUTION – GERSON PATIENT IN MOTION. Just kidding.

Life is beautiful. It hurts, but it's still beautiful.

Everyone here will tell you I'm crazy, that's why my exit will be under cover. I don't need the flack. I've talked it all out with Lisa, Joan and Beverly. My accomplices will each receive a souvenir of that inimitable city we call Paris – the city of romance, light, love and laughter. Do I hear 'inimitable' city – or how about just plain 'city'?

Just remember I am protected. I'm doing what I'm driven to do. It could never be any other way. I'll leave a note for Narelle. She's still on crutches and doesn't move around much.

Trust me Mum, I'll see you soon. I intend staying only two or three weeks or to an outside of four weeks, assuming my visit will be a welcome one. I'll call André when I get there and not before. I'll call you when I get there too.

I anticipate being here when you arrive, but I'm not sure yet. Telegram your arrival details to Beverly Smith, Apartment E (my flat-mate), she knows all about it and will fill you in when she picks you up from the airport if I'm still in Paris. Beverly said she'll be holding a sign with your name, so look for it. She is petite with short cropped reddish hair.

Everyone is waiting for you Mum, I can't wait to see you, but I have to do this first for myself. It really is not as drastic as you probably think. Since I've made the decision to go, I feel a weight has been lifted. The first afternoon and night I'll stay at Brigitte's house, and I'll call you when I get there. This reminds me of *Mission Impossible*. When I was younger I played musical chairs; I've since graduated to musical countries, and I'm not out yet. Remember I'm a winner and a survivor. My health is taking top priority. Don't worry, I'm not stupid.

I had a good report from the doctor today. I still have to get the results of the blood test, but all else is great. My medications have been modified a little. I've cut back on some things, but everything else is the same. He offered me a job at his prospective halfway house on the beach in Mexico as a consultant to the imported patients, support to newcomers and psychologist (*his* words - not mine), and said he would pay me handsomely. Please don't tell anyone – even in Australia. You know how news travels and I don't want Narelle to know that I've had an offer from them. The Mexicans recognise talent when they see it ... they're not stupid either.

Promise me you won't worry. I leave LA November 10th and arrive in Paris November 11th. That's Armistice Day. Let's hope it's the same for us too.

If you're going to follow in my footsteps, that is, play musical countries, you must first:

- Carry your life in a suitcase
- Give up any notion of a fixed address
- Collect International bank accounts, keeping them perpetually empty

- Never run out of excuses to fly to the other side of the world at a moment's notice with no money
- Learn to play dumb, e.g., 'What! You mean to say I have to actually PAY for my ticket?'
- Label yourself a 'Citizen of the Earth' with no fixed abode
- Adopt the slogan, 'Have Bucket, Will Travel'
- Attend all 'Bucket Brigade Conventions' (with bucket)
- Reply to the question 'Where do you live?' with, 'I live in a coffee shop' (without smiling)
- Always carry a valid air fare in case of a burning desire to skip the country
- Always have a valid excuse on hand to accompany the above – if not, invent one
- Always plant a lover in each corner of the world to avoid over-involvement
- Visit them regularly ... not for too long ... keep them coming back for more, then clear out
- In the case of above strategy backfiring, miss a turn, don't pass GO, and don't collect two hundred dollars
- And if you think you have the necessary qualifications to play musical countries and *win*, then you probably have a fighting chance

Between writing these sentences I went down the street to put my navy blue wool jacket into the dry cleaners. I went into the health food store to get some bits and pieces for Narelle and ran into someone I know, who doesn't even live in this 'coffee shop.' I must be really settling into the place.

Jeanie, the secretary at Hunters Hill Cancer Support Group, wrote asking me to send her pieces of information as I come across them so they can learn extra things, but quite frankly I have enough on my plate, and I'm doing only what's absolutely necessary and no more, at least for the moment. All my headspace is at present taken up with my program and my 'froggy' mate, who seems to have found himself in a puddle too deep to jump out of on his own. He's been swamped.

I'm trying to think of what else you need to know and what I can tell you before you come.

Luke's parents haven't replied to my letter. I hope they will ... maybe they've moved? I'm running out of things to tell you, so I think I'll park this little epic and head for my office ... I mean my bathroom. I don't get out much ... outside of the bathroom that is.

It'll be a long weekend in France when I arrive, so if André is going to skip town I'll wait till he gets back, concentrate on my program and enjoy being in Paris again. Really, I *am* going to enjoy this midnight flit ... I've decided that. My mental space is vitally important and as I said, I'm more in control than you realise. Actually, if the truth be known, *I can't wait.* I'll be back before you know it.

We had a Halloween party last night. Everyone came out of their bathrooms especially for it. The dining room looked fantastic decorated beautifully with Jack-o-lanterns and streamers, and all in darkness except for the candles. There were wonderful tablecloths, serviettes and ghost placemats. The cooks had the night off; they got dressed up and went trick-or-treating while we all stayed home, ate ghost casserole and decorated our enema buckets, (when they weren't in use that is). It really was great though, and I imagine Christmas here will be just as exciting.

Last Christmas I was flat on my back after the surgery; this Christmas I'll be flat on the bathroom floor with my enema bucket. This health program stops for no one, not even for you-know-who's birthday. I haven't received an invite yet, so unless He plans to hold it in my bathroom, I won't be going. Hope He saves me some cake ... how about salad? Every picture you see of Him, He's chugging away on a glass o' wine. If it's good enough for Him ...

I'm going to sign off now and make that tape for André, between enemas, between juices, between making my coffee. I make a coffee concentrate now, every two or (at the outside) three days, and use the concentrate as a base then top it up with hot and cold distilled water. On the last check, I still have a stock. I thought we could start up a sidewalk café when you come, and serve coffee on the footpath; it would probably go over better in a cup though. Have to keep some class about this outfit.

Love you lots and lots Mum and can't wait to see you. I'll talk to you on the phone from Paris next. All my love to Barbie and Jeff.

Love from Rainey FGP (The Flying Gerson Person)

P.S. I've decided to go for only one to two weeks – I'll be here when you arrive.

Letter, 6th November 1983

Dear Mum, Barbie and Jeff,

Paul passed away this morning about 5:30. We all sensed it as he had a lot of oedema and a much-extended stomach. His cancer was very far advanced. He went peacefully, and Susan can rest in the knowledge that she did everything possible for him. I'm glad he didn't linger. He is at perfect peace now. Their son arrived just a few hours after he passed away. I wish he could have been here with his parents. It would have been nice for them to have been together at that time. It certainly brings your own potential death a whole lot closer. Since I've been here, three people who I've been very close to have died. This disease waits for no one.

I think it would be good if we embraced death with as much feeling as we do birth. It is after all, a stage of life, but rarely is it viewed as such. In Tibet, the people are prepared for this voyage so they can accept and embrace it, and in doing so, complete the life spiral.

Today is Sunday and I leave for Paris in three days. This is something I must do; it's *me,* and I *have* to do this. If I don't, it will eat away at me for the rest of my life because I still have hope for us, if and when André gets his act together. That doesn't mean that I'm setting myself up for more hurt. At this stage I don't know if I could be hurt anymore. Let's just say that I *know* I've been given the wherewithal to cope at this point.

As soon as my 'froggy' mate pulls himself out of his puddle far enough to see the light of day, we'll be fine. I love André …

I really do. If my best friend or even my worst enemy did this little number… well, he has his problems. I hope when he gets through his crisis …

It really hurts you know. I'm numbed. I don't think it's sunk in yet. It all seems so unreal – so unbelievable. He must have been pretty far gone to have done this. He's playing the game called 'Let's Be the Victim.' We've all played that game at some time or other, and wised up when we realise it gets us absolutely nowhere. That little process can take anywhere from a minute to a lifetime, and if we learn how to play it really well, we even get to go out playing the same game and still be in! When you get really good at it, that's when you pass GO. But instead of collecting $200 you get a puddle (as deep as you want) to wallow in with a few freebies thrown in for good measure, like resentment, fear, anger, attack and defence weapons – a big shell to hide in, a warped perspective of the world and an even worse one of yourself. Unfortunately, that little number comes with the territory.

A part of me is seething with anger and abandonment (I actually get to play the game too on occasions), but the bigger part craves to reach out and help the man I love, whether I'm part of the plan or not. Happily, this side of the coin is infinitely stronger than the other. Good thing, otherwise we'd both be up shit creek. It's bad enough one of us being there.

I was devastated when I got off the phone with André. That seems much longer than just a week ago. My reaction was apparently an uncontrollable screaming fit, which brought people running from the dining room, to see who was being attacked. Someone brought wet towels, another an electric fan – and somewhere in the ruckus I managed to lose my breath which shut me up for a while, long enough for a cold, wet towel to be draped over my face and the fan to be aimed in my direction. After the crowd dispersed to return to their meal, someone had their arms around me. It was Beverly, my roommate. Oh, how I needed that, and to talk to you. Thank you, pet. You gave me much needed grounding and calm.

For the next two days I walked around in a daze until, as Martin would say, logic began to prevail and I began to put my plan into action.

And to think I was the essence of cool, calm and collected on the phone for 80 minutes. André answered the phone, really indifferent and aggressive, which threw me for one hell of a loop. In the end, the conversation went something like this: "Lorraine, talk to me, please talk to me."

Well, considering I'd just spent the last eighty minutes doing just that... it's hard to converse logically while numb, but I did a good job. That is until I hung up the receiver, then I totally lost it.

My feelings at this point range from kill, maim and injure, to un-conditional love. I'm calm now and have my part of the game under control. I have to this time – I can't go under this time, I know that. This time more than ever I can't go under – I'm not and I won't. Never a dull moment is there? I know I enjoy a challenge, but really this is ridiculous! Who the hell's making these rules anyway? Besides, I didn't even ask to play this game. But neither did my 'froggy' mate.

Sometimes I wonder about me. In all of this, since last December till now, I wonder why I haven't already 'gone off the deep end'. André has – why not me? I've got just as many excuses as he has. It's a question of perspective. I would have gone under long ago if I didn't look to myself for my strength.

I've just finished reading this book, *Love is Letting Go of Fear* – a beautifully written book. Yes, the source is truly within and is uniquely ours to use as we would. I'm working on it.

Letter, 7th November 1983

Dear Mum,

The lady at Air France was very helpful. I told her some of my situation when I made the booking and landed myself with three seats. She couldn't have been more obliging. I feel so much better than when I flew from Australia three months ago - so much better.

This morning I rang Eden perfumery to talk to Brigitte. I'll stay with her when I arrive. I need the space initially, and so does André. I'll hop straight in a taxi at Charles de Gaulle and head for her house, then call André the next day after I settle myself in. My juicer has already been shipped there to his house. I'm so excited ... nervous, but excited.

Brigitte will be interested in Totality House as she is also fighting cancer the conventional way. You didn't meet her. She's the manageress of the other perfumery on *Rue de Rivoli* across from the gardens in front of the *Louvre*. I don't think I took you there. I worked there for a long time back in the good old days. The other Eden shop on *Rue de Helder* near the Opera, we affectionately called the 'Sweat Shop.'

I'll be here when you arrive Mum. I mean let's face it, more than three months in any one country and this lady gets restless. Don't worry. I'm doing what I must do, and no amount of talking can change my mind. I've thought it all out carefully and made my decision. I wouldn't do it if I thought it was a stupid thing to do, and I only have to answer to myself. Now I'm going over to Target to buy a few odds and ends for my French expedition.

Bill came by last night. He knew I was worried and said if I needed to talk he was a good listener, so I talked to him a bit and he said, "If you need anything I'm here."

"I need a hug," I replied.

I didn't realise how much I needed to be held until I was in his arms. I could have stayed there forever. I just closed my eyes and enjoyed his warmth.

I wonder if there would be anyone over at Target who would be prepared to give me a hug – I wonder how that conversation would go. Well, I'm just about to go and find out.

Lisa rang this morning to check on the final arrangements for my pilgrimage to Paris. She said that all will work out for the best, whatever happens. She'll be taking me to the airport. Now I'm going to get ready for the big outing of the day – Target. I'll finish this later.

I just thought it would be perfect if I had a healing reaction over there, then maybe André would have to pull himself out of his pile of misery long enough to help me. I won't hold my breath though. I wonder what other little goodies will be pulled out of the hat for me before this little number is through. I like surprises, but this is verging on the ridiculous.

I would write something funny like in my previous letters, but somehow, I don't find this situation laughable. I have kill, maim and injure symptoms at regular intervals. At other intervals, I say very calmly to myself, 'Who the hell gives a stuff anyway?' Then further along the line I feel sorry for him, or for me, and the unconditional love that usually grabs me at the most inopportune moments fades more often than not to conditional love.

All in all I'm handling my end of the bargain well, even though at this point I don't even know whether it's still my bargain to handle. I'm working on it. Remember no phone calls – I'll call you. Now I'm going over to Target to charge a hug.

Well, I'm back. I stood in the men's wear department with a sign that read, 'Hugs - six for a dollar' but nothing happened. I leave tomorrow. I can't wait!

I love you Mum, can't wait to see you in two weeks' time.

Rainey did not make that trip to Paris. At Lisa's house on the day before her scheduled departure, she decided to ring André to say she was coming and to tell him what flight she would be on. His response was that he would be out of town and did not want to see her. It was another devastating blow, and she writes of her feelings at that time, of shock, complete abandonment and despair.

In retrospect, even as painful as this was, I believe her decision not to go was a blessing in disguise.

While compiling Rainey's story I had written to Lisa asking her if she would write her recollections of that time and of her time in Paris with Rainey. The following is part of her reply, which includes her

memories of this particular episode. Lisa's full letter is recorded at the end of this book.

"... now my memories in California.

Ward and I met Lorraine at the airport when she arrived in San Diego. I remember visiting her at the clinic where she was staying to fight cancer. She was fighting so hard. We visited her often, and I took her some things for the apartment to make it look homier.

Then, one day she tells me she is going back to Paris to see André. The day before she was to leave, she was at my house and I was going to drive her to the airport. She called Andre to let him know she was coming and he told her he was going out of town and did not want to see her. She was going to go anyway and wait for him.

I had to work hard to talk her out of going. This would have been the worst thing for her, and I was afraid the trip would kill her. I finally had to get mean. I told her he did not care about her. If she had a friend who called to say they were coming to see her from another country, wouldn't she change her plans? She agreed that she would. And here this guy wasn't willing to do that. He did not care about her. She was in love. He was not. I had to keep talking and working on her. Finally, she agreed it would not be a good idea to go to Paris. Of course she was devastated. Later I drove her back to San Diego."

While going through Rainey's papers to compile this book, I found the following letter written in English, together with an addressed envelope. I don't know if this was a copy of the letter she had posted to André or if it was the original letter - written but never sent. The following is part of that letter.

You are a beautiful person André. You deserve so much and you will have it, you surely will … not by virtue of where you come from or where you have been in your life, but by virtue of who you are.

Who are you? Do you know? Have you ever taken the time to find out, to get close to yourself? Have you ever taken five minutes to yourself and for that time to let go of the guilt, the remorse, the grief, the pain and incredible sense of loss that has been your life until now?

Take five minutes and set free those feelings that control your life. Allow yourself this time of complete freedom. Just five minutes. Feel it, believe it, know it – you will notice nothing's changed. Tristan is still there; you love him just as much. In fact, you will probably find that there is now more space, more room in your being to love him even more than before. Every time a feeling of loss, grief, pain or fear shows itself, take it and use that energy instead, to love your son and to love yourself.

It is a question of channelling. At this time in your life all your energy, all your thoughts are being channelled into pain, confusion, fear, grief, loss … and for what? In that you have no space to love yourself – no space for peace of mind? Is that where you want to be?

André, you will only find happiness when you find harmony within yourself, when you reconcile the unresolved feelings within you. Let go of them. You don't need them. They drag you down. They drag you down so far that you can't see the road ahead. You will not find solace in other people, other diversions, no matter how fast you run, how hard you play, no matter how deep you bury yourself there.

We can choose which movie we watch André; believe me, we are the director, the producer, and we write the scenario, giving ourselves the lead role. If you are tired of watching this movie, then write another one. The choice is yours.

Look at me. I am in crisis at this point in my life, and something has finally manifested itself, something that is crying out for attention – crying out to be noticed. There comes a point when we can no longer ignore what is actually happening within us. You are rebelling. My body is rebelling against me. You can interpret this however you want to. The fact exists that we can either choose to act or we can choose not to. It's not an obligation.

These past ten months for me have been a period of great introspection. I was forced into it as a matter of life or death. My choice was to live, to re-evaluate my thinking and my attitude. I have been holding in my anger, my hurt, and my pain for a lifetime André, and now I am an expert. I have developed this over a period of thirty years – burying it all, locking it away. I threw away the key long ago and have become so adept at it that I'm not even aware that it is happening.

You know I have two choices at this point. One is to lie down and die; it's crossed my mind. My God, I have that power in me at this point in my life to die now if I want! If I decide that, then that thought that fires my action is the reality. The action is only an image. If we change the thought, we change the outcome. We are only a projection of our thoughts.

I am not a philosopher, but I am stating a truth. Your battle André, is within yourself. Your battle is not with Nicole, her husband or with me. Take charge of your feelings. It doesn't mean that you must be in control, it means you must let go.

To you, I am life-threatening. In me you see perhaps a potential reflection of the last ten years of your life; you loved, and suddenly I am on the other side of the world, like Nicole and your son. And even more, I am a risk to die. Maybe that is why you appear to have labelled me a potential source of pain, loss and grief, 'No more! I can't support it.'

What do you do? Rebelling against yourself is not the answer; neither is running away and finding temporary escape or losing yourself in other people or situations. Do you really think that cutting yourself off from the one person you love in this life IS? It won't stop the hurt.

Let me tell you something. You once said that the last ten years of your life seems like a dream. Well, let me tell you that it IS a dream – you are right. Life is an illusion André, it's an image, it's a dream. The only reality is thought itself. Change the thought, and you change the dream *and* the reality.

Remember the day we saw that poster at the bus stop, and you said, "Tristan would like that."

"How will you get one?" I asked.

And you replied, "I always get what I want." Think about it.

At this point in my life I have a choice: to be buried or to stand up and fight, to face myself. André, you have the very same choice, for it is our thoughts that create our reality. I am responsible only for *me* at this point.

I care so much for you André. I love you so very much and want you to know that I am there for you if at any time you need to talk.

Chapter 14

I had accepted the position at Totality House and in November flew to San Diego to be with Rainey. It was a heaven-sent opportunity to be able to look after her and work in the clinic to pay for her therapy. I was in awe of her courage and strength of purpose and of how she had handled the previous three months without assistance, especially through the recent turmoil and heartbreak she had endured.

The days were very long, and I quickly settled into my busy routine. I was also instructed on how to operate the juicing machine by the young Mexican couple who were employed to do the juicing. It was constant, as the thirteen daily juices had to be delivered to each of the twenty-four patients on the hour.

Letter, 12 December 1983

Dear Barbie and Jeff,

Wishing you lots of joy, love, happiness, cheer, food and grog – nuts pudding and gravy, chippies and lollies on this Christmas day – the anniversary of our Saviour, 1983.

Meanwhile, back at the ranch – or should I say the 'looney bin' – I mean where else does one celebrate the joys of this, our Festive

Season, with five coffee enemas, thirteen juices, a baked potato, steamed carrots and cabbage, sprouts and salad, with an apple for dessert, or a banana or a pear? Those of us, who have earned our graduate status, shall revel in four ounces of cottage cheese; and WAIT FOR IT… yoghurt on their baked potato! My God – the Gerson Gourmands!

What do you mean this place is no fun? All I can say is thank God for the thirteen juices because, by the time the next meal comes around, we can't eat a bloody thing! See — there are occasional blessings in disguise.

Christmas this year is like the Christmases I've spent in France. The one with Madam Gaba was about as exciting as Pitt Street in Sydney on a Sunday; and if Lisa hadn't have whipped off the cap of a gendarme at midnight on New Year's Eve (only to be chased by same down the *Champs Élysées*) we would have had an uneventful Christmas.

Then the other Christmas when I spent a wonderful, sumptuous weekend with my heartthrob of the era, Marcel, on the Riviera at Toulon. That was dreamy – I really loved that – he was a beautiful guy. Then last Christmas … well, you know about that. This one, we will be spending in the land of hamburgers, hot dogs, ketchup, plaid pants and roller skates.

After these last eighteen months, I want to fly away to some peace and quiet, away from trauma to a change of scene. I plan to go to Capri for a while – I'll work there and just soak up the sun, the smiles, the sea, and the sparkles and do some writing. I don't want a big city. It's too much hard work – too tense. I just want some lovely safe place … an island away from it all will be fine. It costs $350 from New York to Rome, and I know enough people on Capri where I can work for six months and take six months off – that's how it is on Capri. Then I want to work in healing somewhere in the world. Australia needs it badly. I need a break before I do that, so that's my goal.

When my world crashed around me a month ago, I was desperately lost and numbed; I still hurt. I wake up some mornings thinking I've been dreaming – it's too much. I needed to hang onto myself and then sometime later I needed a goal. Without a goal, especially in my situation, I asked myself, why am I doing this therapy, so I can do WHAT exactly? If you see my point? I need to know that I am working toward something. So that's my mountain, and I'm climbing it.

This year will be a very sober Christmas – yes, even more sober than mine was last Christmas, and no, that doesn't mean to say we won't be having one, we will. We'll have a little Christmas tree with my tall, dark and handsome man tied to its trunk and a card around his neck that says, "To Rainey from Santa." See what you get when you write him letters? He wrote back and said Rudolph went in for his 50,000 mile grease and oil along with the rest of the clan, so guess what ... he's walkin'. Says he'll hit Sydney around Easter, so he and the rabbit have done a clean swap. I bet they have already put up the tree in Martin Place. 'Ya win some, ya lose some.'

Now I'm on the loo. My back is killing me – the pain is referring like crazy – it must be some tension that I thought I'd dealt with in all of this turmoil. It's freezing my back up. Not to worry, a few contortions with the chiropractor should do it. Hope he gives me a few adjustments while I'm there too. He's quite a bit older than me, so I told Mum already that I saw him first. I'm going in for the kill and then failing that, Mum can try her hand. (Just kidding.)

William called and wanted to send me a ticket to London for Christmas. Failing that, he said he would come to the states mid-January to see me. I cried when I got off the phone, wishing that André would have cared even half as much to send a letter. Well, there will be no more long-distance relationships for me. I'm burnt out.

The good news now. Lisa is pregnant! They are so excited they're bouncing off the walls. It's great. They will come down to visit on Saturday. Joan rang to say that she and her boyfriend will be going to Catalina Island (just 25 miles due west of LA) where an ex-bucket brigadier lives with his Norwalk juicer and family.

Next Sunday we are all going on an excursion to the zoo in a van complete with a Norwalk juicer. God, the animals will think all their Christmases have come at once when they see us. I wouldn't miss it for the world. I'll take photos. It will be history in the making – a real first. Who the hell would be silly enough to do it twice?

We are thinking of you and love you both lots. Merry Christmas and have a lovely day. You are with us in spirit.

Love,

Rainey

Rainey kept a journal in which she recorded her dreams. Here is one of those entries. It was dated 11th January 1984.

I dreamed I went back to Paris to my apartment. I was confused as to how many rooms it had. I thought it had only one, but I found more, two or three, and in one there was a gift from Denise – a tall plant in a pot with a personal note, but she didn't say anything about André.

In one of the rooms was a young child, a little girl. She must have been waiting there in that room for a long time … alone, lost, sad, and forgotten. When I entered, she came to me. I didn't know who she was at first. But I knew that she belonged to me, that she was an intrinsic part of me that I must have left behind. She was a pathetic figure, empty, sad, alone, but filled with so much beautiful warmth and love. She put one hand on my stomach and the other on my back. It was as if she had been waiting for me for so long, broken-hearted, helpless, but when she saw me, it was like she had come home.

It seemed she was a part of me – the child I had lost. It scared me at first; it was eerie, but her warmth and love dissolved that feeling and it became a beautiful reunion. She seemed to know more about it than I did. She had obviously been through incredible suffering, and I could feel innately all that she felt. It defied words ... there were none. She had so much patience, so much love and warmth. It's hard to put an age to her. She had a beautiful innocence, even amid her suffering. I think she was seven or eight and made of pure feeling.

About a month after I had arrived, Rainey began experiencing acute pain in her back. She couldn't sleep, and nothing seemed to give her relief. I called her doctor in Mexico and was told it was only muscular, but found that very hard to believe given the circumstances. I began searching the phone book for an acupuncturist in the area. It was about 8 pm when I rang Jacques MoraMarco, and he came with his wife, Jill. After he had treated Rainey, she was able to sleep through the night without pain.

That meeting was the beginning of a lasting friendship. Jacques came to the clinic several times to give lectures. Both he and Jill were very supportive of Rainey, and I could call on him at any time. He continued to follow her progress, treating and advising her over the following months. Jacques was an incredible support to us both, and for that, I will be forever grateful. He and Jill were to play an ongoing part in our lives, and even now they remain dear friends.

Today, Jacques is Dean of the Emperor College of Oriental Medicine in Santa Monica, California.

One morning after Rainey had showered and dressed, she sat on the side of the bed and said, "Mum my legs won't work, and I have pins and needles in them."

She couldn't walk. It happened so suddenly while we were getting ready to go to Mexico for an appointment with her doctor. Someone carried her downstairs to the waiting car.

After the consultation, I went back into the room because I was not satisfied with the doctor's findings and had more questions. I asked him to speak to me, not as doctor to patient, but as parent to parent. I began by asking him questions, "Do you have a daughter? How old is she? What is her name? What would you do if Emilia was in Lorraine's situation?"

He didn't answer straight away. He gave me a thoughtful look, then said, "I'll be honest with you. We have done all we can here for Lorraine. Her cancer is now moving up her spine towards her brain when the pain will become excruciating. Lose no time in taking her back to UCSD hospital where they have every modern facility."

He arranged to have an ambulance take us back.

At the border station, the ambulance was stopped and pulled aside. It was thoroughly searched, and the driver was taken for questioning for over an hour. I pleaded with them to let us through, but they were in no hurry and we were losing even more time.

When we finally reached UCSD Hospital, Rainey was admitted to Neurology, and after being examined was told she would never walk again. At first, she would not accept this. She was determined to walk again and struggled day after day along the parallel bars, refusing to give up.

In the months that followed, she was admitted to UCSD Hospital on several occasions where she became a familiar face to many of the medical and nursing staff. They would often come by her room just for a chat. One day a nurse drew me aside and said, "I've never seen anything like this before; I've never seen so many doctors and staff members take such a personal interest in a patient. It's most unusual."

One morning, a group of interns came into the room on their regular rounds and were chatting together with her. I heard her say, "Yes, I know I'm being treated palliatively. Thank you, but I'm going to prove you all wrong. I will win this battle, and I will walk again. You'll see."

Journal entry, May 1984

I have been told twice now that I have only six months to live, the first in Sydney in December 1982, and again now, May 1984. I sometimes thought, in what seems another lifetime, what I would do if I were ever given this information before the event. Would I tell my family, my friends? How would I react, and what would I do with my time? I thought I would run as fast as I could in the opposite direction, snatching as many unfulfilled hopes and dreams as I could along the way. I must admit it never entered my mind then to look at the situation squarely and fight tooth and nail for my life.

My thoughts wander for a moment and find themselves in Paris, that legendary city of light, love and laughter and my home for three years. Afternoons would find me in the Latin Quarter. How best to immortalise my memories of this fair city?

My thoughts are running a mile a minute. I remember it well. Sitting in a café, I had just finished another café crème, and with the biting cold wind that December in Paris brings, I headed home along the Quais de la Seine. Next day at 1:30 pm I would be winging my way to Sydney not suspecting that forty-eight hours later I would have already undergone major surgery at Sydney Hospital, and would be told I had six months to live.

But in that moment, I knew nothing of this and was already planning my return to Paris. My work there was secure – I had managed to renew all contracts with my companies – Fiat, CBS, Van Cleef & Arpels and Minolta. I smiled to myself as I remembered 'the infamous seven' ... my class at the Fiat Company, just the day before my departure when they announced that their class had been cancelled, and in its place would be a champagne Christmas party. It was wonderful – they were wonderful - and so were the Christmas decorations along Boulevard Haussmann – an intoxicating mélange of colour, music, movement and light. The huge strobe lights strung high above the Boulevard gave an almost surreal, magical effect. A child at heart, I revelled in this, wished the whole city a 'Happy Christmas' and floated home to do my packing.

I was not aware of Old Father Time at my heels. Had I mistaken the light dancing from his scythe for the runaway Christmas lights in my imagination? And had I heard him say that a little more than a year from now would find me in a hospital bed in San Diego listening to my neurosurgeon telling me gently that I would never walk again and that I probably had at best, six months to live? No, I knew nothing of this.

Now, I'm trying to walk again along the parallel bars, trying to sit and to stand. I'm learning to adapt to my new situation, but more importantly, I'm learning to live in the moment, to give my best to it and to move forward.

TIME.

Time asks no questions
Avoids no problems
The cold truth unfolds with seamless ease
Devoid of reflection or sentiment.

-Lorraine, 1984

Letter to a patient in Totality House, May 1984

Dear Loretta,

It was lovely talking to you on the phone this morning while Beverly was visiting me. In fact, being in this hospital has almost been for me, a stolen holiday and has pepped me up when all the old friends visit and bring with them so much love and encouragement. It lifts me high enough that I feel so different – lighter, uplifted and stronger. I can feel that strength and positivity being roused deep within me through the wonderful interaction with our friends, then I work at cultivating that within myself as my own fortress. But I know I need the support – me, who has always been so self-sufficient and independent of others.

I loved sharing thoughts and feelings with you this morning; especially to know that for all our clamouring and grasping for light, love, life and health, that at times to have feelings like, 'How can I go another step? Where is the energy? I have none. Wouldn't it be a whole lot easier to roll over and slip out of this life?' ... at those times I try desperately to be excited about whatever I would like to do ... to be. But then these moments melt in the wind. I'm too tired ... I'm just too tired. But Loretta, I allow myself those feelings of anger and frustration and I don't reproach myself as I no longer find conflict in those feelings of pure exhaustion and emptiness. I try not to wallow in them either, but rather accept them as normal and move on.

March of this year found me paralysed from the chest down due to a tumour on my spine and intensive radiation has not changed my situation. I tell myself that I will walk again and that I will live, and that in due course I hope one day to share my story in the hope that it may inspire and encourage others travelling the same path. However, it would seem that the odds are stacked heavily against me, so unless my shoulders suddenly sprout wings, it feels like I'll be grounded for a while.

If our situation is an inexplicable intensity, then so too must our emotions be, and that's okay but we must have a greater goal and know it will be ours. We must believe in it, expect it, and settle for nothing less than our highest aspirations for ourselves. You can do it Loretta. I can do it, and we will.

I have included with my letter, a little book that has given me motive and new insight into what I can do for myself and how to do it. It has been a real source of inspiration for me and I'm happy to share it with you. Please know that you are in my thoughts and prayers.

Much love,

Lorraine

In July, Barbie came over to spend some time with us. It was wonderful to see her and for the three of us to finally be together again. Soon after she retuned to Australia, Rainey was admitted again to UCSD Hospital.

As before, I was allowed to sleep in her room. One morning she said, "Last night I was so afraid ... I was struggling to breathe." When I asked her why she didn't wake me, she told me she didn't want to worry me. As the days passed, her pain was becoming intolerable, and the doctors increased her doses of morphine. I was with her day and night. One day she asked, "Mum, God won't give me more pain than I can handle, will He?"

Against such insurmountable odds, I still clung to the possibility ... or was I beginning to question my faith and belief that she would be well? This time in the hospital, my thoughts were very disjointed. I remembered a conversation we had ten years earlier when she was home from teachers' college for the Easter holidays. One day we were sitting quietly together when she said, "Mum, I wonder who will go first."

Thinking I had forgotten an appointment, I asked, "Go where, love?"

"You know Mum. Who will die first, you or me?" I was so shocked to hear her say that.

"Of course, I will go first. You are young; you have your whole life ahead of you. Why would you even ask such a question?"

Very seriously and very quietly she had replied, "Mum, I don't want to be last; it would be too painful to be last."

My tears are flowing now as I write, remembering that time. In retrospect, it was as if she had a glimpse into the future. Her fascination with TIME and her thoughts of dying ... I didn't realise before going through her diaries and letters, and my recollection of conversations in the past, but I feel she knew on some intuitive level, even back then, that her time would be short. Is that why she lived her life to the fullest, especially in Paris? Striving to BE and to LIVE and to experience as much living as she could? And is that why she held onto life so tenaciously at the end, against such insurmountable odds – not wanting to cause ME the grief of being last?

My thoughts were running riot. What are we doing here? This is not where we should be. I should have taken her home months ago to be with Barbie, and now it's too late.

Several months previously she had told me that she didn't want to go home because she saw that as a failure, to return home still fighting, and losing her battle. From previously going from strength to strength and inspiring others to overcome and win their fight against this terrible disease, how could she now help others in her present situation? She felt she had to keep on fighting, to win, and be able to continue to support and motivate others on this journey.

The days passed, and I was always by her side as I watched her body become weaker and her spirit quieter. One day she roused to ask me, "Are my guides here Mum?"

"Yes, love, they are at the end of your bed,"

"Can you see them? How many?"

"There are three," I replied.

She smiled.

On August 2nd, 1984, I held Rainey as she left her earthly body, and slipped quietly out of this life, to continue on her soul's journey.

Everything moves in time and space. The clock ticks, the pendulum swings punctuating time continuum, even the air we breathe continually moves around us. But for this moment, listening to Rainey's last breath, time stood still for what seemed an eternity. There was no movement, no sound. It was as though the very air was frozen and I became far removed from the scene … as if I was viewing it from a great distance. There was total silence, then a loud swishing sound … and I left with Rainey.

Together we travelled swiftly through time and space … where time had no meaning … where the silent void became a wonderful eternity and peaceful beyond description. I was with her, and I would never leave her.

Then suddenly I was jolted back to reality by a loud voice, a friendly voice, as if announcing a popular guest speaker.

"Miss Lorraine Walton!" and I was immediately back, sitting by Rainey's bedside.

Looking up, I saw that the room had somehow changed shape. It was now very long and narrow, and in the distance I saw a white coated figure enter in slow motion, very slow motion. The figure seemed to take forever to reach the centre of the room where it stopped, and all was silent.

Slowly the room recovered to its normal size, and I recognised the figure in the white coat. It was Rainey's neurosurgeon. He often dropped by her room just for a chat. I rose from the chair and heard myself say, almost accusingly, "You are too late! She left several messages for you to come and visit, but you didn't come, and now you're too late … you're too late!"

It was only in that instant that the reality fully registered. My knees buckled, I sank back onto the chair. Then he was crouching down in front of me, speaking to me, but I didn't hear a word he said.

Later that night at Lisa's house, I stepped outside into the cool night air and looked up at the night sky. I had never seen so many stars – billions and billions of brilliant, gleaming, twinkling stars – so close I could almost reach out and touch them, and for a moment I didn't feel alone. I felt somehow connected to those stars. They seemed to be darting around and having excited, animated conversations, perhaps welcoming Rainey home, and I felt a real part of their excitement.

"I wonder which one of those stars is my beautiful Rainey? I know she is at peace now – no more pain – but she has gone. I will never see her again. That was the unbearable reality; I would never see her again, and my grief knew no bounds. I sobbed for her incredible courage and dedication. I sobbed for her grief in the loss of her unborn child and for the loss of her one and only real love, and I sobbed for Barbie on the other side of the world and longed for her to be with me and to feel her arms around me.

Then I heard Rainey's voice, so clearly, and once again I was back re-living that Easter long weekend ten years ago, and hearing her say, "Mum, I don't want to be last. It would be too painful to be last."

Time and the passing of the years do much to soften and temper the pain of grief. The heart still aches, and the sadness remains, gently tempered by the beautiful and happy memories that Rainey has left us: her laughter, wisdom, humour, thoughtfulness, and her love.

"*Death teaches us (if we are prepared to listen) that the time is now. The time is now to pick up the telephone and call the person you love.*

Death teaches the joy the moment. It teaches us we don't have forever.

It teaches us that nothing is permanent. It teaches us to let go ... there is nothing you can hang on to, and it tells us to give up expectations and let tomorrow tell its own story because nobody knows if they will get home tonight.

To me, that's a tremendous challenge. Death says, "Live now," and I know we have a lot of living, loving and learning to do. We must live in the moment."

-From 'The Joy of the Moment' by Leo Buscaglia

Epilogue

*K*nowing how much Rainey loved nature and the outdoors, I chose a serene space in the beautiful grounds of San Diego's Greenwood Crematorium for her final farewell; a gazebo jutting out over a lake that was covered in lilac coloured water lilies. She would have loved that, especially all the ducks that came to the service uninvited, swimming between the water lilies. How wonderful! Rainey loved ducks.

We scattered some of her ashes on San Diego Bay. Jill and Jacques had hired a sailing boat and its crew, and with Lisa and Ward, we sailed out at sunset. Rainey loved sunsets.

The next day Jill, Jacques and I were walking along the beach when suddenly Jacques stopped and said, "Let's go in and swim for Lorraine."

Without hesitation, fully clothed, we ran into the surf.

"This is for Lorraine!" he shouted. What an incredibly joyful feeling that was. It was as if she was right there with us, revelling and playing in the waves. That magical moment will remain with me forever.

I felt that I could not go home yet; I wanted to fulfil Rainey's wish. At Totality House one day, she had said to me, "Mum, when I get well, the first thing we are going to do is go to Yasodhara Ashram in British Columbia. I want you to meet Swami Sivananda who was here caring for his father. We had many long conversations, and I was so grateful for his friendship and guidance."

I spent three months at Yasodhara Ashram in Canada, on the shores of Lake Kootenay. Swami Sivananda met me at the bus station, and as we neared the Ashram, I was moved to tears on seeing the beauty of the scenery. It took my breath away, but Rainey was not with me to share it.

Those three months were the healing time and space I needed. I attended daily prayer meetings, made some wonderful friendships, and Swami Sivananda was my guide and mentor. I worked with others in the orchard picking the fruit, in the huge vegetable garden tilling the soil and gathering the vegetables for the big kitchen, and I was there to witness a cow give birth to her calf.

There was time to walk through the beautiful surrounding woodland down to the water's edge of Lake Kootenay, and this was my favourite time when I could be alone. The Ashram was my healing haven where I slowly began to find some semblance of calm, peace and acceptance.

I remembered nothing of the long flight home, only Barbie's arms around me at the airport. It was wonderful to be with her again. I was home, but Rainey was no longer with us.

Barbie, Jeff, David and I scattered some of Rainey's ashes from a boat at the Heads of Sydney Harbour – a very special time for Barbie – a time for her and Jeff to say their own goodbye and for David too. I scattered the rest of Rainey's ashes on the River Seine when I returned to Paris in 1986. I think she would have liked that. She did, after all, call herself a 'Citizen of the Earth.'

Addendum

The following two letters are from Lisa and Suzi on their recollections of Rainey.

My Dear Yvonne,

I am finally writing to you. I'm not going to let myself up till I'm done. I have been thinking about my time in Paris since I received your first letter. I just didn't know what to write. It was another life, another time, so long ago. Ward and I will have been married for thirty years this August. When we spoke on the phone, you sounded so much like Lorraine. She would always say 'lovely,' or 'uh huh,' when agreeing like you do. I suppose it's an Australian thing.

I just received your second letter. It did help to jog my memory, so here goes. I will just jump around and try to tell you what I remember of my time with Lorraine.

I met Lorraine at the perfume shop. That's right, it was called Eden. Monsieur Ricard hired girls that spoke different languages. Denise was also working there. I think most of us were illegals. The Argentinian girl would always tell us that if the *gendarmes* came into the shop, we had to hide in the basement. I think we worked six days a week and eight to ten-hour days. I think I was paid two dollars an hour.

I don't remember how we found Madame Gaba – I think we answered an ad. It turned out that she knew Monsieur Ricard and he vouched for us. She only wanted one person, but we said we came as a pair.

Madame Gaba was old and crabby. The room we shared was the one she had shared with her husband when he was alive. Lorraine and I used to laugh because the mattress was worn down on both sides and there was a huge mound in the middle.

Living with Madame Gaba became very difficult and we couldn't take it any longer. Lorraine found a studio on the eighth floor, but it did have an elevator. It had a beautiful bathroom with a big bathtub, a living room and a small kitchen.

At that time I had a student visa, so I was legal to live there and I think Lorraine had a work visa. Together we made one legal person. I must have been tutoring at the American school because it was the only way I could have paid my share.

During this time we met the Iranian boys. I remember we did joke about them being our hostages. I met Ward in the spring of '81. He was not comfortable being around Iranians because of his clearance and his job at the Embassy, plus he had friends who had been taken hostage in Iran. I ended up breaking away from them because I wanted to see Ward.

Somewhere during this time, Lorraine finally told us that she was fighting cancer and having chemotherapy. I remember that I had talked Lorraine into letting me go with her for the next treatment; it was a rough taxi ride back. She kept throwing up. I could not go again because I left town with my parents. They had come with friends for a visit, and we were booked to leave for Nice.

Lorraine was always living each day to the fullest. She enjoyed life and got so much pleasure out of everything. Ward and I would often comment on this. When we learned she had cancer, it made sense to me.

Yvonne, you mentioned Lorraine's letters. I remember she and I talked about the movie *Out of Africa* which was based on Isak Dinesen's diary and letters, and we would joke about *our* letters becoming a book and a movie. I'm glad you are doing it.

In California, Ward and I met Lorraine at the airport when she arrived in San Diego. I remember visiting her at the clinic where she was staying to fight cancer; she was fighting so hard. We visited her often, and took her some things for the apartment to make it look more 'homey.'

Then one day she tells me she is going back to Paris to see André. The day before she was to leave she was at my house and I was going to drive her to the airport. She called André to let him know she was coming and he told her he was going out of town and did not want to see her. She was going to go anyway and wait for him.

I had to work hard to talk her out of going. This would have been the worst thing for her and I was afraid the trip would kill her. I finally had to get mean. I told her he did not care about her. If she had a friend who called to say they were coming to see her from another country, wouldn't she change her plans? She agreed that she would. And here this guy wasn't willing to do that. He did not care about her. She was in love, he was not. I had to keep talking and working on her. Finally, she agreed it would not be a good idea to go to Paris. Of course, she was devastated. Later I drove her back to San Diego.

I don't remember too much about the last day in the hospital. I remember you telling me that Lorraine was in so much pain. She had told you that no one should have to live with that much pain. When she did pass on that day, you wanted me to come into the room afterwards. When I saw Lorraine, I could immediately see that she wasn't there, that she had gone on. You and I talked that night. On the doctor's advice you had agreed to increase Lorraine's morphine to ease her pain. I told you then, and still today, I *know* you did the right thing.

I remember going with you to the funeral home and trying to decide what to do. Finally, the decision was made for cremation. It was the only logical choice. I remember the service in the gardens at the crematorium. Ward and I went out on the boat to spread Lorraine's ashes. Didn't you take some back to Australia?

I remember meeting David, the Australian boyfriend. Was that in Paris? He was nice enough I guess, but he wanted to control Lorraine too much. She was such a free spirit.

I remember Lorraine had taken pictures of the same location in Paris at different times of the year to show the changing of the seasons. Do you have those pictures? I thought it was so neat that she would think to do that. She loved life and enjoyed each and every moment.

Well, that's it for my memory. Ward is going out of town on business this week. I told him to think about memories of Lorraine while he is driving. He will, and I will pick his brains when he comes back.

Thank you for making me take this trip down memory lane, Yvonne. I was so fortunate to have had that time in Paris and to have known Lorraine. We became such good friends. She had a great life – even though it was short, she lived it to the fullest.

Love,

Lisa

Dear Yvonne and Barb,

It is so amazing to be able to remember that experience with Lorraine in Paris and for her to have documented it at the time, and it is just as I remember!

Lisa met me at the train station with her sign, and I felt so embarrassed, but it was probably the only way we could make contact. The next embarrassment was her speaking loudly on the metro saying slightly negative things about French people, not a good idea as we were surrounded by French people! We were in Paris!

The apartment was tiny, just big enough for the queen size futon I think, and room for suitcases which were storage containers and a tiny kitchenette, a sink, a cooktop, a small cupboard above the sink, I think! I don't remember the bathroom. There was a lovely French window with a view of roof tops I think! We all slept on the futon. It was folded up to be a seat during the day. Lorraine and Lisa were very tidy as there was no option to be otherwise. There was a supermarket nearby, and we bought yoghurt and eggs (we boiled them) and baguette (with butter and conserve) for our breakfast.

One of the places we had dinner at was an old library building which was now a massive restaurant. The tables had white paper tablecloths which the waiters wrote your order and bill on. You tore the bill bit off when you went to pay. It was a three-course meal for a fixed price, and you ordered all the courses, and they were all delivered at the same time. It may have been because we were there late. Some of the waiters were packing up the other tables and putting the chairs up on them, as we made our way through our three courses – a unique dining experience.

Another place was a bistro with musicians playing the ubiquitous French accordion music, and some other diners got up and danced in the aisles. So lovely, so French! I vaguely remember the dark downstairs jazz club with its fabulous music and atmosphere and jazz-loving patrons.

Lorraine was so alive and full of mischief and daring. She had a wicked sense of humour.

She told me stories of her tour guide exploits and running to catch the shops to buy bread and meat before they closed for the evening, and being chased by the worried suitcase-carrying English tourists she was escorting to their hotels in the narrow alleyways, and seduction experiences including a Frenchman with a bear skin rug! She looked chic in her tight pants and tailored shirts and low heeled black court shoes, maybe also a silk scarf and her long blonde hair. I also remembered the phone box incident, all those free international phone calls late in the evening!

My other experience which happened in Sydney was synchronicity. I had flown to Sydney to visit my mother and was on the airport bus going into the city to take the train from Central to Emu Plains. I looked up at an advertising sign in the bus for the airline that Yvonne worked at, and thought of her and Barbie and Lorraine. Then I looked down and to the front of the bus and there was Yvonne. I talked to her and asked about Barb and Lorraine, and she said Lorraine was currently in Sydney being reviewed for her melanoma and having some treatments. I delayed my trip home and went with Yvonne instead to her home, to spend a lovely evening with her and Lorraine, my last encounter with her as it turned out, but so special and serendipitous.

I remember Lorraine's gorgeous humour about her cat, Dooppy.

The piece of Lorraine's writings, saying she feels other people will read her diary is so amazing, so poignant.

Thanks again for contacting me and rekindling all these wonderful memories. Well done for this beautiful project. I am sure Lorraine's life will inspire others when they read her story. Mindfulness is all the go these days, and that is exactly how Lorraine lived.

Love,

Suzi

CPSIA information can be obtained
at www.ICGtesting.com
Printed in the USA
LVHW02s1744210818
587651LV00013B/1148/P